Ken Anderson (signature)

Mayberry Reflections

The Early Years

by
Ken Anderson

WESTVIEW BOOK PUBLISHING, INC.
Nashville, Tennessee

First edition September 2006

Printed in the United States of America on acid-free paper

ISBN 1-933912-33-2

Cover design by Hugh Daniel

Prepress and typography by Westview Book Publishing, Inc.

WESTVIEW BOOK PUBLISHING, INC.
PO Box 210183
Nashville, Tennessee 37221
www.westviewpublishing.com

For Linda Anderson

Wonderful Wife, Great Companion
My Best Friend

Contents

Foreword

We are living in times when Americans spend millions of dollars each year in search of something to help reduce stress in their lives. We try everything from medications to therapy to alcohol and illicit drugs. Yet many of us continue to live each day feeling unfulfilled and totally stressed out.

We find that our lives are so filled with work, meetings, family events, school activities, church obligations, and social responsibilities, that we rarely find even a few moments of quiet time when we can escape and forget all those pressures that seem to follow us each waking minute of every day.

Many believe that a few moments at the local watering hole after work might help. At least some familiar faces and friendly smiles might be found there. Instead, the very same things seem to follow. People are complaining about their jobs, their spouses, the economy, and the politics in Washington. Upon leaving, one feels no better, and the only thing accomplished is that there are fewer dollars in the pocket and a few less hours in the day.

I am no different from anyone else. My life is also filled with many stressful moments. But unlike many, I do not seek relief at the local watering hole. Nor do I see a therapist or use drugs. Nor do I try many of the other self-help programs that we see advertised all around us. No, I have a very different temporary cure for my anxieties and stresses. I find my relief by visiting that wonderful friendly fictitious town of Mayberry, North Carolina. For you see, like thousands of others throughout our country I am one of those people who loves to visit Mayberry through the wonder of television. And for me, it works. For a short time each day I can go back to a much simpler and innocent time and place where everyone knows everyone's name. I find that my blood pressure drops, my breathing relaxes, and my entire mood changes.

I have come to know many people like me through the many websites that are dedicated to that wonderful place called Mayberry. I teach the Back to Mayberry Bible Study, and I hear the laughter, and I see the smiles when discussions begin about the people in Mayberry. Yet, I must admit, I do take ridicule from family and friends. For like many people, they do not understand the appeal of an old black and white television program that made its debut in 1960. My family and friends often laugh at me and ask why a fifty-nine year old retired teacher spends so much time watching a corny old television show like the Andy Griffith Show. They want to know what I see that they don't. So I try to explain in a very simple way.

When I see Opie and Andy sitting out on the porch having one of their man-to-man talks, I see the father I never had. When I see Ellie Walker behind the soda fountain at Walker's Drug store, I see Mr. and Mrs. Weix behind the soda fountain of the drugstore that I frequented as a young boy. When I see Opie and his friends frolicking through Crouch's Woods and fishing at Myer's Lake, I see my brothers and me fishing at the old Mill Pond and playing out in Rau's Woods. When I see Floyd cutting hair and talking to the town cronies, I see myself sitting in Virck's Barbershop and I am listening to the men folk telling their hunting and fishing stories while I read comic books and enjoy the smells of the witch hazel and other manly scents. Or when I see Miss Crump encouraging Opie to go outside to play football, I see Mr. Eiden, my seventh grade basketball coach, laughing and encouraging us after we just lost a basketball game by a score of 88-0. After all, it was just a game back then. And when I see good old Mr. Foley working in his little grocery store on Mayberry's Main Street, I remember Mr. Krueger who rigged a contest in his grocery store in order for a little boy to win a beautiful new cowboy outfit because his parents didn't have any money to buy one. That little boy happened to be me.

When I see Andy and Barney welcoming Otis each Friday night and treating him with dignity, I recall very vividly our small town police officer that would follow my dad home when he had a snootful, to make sure he got home safely to his anxious and awaiting family.

These are just some of the things I see whenever I visit Mayberry. And I see much more. For you see, I was very fortunate to have grown up in a very small town during a wonderful time when my friends and I were safe and secure knowing that we could roam around town, just like little Leon and Opie, and we could really get to know all those wonderful people who are no longer there.

The purpose of this book is really quite simple. I hope as you read each reflection you will take a few minutes to pause and be transformed back to another time and place. As we all know, Mayberry is a fictitious place. But the ideals and values that were instilled in the people that lived there are very real. They were important to the people of Mayberry, and they should continue to be important to each and every one of us no matter whom we may be or where we might live.

I chose to write about the years 1960-1964 because those were my high school years. They were also the first four years in the lives of the people in Mayberry. Hopefully, when a little time has passed, I will write another book of reflections for the next four years in the life of Mayberry. After all, I wouldn't want any of the wonderful stories of Mayberry to be left untold.

Acknowledgments

I would like to thank the many people who have helped to make this book possible. So many people through the years have encouraged me to pursue my writing. First, I thank the many educators who helped to instill in me a love for the written word. Without their guidance and inspiration, I would never have acquired my passion for reading and writing.

A special thanks to Kathryn Dardin, my author representative from Westview Book Publishing. Kathryn was instrumental in helping my dream become a reality. She encouraged me by posting many of my writings on her website, *Christian Activities Online*. When I first approached her about writing this book, she gave me the encouragement and confidence needed to pursue my project. She guided me through many of the preliminary steps involved in getting a new book published. Without her help this book would have not come to be.

I would also like to thank Hugh Daniel, General Manager of Westview Book Publishing. Like Kathryn, Hugh was a tremendous help. He guided me through much of the technical aspects of putting a book together. His frequent correspondence answered my many questions, and his skill in putting my book together into the format it has now become is much appreciated.

Dave and Marsha Scheuermann deserve special thanks. They allowed me to photograph many parts of their beautiful Taylor Home Inn Bed & Breakfast at Clear Lake, Wisconsin, and they gave me permission to share my story and pictures about our wonderful visit at their Inn. It gave me a very personal and close look at a little part of Mayberry. Being in the Taylor Home Inn inspired me to work hard to help others enjoy the many wonderful attributes of Mayberry, North Carolina.

To Alan Newsome from the "Who's Been Messing up the Bulletin Board" chapter of the "Andy Griffith Show Rerun Watcher's Club", I would like to say "thank you" for all your daily digests that so many of us receive every day. I want to also thank Alan for providing the pictures of the Mayberry squad car.

Lastly, I would like to thank my wife Linda. Without her patience over the thirty-six years we have been together, I would never have been able to pursue my passion for Mayberry. I want to thank her for her constructive criticism and her editing abilities. But I want to especially thank her for enduring the thousands of hours that I have spent watching the wonderful people of Mayberry. She is also responsible for many of the Mayberry collectibles that I have received as gifts over the years. She may not have quite the same passion for Mayberry as I have, but she certainly could give me a run for my money.

Mayberry Reflections

Season Number One

Episode 1
"The New Housekeeper"

Taylor Home Inn Bed & Breakfast, Clear Lake, Wisconsin

"Paw, what are you talking about? Why won't I ever see you again?" - Opie

When Aunt Bee arrives at the home of her nephew Andy Taylor, she is seeking to fulfill one of life's most important goals. She wants to feel needed. It has been many years since she has raised Andy and now she has been given the opportunity to help raise little Opie. For this she is very grateful. So she eagerly moves to Mayberry to make a new life for herself, and takes on the responsibility of raising a motherless little boy.

All of us want to feel needed and useful. We need a purpose in our lives and we need a reason to get up each morning. Many people have their careers, which quite often more than adequately gives a feeling of being needed. Add to that a loving spouse and children, and that feeling of worthiness is multiplied greatly.

3

However, for people like Aunt Bee, fulfillment is at times difficult to find. She has no career, and no spouse or children. She has spent her entire life caring for others. She comes to Mayberry expecting to once again find that fulfillment that is so important to her. When Opie rejects her because he misses Rose, it is more than Aunt Bee can bear, so she decides to leave. Her mind is made up when she listens to Opie say his nightly prayers, and he remembers everyone but her. It is only when Opie realizes that Aunt Bee needs him as much as he needs her that he is ready to accept her into his heart.

Change is always difficult, but especially for children. Security in a home is vital for a child's well being. When that security is threatened, children can become insecure and frightened. Fear of the unknown becomes very real to them.

Aunt Bee tries so hard to be accepted by Opie. She is willing to learn how to play baseball, and she even tries fishing. She makes special foods for Opie and Andy, but Opie just can not find room in his heart for both Rose and Aunt Bee. Aunt Bee does not cook fried chicken like Rose did, yet when sent to his room for not eating it; he sneaks some to his room and devours it like candy.

Opie is not the only person who is facing a major change in life. Andy is also losing Rose, and after taking care of Opie for so long, he will miss her very much. Aunt Bee, although an aunt to Andy, is a new person in the household. It will be an adjustment having her with them, and getting used to her ways. Aunt Bee also has a major adjustment to make as she moves to Andy's house. She is coming to a new town where she knows few people. She is leaving behind a sense of security as well as friends. Even Rose's life will no longer be the same. She is leaving Andy and Opie who she has grown to love very much.

As we go through the busy days of our lives, we need always be mindful of the needs of others. We never know when we will come across people like Aunt Bee who need us, as much or perhaps even more, than we may need them.

"If she goes, what'll happen to her? She doesn't know how to do anything, catch fish, play ball, hunt frogs. She'll be helpless." - Opie

Episode 2
"The Manhunt"

"Sheriff, you'll never guess what's happened. Something big; biggest thing that's ever happened in Mayberry, real big, big, big, big!" - Barney

There is no doubt that Opie truly idolizes his father. He believes Andy is the most important person in the whole world. But Andy tries to explain to Opie that there are a few other people in the world who might be a little more important. Like the President of the United States, or perhaps the Queen of England.

When the State Police come to Mayberry during a search for a criminal, they ask Andy and Barney to stay out of the hunt. Opie cannot understand how such a thing could possibly happen. After all, his father is the sheriff and the state policeman is only a captain. His father should be the one in charge of the search, not the captain.

It is very important for young children to have role models. And what better role model for a little boy to have than his own father? What boy hasn't said those immortal words, "I bet my father can lick your father?" Every young boy wants to believe that his dad is the smartest, the toughest, and the best father in the entire world. Opie does not have a mother at home like most children his age. So rather than going home after school, he quite often stops at the court house and spends time with his paw. Andy does not mind this one bit. In fact it is his favorite time of the day. How fortunate for Andy to have a job where he can spend time with his son.

Unfortunately many young boys today are growing up without fathers in their lives. However, it does not mean they cannot have an older person who will be a role model for them. It may be an older brother, an uncle, a teacher, or a next door neighbor. Boys enjoy having someone teaching them the important things in life - like how to fish, throw a baseball, build a campfire, or how to deal with a bully from school.

Andy does not let Opie down. He decides that it is his sworn duty to protect the citizens of Mayberry. So he and Barney go in search of the convict. They know the lay of the land around Mayberry. While the State Police are setting up roadblocks on the main roads, Andy

5

and Barney do a little search of the lesser known areas. Andy knows the people of Mayberry so well that he is able to recognize clues that the State Police would miss. Clues like Emma Watson not complaining about her pain and not having any pies out to cool. When Andy discovers these two little bits of information, he knows something is indeed amiss.

Because of his determination and expertise of the Mayberry area, Andy is able to capture the crook, and he restores Opie's faith in him as a sheriff. Every boy and girl deserves to have a positive role model to guide them through life. Opie had one, and isn't it wonderful that it was his own father?

"Nooooo, that won't be necessary. Course, if you could see your way clear to send me one of those maps with the sticky buttons on it, I'd appreciate it." - Andy

Episode 3
"Guitar Player Returns"

"Jim, why in the world don't you do something about yourself? Why you've got a fine talent there." - Andy

*J*im Lindsey is a very talented musician. He plays the guitar and he enjoys performing on the sidewalks of Mayberry. However, not all the people enjoy having him play outside their places of businesses, so several times Andy has had to arrest Jim for disturbing the peace. Orville Monroe is one businessman who especially dislikes Jim's sidewalk concerts. Orville is Mayberry's undertaker, and he considers it undignified to have loud music being played outside his funeral parlor.

It is a wonderful thing to have a special gift or talent. Whether it is singing, writing, dancing, or athleticism, we should try to develop our talents to their fullest. But Jim Lindsey doesn't do that. Rather than pursue his musical abilities and make something of himself, he takes the easy way out. He stays in Mayberry and plays for the simple enjoyment of it.

Using a talent for simple enjoyment in itself is not wrong. What is wrong is when we do not use our talents to better ourselves. Too often we sit back and do nothing about it. It may be because we have no ambition or because we do not have confidence in our abilities. Jim Lindsey exhibits some of both. He has little ambition, and he lacks confidence in himself as a musician. Perhaps he doesn't pursue his gift of music because he is afraid of failure. After all, if he doesn't attempt new things, then he doesn't have to worry about failing. On the other hand, if he does not attempt new things, he will never experience the joy and satisfaction that comes with success.

Andy knows Jim has a great talent, and he also knows Jim has little ambition. Not wanting to see Jim waste his life, Andy comes up with a plan to get Jim an audition with Bobby Fleet. He knows that Jim will never consider auditioning for Bobby, and he knows Bobby is not interested in listening to Jim, so he must somehow get Bobby and Jim together without either of them knowing the reason.

Andy and Barney arrest Bobby Fleet and his band on a phony parking violation. He puts them in jail, and tells Barney to get Jim and bring him to the courthouse. Jim is also brought in on a phony charge. When he sees Bobby Fleet, he becomes angry with Andy for being so underhanded. Although he lacks ambition, Andy knows that Jim has pride. He tricks Jim into playing the guitar by telling him it needs tuning. When Bobby Fleet hears Jim tuning the guitar, he starts giving him a bad time about his playing. Jim can take just so much, and before he realizes what's happening, he is playing a great song with Bobby Fleet's musicians joining in. Thanks to Andy's trickery, Jim joins Bobby Fleet's band, and leaves Mayberry to pursue his musical talents.

We all have been given various gifts and talents. Sometimes it takes a long time to discover them. It may even take longer to pursue them. To not use the talents we have is a terrible waste. Whether our talents are athletics, music, academics, or public speaking, we can never reach our full potential as a person until we have pursued those talents in some way. Thankfully, Andy helps Jim Lindsey discover this very thing.

"Ah, he digs you, so you be nice and dig him back, you hear?" - Andy

7

Episode 4
"Ellie Comes to Town"

"Just call her a lady druggist, Barney, and if they're all as pretty as she is we sure could use a lot more of them, couldn't we?" -
Andy

Ellie arrives in Mayberry to help her ailing uncle in the drugstore. She has just finished pharmacy school, and she is determined to do her job well, and to do it by the book. There are rules and regulations that she must follow, but she soon learns that the easygoing people in Mayberry don't always follow the rules as other people might.

When Emma Watson wants to buy her pills for ten cents, Ellie refuses to sell them to her because she does not have a written prescription. Emma is convinced that without her pills she hasn't got long to live. Ellie sticks to her rules, however, and before she knows it people are beginning to take a dislike to her. Even Andy accuses her of being heartless, and seems to lose his usual easygoing manner. But Emma is an old lady, and has lived in Mayberry for a long time. Certainly Andy is going to be more sympathetic toward her need. Andy isn't known to be one to adhere strictly to rules, so he thinks Ellie should bend them when necessary, just as he often does.

It is important for people to stick to their principles when they believe they are right. After all, rules and regulations are what make our society run smoothly, and they are usually put into place to help people, or to protect them from being harmed. Without rules and regulations, we would have total anarchy. Ellie has a very important job being a pharmacist. Failure to follow the rules of her profession could easily jeopardize the lives she has sworn to help.

However, we sometimes forget that people are human, and that sometimes rules need to be bent a bit in certain circumstances. If there were a "no swimming" sign by a lake, and a person was drowning, we would not let that rule against swimming prevent us from diving into the water in order to save a life, would we?

Andy refers to this as the "human equation". When our principals are challenged, we need to closely examine whether or not those principals are a true help or a hindrance. Ellie knows that Emma's pills are nothing but sugar, a placebo, so when she refuses to sell them to Emma, she is not endangering Emma's health in any way. Yet she has a code of ethics that she must uphold. She is also new to Mayberry, and she needs to set her standards, and let people know what those standards are.

In the end Ellie gives in and brings Emma her pills. Despite her own principals, she decides Andy is right. Perhaps it is wrong to allow poor old Emma to suffer without her magic pills. Emma takes her pills and immediately feels better.

Now it is Ellie's turn to teach Andy a lesson about the "human equation". When Ellie came to deliver the pills to Emma, she illegally parked her car in front of a fireplug. When Andy takes out his ticket book, not knowing it is Ellie's car, Ellie asks him what happened to his "human equation." She gives Andy a list of reasons why the person may have parked in front of the fireplug. Andy decides that Ellie is right, so he puts away his ticket book, and Ellie gets in her car and drives away.

"Ah, Miss Walker, them pills, you sure they won't hurt her no matter how many of them she takes?" - Andy

Episode 5
"Irresistible Andy"

"How dare you thinking I'd want to marry you. Who do you think you are?" - Ellie

Ellie Walker is the new lady druggist in Mayberry. She is an attractive, young woman. Andy is the sheriff in Mayberry. He is relatively young, attractive, and unmarried. Wouldn't it be wonderful if these two nice people could somehow get together? Andy can certainly use a wife, and Opie sure would like a mother.

Andy is at Walker's Drug store buying a hot water bottle. It is a prize for Saturday's church picnic and dance. While explaining the water bottle to Ellie, Andy discovers that she is not going to the picnic. He cannot understand why an attractive young girl like Ellie hasn't been asked. He decides that the friendly thing for him to do would be to invite her to go with him. After all, it would be more like a neighborly call than actual "buzzing." Buzzing is Fred's way of saying going after a pretty young girl. Andy hems and haws while trying to ask Ellie for the date, so Ellie makes it easier for him and tells him she would love to go if he is asking her.

Aunt Bee is delighted to hear that Andy is taking Ellie to the church social. He is telling her how he came about to ask her. Suddenly he realizes that he never did quite get to actually asking her. She asked him. Then he remembers that her Uncle Fred was the one to suggest he take her. Andy is beginning to think the entire episode was a set up to get him to take Ellie. When Opie comes home and tells Andy he got a free ice cream cone because he was "Sheriff Taylor's little boy," he is convinced that he is a victim of a conspiracy to get him married off to Ellie.

Men like to think of themselves as the pursuer when it comes to romance and courtship. We like to be the ones in charge. Most of us don't like being pursued by a woman, although personally speaking, I do have to admit it isn't one of the pleasures I experienced very often in life. We may feel intimidated or threatened if we are the one being pursued. It might make us feel like the woman is trying to catch a husband, and we just might not want to be caught. At least this is how Andy sees it.

When we enter into new relationships, whether they are friendships or romances, we need to be careful not to jump to conclusions about another person's motives. Too often simple acts of kindness or words of endearment can be misinterpreted to mean something else. Ellie likes Opie because he is a cute little boy. She gives him an ice cream cone because she is a kind, thoughtful person. She is giving ice cream cones to many of the children who are coming into the store.

Andy sends other young "bucks" to the drugstore to flex muscles, wiggle ears, and twitch a nose at Ellie. He is sending new game her way. His plan fails when Uncle Fred makes an appearance and they skedaddle out of the store as fast as they can. Ellie realizes what Andy is doing, and soon tells him in no uncertain terms what she thinks. She tells Andy that she will not go with him to the dance, and furthermore she will ask the first eligible man who comes in the store. Well, Barney enters almost immediately, and Andy now has a whole new problem to deal with. Fortunately, Andy sees the errors of his ways, and he persuades Barney to be on duty the day of the picnic, and he ends up taking Ellie. He sure goes about it the hard way, doesn't he?

"Howdy Miss Ellie, Opie tells me you think I got a nice smile." - Andy

Episode 6
"Runaway Kid"

"When you make a solemn promise to a friend, it ain't right to go back on it. Never let your friend down. Never break a trust. And when you give your word never go back on it." - Andy

Promises are very easy to make. Often times, especially among children, we are asked to keep a promise before knowing what we are promising. How many of us have heard the question, "If I tell you something, do you promise not to tell anyone?" And in many cases, without thinking, we say yes. We are then faced with the predicament of whether or not we will be able to honor that promise.

Opie promises his friends that he will not tell the sheriff that they pushed his car in front of a fire plug as a joke. Yet when Andy tells Opie about it, Opie immediately admits that he and his friends had pushed the car as a joke. He feels he needs to tell his father. Of course he does not think he should get into trouble for it because he has only pushed a little.

When Andy finds out that Opie has made a promise to his friends, and then breaks that promise, he sits Opie down for a talk about the value of keeping promises. He tells Opie the importance of never letting a friend down. Andy reminds him that he should never go back on his word. Yet before long Andy finds himself doing exactly what he tells Opie not to do.

Opie brings a new friend, Tex, home with him that very day. Tex is running away from home. His parents have no idea where he is. Andy makes a promise to Opie that he will not tell Tex's parents that he is with them. Andy is now faced with a difficult decision. Should he go back on his word he gave Opie and take Tex back to his parents, or does he honor his promise he made and do nothing? As a father he is obligated to do one thing, but as a sheriff he is obligated to do quite another.

We need to be mindful that promises should not be taken lightly, nor should they be made lightly. A promise is a type of oath, especially when made between close friends. If we make a promise we are saying we are going to honor our word and we can be trusted. If someone promises us something, we are placing our trust in them that they will keep their word.

Promises should be taken very seriously. When Cub Scouts join a pack, the first thing they learn to do is recite the Cub Scout Promise. If called to be a witness in court, we promise to "tell the truth, the whole truth, and nothing but the truth, so help me God." When the day of our wedding comes, we make one of the most important and cherished promises of all. We promise to love and honor our spouse until "death do us part".

Andy wants Opie to learn how important it is to keep a promise. How can he expect Opie to learn this important value if he breaks a promise to him? Andy does find a way to explain the reason why he has to take Tex back home. As important as promises are, Andy lets us all know that they cannot stand in the way of helping someone who could possibly be hurt.

"Opie, I got an idea. Let's push Barney's car in front of the fireplug and I'll write him out a citation like he done me." - Andy

Episode 7
"Andy the Matchmaker"

"You're putting me on. Who'd want me?" - Miss Rosemary

*M*iss Rosemary is a very insecure person. She has a low opinion of herself, and it is very apparent whenever she speaks. She is also a kind person who enjoys doing things for others. She takes great pride when she is given the task of mending Andy's Justice of the Peace robe. She returns the robe to Andy just as Barney is handing in his resignation. He is resigning as deputy because his pride has been hurt. He is being teased. Someone writes a poem on a wall that ridicules Barney's policing abilities.

Barney is also a very insecure person. While often times he acts as if he knows everything, it is apparent that he is very uncertain about himself. He is new as a deputy, and he wants to do his job well. Yet the children in town tease him, and even the adults who are supposed to be his friends enjoy poking fun at him from time to time. Sure he has never made an arrest. But that isn't his fault. There just isn't anyone to arrest. Barney even suggests that if two strangers happen to be around, and one of them is determined to kill the other, the least they could do would be to do it in Mayberry.

Andy discovers that Barney has been walking Miss Rosemary to church on Sundays. Barney even notices that she wears a different waistcoat each week. Rosemary is a bit smitten by Barney too, but both of them are too shy and insecure to do anything about it. Andy decides it is time to boost Barney's ego a few notches, so he and Ellie manufacture a fake robbery to give Barney some policing to do. While attempting to find the robber, who does not exist, Barney brings in a stranger for questioning. Knowing the man is innocent; Andy calls Chattanooga to see if he can clear the man. As it turns out, the man is wanted for more serious crimes, and Barney turns out to be a big man in Mayberry when the story hits the newspapers.

For people like Barney and Rosemary, developing a meaningful relationship can be a difficult thing. The right words just don't seem to come. They may be afraid of expressing their true feelings because of a fear of being rejected. They cannot believe that someone might actually want them. Sometimes it takes a third party to act on behalf of one of the people involved. We all remember the story of Miles Standish, John Alden, and Pricilla. Maybe the same thing would work with Barney, Andy, and Rosemary.

After seeing his name in print, Barney's ego does get a boost. But perhaps it is boosted a bit too much. Now he is not sure if he wants Rosemary. After all, he is now a celebrity of sorts, so why not play the field. Andy steps in once more. Pretending to have been keeping silent for Barney's sake, he tells Miss Rosemary how wonderful she is, and how he admires her, and how he wants to court her. Barney realizes that he is about to lose his chance with Rosemary, so he finally speaks up and asks her for a date. The romantic scene closes with Rosemary's acceptance, and the two of them shaking hands on the deal.

"I want you to look at that there blueberry pie. Ain't that pretty? And my favorite kind too. Miss Rosemary, you are one for putting a glow in a man's day." - Andy

Episode 8
"Opie's Charity"

"I'm a proud woman Andy. I can't help it. I was reared that way." - Annabelle Silbey

Pride can be a double-edged sword. It is a good quality. We encourage pride in one's work and in one's country. We show pride when friends and family do good things. This is good. But pride can also get in the way of honesty. Pride can prevent us from admitting mistakes or guilt. Pride can cause us to believe we are better than others, and it may cloud the way we treat others. We need a proper balance of pride and humility.

Annabelle Silbey is a proud woman who spends a great deal of her time helping out with various charities in Mayberry. One of her favorites is the Underprivileged Children's Drive. She goes to the schools to ask the children for donations to help other less fortunate children in Mayberry.

Annabelle is an extremely proud woman. She and Andy enjoy talking about the funeral she gave her husband Tom after he was run over by a taxi in Charlotte. There is one slight error in Annabelle's story. Tom is not dead. He shocks Andy by showing up at the courthouse shortly after Annabelle leaves, and he explains the whole thing to Andy. He had gotten so fed up with his wife's nagging him about his drinking that he just up and left her. She was too proud to have people find out the truth, so she went through the pretence of his dying. She made up the story about his being run over by a taxi in Charlotte. Then she had a box shipped back to Mayberry which was supposed to have contained Tom's broken body. She had a funeral, and she even put up a headstone at the cemetery.

When Andy finds out that Opie gave a mere three cents to the Underprivileged Children's Fund, he becomes very upset. He does not understand why Opie would not give more than he did when he

14

knows Opie has money in his piggy bank. He is very disappointed in Opie, and it is an embarrassment to him, as sheriff, to have a son who is so stingy when it comes to helping others. Aunt Bee points out to Andy that Opie is a good little boy, and the only reason Andy is so disappointed in him is because his own pride has been hurt. She even calls him Annabel.

Andy criticizes Annabel for being so proud she could not admit that her husband left her and was not really dead. She was so proud she staged a phony funeral as a way to save face. It is only when her husband suddenly reappears in Mayberry that she finally has to live up to her deception. But Andy realizes he is no different than Annabel.

Andy's faith is restored in Opie when he finds out the real reason he only gave three cents. He is saving his money to buy his girlfriend Charlotte a present. He is going to buy her a coat for winter because the one she now has is all torn and patched.

When we give to others, we should give out of humility and love. We should not give out of a feeling of pride, but rather in the good that comes from our actions. Opie does not tell Andy what he was going to do with his money. He does not brag about buying a coat for a needy girl. He keeps it a secret. He is giving in a way that we all should. He is giving from the heart.

"You know this morning Annabelle and me we took a walk over to the cemetery where I'm buried." - Tom Silbey

Episode 9
"A Feud is a Feud"

"You let them scare you Paw. If they wanted hitchin' then it was up to you to hitch them." - Opie

M arriage is something that no two people should ever enter into lightly. When a couple marries, they are making a lifetime commitment. An important part of entering into a marriage is to have the blessing of one's parents. If the parents of a young couple approve of the marriage and embrace the union, the marriage stands a much greater chance of being a happy and successful one.

As Justice of the Peace, Sheriff Taylor is often called upon to marry couples. As long as the couple is of legal age and has the marriage license, he is obligated by law to perform the marriage. They often came to his house in the middle of the night. Andy dons his nightcap, and Aunt Bee plays the piano. It is what people expect an elopement ceremony to be like. In most cases people come to Andy to be married in order to save money. They want a simple wedding. They have their parents' consent, and few problems are ever encountered. But what will happen if two fathers oppose a marriage that Andy is about to perform? Will Andy go against the parents' wishes and perform the ceremony when there are shotguns pointing at him?

Family feuds occurred throughout history. In some cases the feuds were carried on for generations, even though the instigators of the feuds had long since been dead. Perhaps the reason for the feud is no longer important, and may even have been forgotten. The Carters and the Wakefields are involved in just such a feud. They have been shooting at each other for years, and no one seems to even know why. Now a nice young couple from those feuding families wants to get married, and they want Andy to perform the ceremony.

It is a tragic waste when people carry grudges throughout their lives. Friendships and families can be divided because unforgiving people are not willing to forget their differences from the past in order to move on to a harmonious future.

Andy knows if he marries Hannah Carter and Josh Wakefield without their parents' blessing, it will only bring unhappiness to the young couple. He needs to find a way to end the feud. Enlisting Hannah's and Josh's help, they go to the library to study the history of the feud. They find nothing mentioned about anyone ever being shot during the lengthy feud. Andy informs Mr. Wakefield and Mr. Carter about these findings and tells them it is time to change things. He gets the two men ready to face each other in a one on one duel. Andy, however, makes sure they are using empty guns so no one gets hurt. When the men are supposed to turn and fire, Andy fires his gun in the air, and the two cowards take off running like scared rabbits.

Andy once again uses his common sense and creative ways to bring together the Carters and Wakefields. Shaming the two men for their cowardice, and pointing out the bravery of their offspring, the Carters and Wakefields finally agree that the wedding should take place. Because of Andy's ingenuity, peace and harmony is once again found in the mountains near Mayberry .

"I declare I had better get out of this outfit. I'm beginning to feel like Dopey the dwarf." - Andy

Episode 10
"Ellie for Council"

"Oh Ellie, you don't want to concern yourself with government business. You want to let the men worry about that." - Andy

Throughout Mayberry's long history, men have always been in charge of its government. In fact no woman has ever run for town council. That is, not until Ellie Walker comes to Mayberry. When she decides it is time for a woman to be on the town council, the entire town becomes divided. It is the men against the women in one of the most heated political events in the history of Mayberry.

In Mayberry the roles of the sexes are quite clear. The husband is the man of the house who earns the money and controls the purse strings. The wife, on the other hand, stays at home to raise the children. She does the cooking and the cleaning. She attends garden club meetings, does the marketing, goes to the beauty parlor, and works on various committees for the church and school. But she stays clear of political issues.

It is very easy to stereotype people. We all do it at one time or another. Whether it is stereotyping the role of a man or woman, a certain ethnic group, or any particular group of people, stereotyping can be a very unfair practice. We place a person in a particular group, and then we expect that person to act according to the norms of that group. Fortunately over time stereotyping has become less noticeable. We have learned that a person's role in life is not fixed simply upon a person's given sex, race, or age.

The men of Mayberry do not want Ellie to run for the town council. They don't want her to run for one and only one reason. She is a woman. No woman has ever run for town council before, and the men do not want that changed. The women, on the other hand, want Ellie to run, and they want her to win. Mayberry is divided as the campaigning for Ellie grows. Each side is developing a strategy that it hopes will work to its benefit. Husbands have cut off their wives' charge accounts, and wives have stopped cooking, sewing, and ironing. It is a tossup as to who will give in first.

Ellie decides to drop out of the campaign. She is saddened to see the rift she has created among her friends. When she tells Andy that the men have won, Opie is overjoyed to know that the men have won, and they are keeping the women in their place. Opie has certainly learned a lot from Andy's example, hasn't he?

It takes Andy a while to realize it is not right to oppose Ellie simply because she is a woman. But when he hears what Opie says about keeping women in their places, he realizes how wrong he has been. He decides he will support Ellie, and he urges Mayberry's male population to do likewise. His little speech is about to make history. Mayberry is about to have its first councilwoman. Andy personally also makes history. It is the first time he has ever been kissed by a councilman.

> *"There's one for the books, ain't it? Sheriff being kissed by a councilman and speaking for sheriffs everywhere, I'm for that."*
> *- Andy*

Episode 11
"Christmas Story"

> *"Oh boy, are we going to have a good time tonight. Aunt Bee's got everything. We're gonna sing, laugh, and you'll be Santa Claus." - Andy*

Christmas is a wonderful time in Mayberry. Andy is anticipating a fun-filled Christmas Eve. Aunt Bee made a turkey dinner, the eggnog is chilled, the presents are wrapped, and Barney is ready to be Santa. But their plans are suddenly changed when Mayberry's grumpiest citizen, Ben Weaver, causes trouble for Andy, and he has to spend Christmas Eve at the courthouse.

For some people, Christmas is not joyful. The music, the cards, the stores, and the holiday specials on TV all portray Christmas as "the most wonderful time of the year." To many people, it is anything but joyful. For some, it is the loneliest time of the year.

Ben Weaver is one of Mayberry's wealthier citizens. He owns Weaver's Department Store, and he makes a great deal of money. Yet he is also one of Mayberry's unhappiest citizens. He has no friends, and he lives alone. He shows little sympathy for people who are going through hard times. So Christmas for Ben is just another day of the year. He may even resent it because his store will be closed, and that will cost him money. He doesn't like Christmas, and he does not like seeing others enjoying it.

It is never revealed why Ben Weaver is the way he is. What makes him so miserable is a mystery. Was he always this way? Did he enjoy Christmas as a child, or were his childhood Christmases unhappy times for him? It is easy to dislike Ben, but we do not know what emotional garbage he is carrying within. There are usually many reasons why people become angry and disgruntled. But Ben keeps his reasons to himself.

We all know people like Ben. But what we may not know is that if given the opportunity, they might very well enjoy Christmas as much as others. If we would make an effort to reach out to these people at Christmas time, or at any other time, we might make a difference in their lives. They may just be waiting for an invitation to be a friend. They just might not know how to take that first step. As we watch Ben Weaver in this episode, we see a lonely old man who wants to be a part of Andy's Christmas celebration. His problem is that he does not know how to go about being invited.

We know if Ben were to ask Andy to be included, he will be welcomed to join the Christmas festivities. But Ben is either too proud or too ashamed to admit that he is lonely, so he must do something else. Ben goes on a crime spree hoping to get arrested. He tears up a ticket he received from Barney, and he steals the courthouse bench. When he refuses to pay the ticket, Andy does exactly what Ben wants him to do. He puts him in jail. Because it is Christmas, Ellie pays his fine, and Andy lets him go. While watching the festivities through the jail window, Ben makes a loud noise when he falls. When Andy finds him lying on the ground beneath the window, he realizes what Ben is trying to do. He arrests him, and puts him in jail, but not before allowing Ben to go to his store to get some very important items. Poor Ben, even when he wants to do

19

something kind, like give Christmas presents, he does not know how to do it. He pretends that the presents are mistakes. Perhaps this is the first time in his life that Ben has given anyone a Christmas present. Maybe now, it won't be his last.

"Hey Sam, you'd better wake the young'ins up and take them home and put them to bed." - Andy

Episode 12
"Stranger in Town"

"I was from no place, living alone, hotel, no family. That's like being no place." - Ed Sawyer

*E*veryone in Mayberry knows one another, and cares about each other. It is a small town, and the folks who live there are very friendly. They greet one another on the street, they enjoy gossiping at the barber shop or beauty parlor, and they worship together come Sunday morning.

But how will Mayberry welcome an outsider? I don't mean just an ordinary outsider. I mean someone who knows everyone's name, business, and personal habits. How will the friendly folks of Mayberry react when a total stranger suddenly appears in their midst, and begins to act just like one of the town's people?

This is exactly what happens when Ed Sawyer gets off the bus in Mayberry one warm summer day. He walks right into Floyd's Barber Shop. He calls everyone by name. He asks Floyd about his rheumatism. He tells Andy to say hello to Aunt Bee and Opie. He calls Mrs. Buntley by name, and he knows the name of her twins, Robert and William. He even knows that William has a mole on his right ear. When he goes to the hotel to get a room, he calls Jason by name. He does not want to have room 209 because he knows that is the room Wilbur Hennessey got drunk in, and fell out of the window. He takes room 216 instead, even though it is green. He knows it is freshly painted so that will be nice.

The people of Mayberry are afraid of Ed Sawyer. How is it possible he knows so much about them? No one has ever seen him before, yet it is as if he has lived in Mayberry his entire life. Barney suspects he may be a spy of some sort. Mrs. Buntley thinks he may even be something from the supernatural world. He is indeed very peculiar.

We all form first impressions of strangers. But when we think about it, how many of our first impressions are accurate. Once we get to know new people, and we learn things about them, we slowly begin to accept them into our communities. This is what our friends in Mayberry do to Ed Sawyer once Andy shows them the error of their ways. Andy sits down with Ed, and Ed tells Andy quite a story.

Ed has been in the army, and one of his buddies is from Mayberry. He read Ed the letters from home. He would tell stories about the people and places of Mayberry. When Ed got out of the army he continued to get the Mayberry newspaper and he read everything he could about Mayberry. Before long he began telling people he was from Mayberry. He almost began to believe it himself. Then when he read the filling station in Mayberry was for sale, he decided to move to Mayberry, his hometown.

Andy tells the people Ed's story, and they realize they were wrong when they refused to welcome Ed into their tight knit community. Before he knows it, Lucy Matthews is asking him to call on her, and George Safferly tells him he can buy his gas station. It looks like Ed is finally accepted by Mayberry, and he will stay where he has always wanted to live. The one strange thing is that we never see Ed Sawyer again. He leaves Mayberry just as mysteriously as he entered, and we never learn why. He is indeed a peculiar fellow. Maybe he was from the supernatural world. One never can tell.

"It didn't work. It's as simple as that. It just didn't work." - Ed Sawyer

Episode 13
"Mayberry Goes Hollywood"

"Poking fun? Why I should say not. They're charming, natural. They are very nice people. I could never poke fun of them." - Mr. Harmon, Hollywood Producer

*O*ne important thing that makes Mayberry such a delightful town is its people. They are neither flashy nor pretentious. The citizens of Mayberry are a simple, down to earth, and easygoing people.

They love to wear simple clothes and eat good old-fashioned southern food.   The old timers enjoy sitting on the benches along Main Street whittling their wood. Playing checkers at Floyd's Barber Shop is a popular pastime.   Then they discover that a Hollywood producer is coming to town to make a movie. Suddenly the town of Mayberry and the people who live there are transformed totally   from who they really are.   They decide it is time to gussy up the entire town.

All of us at some time or another probably pretend to be someone we really aren't. Perhaps it is to impress a prospective employer, or maybe we are about to become reconnected with an old acquaintance. So we decide that we need to change who we are. Or at least we need to change the appearance of who we are.

When the movie producer first meets the delightful people of Mayberry, he immediately likes them because they are so charming, natural, and nice.   They are most likely totally different from the people who live in Hollywood, and this is a refreshing change for him. These are exactly the type of people he is looking for to be in his movie. Everything is perfect and nothing needs to be changed.

However, like most people would probably do, the natural, simple people of Mayberry decide that they need to "gussie" themselves up for the movie. So they buy new clothes, redecorate their places of business, and change their hairstyles. They now look like the people of Hollywood should look.   They plan a big welcome for the movie people, complete with pies and singing by Mayor Pike's daughter. To complete the celebration the oldest tree in Mayberry is about to be cut down.

When the movie people arrive in Mayberry, they find everything changed. Gone are the natural charming people. No longer do the storefronts have their simple appearance typical in small town Americana.   The people are told to get out of their trick or treat costumes and are asked to change their delightful town back to the way it was.

When we try to become something or someone that we aren't, we are only deceiving ourselves. It doesn't take long for others to see through our façade. If people are going to like us, isn't it best for them to like us for who we really are and not because we are only someone we are pretending to be? Mayor Pike and the town council thought the movie people might make fun of them. It was almost as if they were ashamed of whom they were.

I have lived most of my life in small rural communities. I am not a sophisticated worldly person, and anyone who meets me can see that immediately. I am proud of who I am and where I came from. I hope my small town values will continue to stay with me all the days of my life. They are an important part of who I am.

"Yes sir, Opie, everything's back to normal in Mayberry." - Andy

Episode 14
"The Horse Trader"

Mayberry's Famous Cannon

"The golden rule says that you're supposed to be honest and square dealing when dealing with other folks." - Andy

What small child hasn't been involved in a trade only to discover later that he has been cheated? It is one of those early lessons in life that we all learn. Unfortunately we sometimes lose a valuable possession while learning this important lesson. I remember playing marbles for keeps and trading away some of my best "glassies" for something far less valuable. For some reason I always seemed to come out on the short end of all my trades.

As a single parent Andy has a difficult job raising Opie. He faces many challenges. He wants to raise Opie so he will grow up to be a fine young man. Many times we see Andy and Opie sitting on the porch or in their boat, and they are having one of their man to man talks. One of the things Andy always tells Opie is that honesty is the best policy. Whether it's admitting to a wrong when he makes a mistake and gets into trouble, or making excuses for not doing chores, Opie is frequently reminded about the importance of telling the truth.

One day Opie comes into the courthouse with a bagful of licorice seeds. He got them on a trade. He traded his new cap pistol for the seeds. But he knows he has been gypped, so now he plans to trade the seeds for a pair of roller skates. Andy reminds Opie of the golden rule and tells him to forget about trading off his worthless licorice sticks. But Opie tells Andy that he is practicing the golden rule. He tells Andy that Tommy did it unto him and now he is going to do it onto Jerry.

What will happen when Opie hears Andy tell lies about the old town cannon when he is put in charge of selling it? Should Opie do what his father says or should he do as his father does? Both Opie and Barney become dismayed when they witness Andy telling untruths to a possible buyer. The antique collector ends up buying an old worthless cannon from Andy thinking it was once used by Teddy Roosevelt. Andy justifies his actions by saying he is doing it for the good of the town and not for his own personal gain.

Andy catches Opie in another shady deal when Opie trades an old button for the roller skates. He says the buyer might have gotten the idea the button once belonged to George Washington. It doesn't take long for Andy to find out where Opie learned that method of "dickering".

As parents and adults, we must be very careful what we say and do in the presence of children. We may tell them the right things to do, but if they see us doing the opposite of what we say, what then should they believe? Actions do speak much louder than words.

Andy, however, once again redeems himself and tells the antique dealer that he made up all the stories about the cannon. And although the town of Mayberry may have come out short on the deal,

Opie was the one who really comes out ahead, for he once again learns that honesty is indeed the best policy.

"If honesty is the best policy, then how come I'm out a cap pistol?" - Opie

Episode 15
"Those Gossiping Men"

"We don't gossip. We just pass along news." - Emma Watson

*F*loyd's Barbershop is an important institution in Mayberry. For many years the men folk of Mayberry have gathered at Floyd's to get their haircuts and shaves. They have also gathered at Floyd's for other important reasons. They gathered to tell fishing stories, to play checkers and to share stories about the many people and events in Mayberry.

The dictionary defines gossip as: "a person who habitually reveals personal or sensational facts about others, a rumor or report of an intimate nature, or chatty talk." In many cases gossip turns out to be mean and unsubstantiated bits of information about people, and in many cases the gossip can cause harm to the person talked about.

Small towns are notorious for gossip. Mayberry is no different. Both the men and women of Mayberry often spend a good part of each day talking about the goings on and happenings with their neighbors and friends. However, they often do not consider it to be gossip. Rather, they say they are just passing along news. No one is exempt from the gossip in Mayberry. Whether you are the preacher, a teacher, or even the sheriff, one never can tell when an interesting story will start its journey through the homes and businesses of Mayberry.

For some strange reason we all seem to enjoy a good tidbit of gossip from time to time. We enjoy it even more if it happens to be something controversial about someone we know. Why we seem to enjoy gossip is an unknown, but since early times people seem to thrive on the misfortunes of others. Bad gossip has a way of really traveling fast. Too often it changes and grows each time it is passed on to another person. Once it starts, it is almost impossible to stop. This is especially true in the town of Mayberry.

Barney has a small cut on his trigger finger, so Andy goes across the street to Walker's Drug Store for some sulfur powder. When Aunt Bee and Emma hear that Barney cut his finger while cleaning his gun, they begin to pass along the news. By the middle of the afternoon Orville Monroe appears at the courthouse offering Andy his services during his time of sorrow. Orville is Mayberry's undertaker. In a very short time Barney's little cut grew to a bullet hole in the chest. In other words, "Barney is dead."

Aunt Bee and Emma decide to get back at Andy for giving them a bad time about their gossiping. They have a bit of fun as they start a harmless rumor throughout Mayberry. They suggest to Andy that a shoe salesman might not really be who he says he is. By the end of the day the men of Mayberry have a rumor going around that he is a Hollywood talent scout. They fall for Aunt Bee's scheme hook, line, and sinker. They decide to audition for the man while ordering new shoes. So one by one they visit his hotel room and entertain him while trying on shoes. Andy and his friends look mighty foolish when they discover that the man from New York City is really a shoe salesman. It will be something they will think about quite a bit each time they put on their new pair of shoes.

"Why Sheriff Taylor, where is that famous sunny disposition, the cheery smile, and the twinkling eyes? Oh I know now, don't tell me. I should have understood. It's the natural disappointment in realizing you're not going to play the guitar on the Manhattan Showtime Program after all." - Aunt Bee

Episode 16
"The Beauty Pageant"

"For doing such a beautiful job with this year's pageant, and for just behaving beautifully through the whole thing, I crown thee Miss Mayberry." - Andy

Founder's Day is a very special day for the people of Mayberry. It is a day set aside to remember the founding fathers of their wonderful close knit community. For years now the day is spent with picnicking and parades. But this year there will be something different. There will be a beauty pageant, complete with girls. Where there is a beauty pageant, there must be a judge, and who else but the honest, fair-minded Sheriff Taylor can do a better job as judge?

Beauty pageants have always been popular events. What man doesn't enjoy seeing a contest where all the entries are beautiful young ladies? However, like all contests, beauty contests have a tendency to become very competitive. After all what is beauty? Beauty is in the eye of the beholder, as the old saying goes. So when Sheriff Taylor finds himself appointed judge, little does he know the problems that he will confront.

Andy learns in a hurry that being a beauty contest judge is not going to be easy. Everyone in town is pressuring him to select a relative or friend. Girls come to his house to show off. His good friend Floyd wants favoritism because he is writing the Miss Mayberry song. Aunt Bee is pressuring him to get Ellie in the contest. Even his own son pressures him to pick his girlfriend, Mary Wiggins. It is especially difficult for Andy because he admits that he thinks all girls are beautiful. He can hardly wait for the contest to be over.

One of the qualities any judge must possess is fairness. A judge must not let personal bias and prejudices enter in his decisions. He must consider all the entrees fairly without favoritism and then make his decision based on the criteria set before him. But Andy Taylor is only human, and when Ellie Walker is unknowingly entered into the contest, he faces a very difficult decision. Ellie is by far the obvious winner, but she lets Andy know that if he picks her, she will never speak to him again.

Our society is obsessed with outward beauty. Cosmetic surgeries and products are a billion dollar industry in our country. Americans want to be a beautiful people, and we often lose sight of the importance of our inner beauty. When we watch movies or television, it is the person with the best looks who often has the leading roles. Magazine covers feature young, thin, girls who have perfect hair and lovely complexions. There are even beauty contests for preteen girls and babies. Somehow we have been taught to believe that what a person looks like is the most important attribute in life.

The time has finally come for Andy to announce the winner of the contest. After stalling as long as he can, he names Miss Mayberry. He chooses none of the regular entrees. He bestows the honor upon Miss Bishop. She is truly a beautiful person. She worked so hard and so unselfishly getting the pageant all ready. She is always willing to help others and she treats everyone with kindness and love. Of all the ladies in Mayberry, she exemplifies the meaning of true beauty.

"Listen to this Floyd. 'And the climax to yesterday's proceedings came in the form of a special song for the occasion, written, composed, and rendered by our own Floyd Lawson.'" - Andy

Episode 17
"Alcohol and Old Lace"

"Jennifer, you'll be the death of me yet. How many times must I tell you? A lady never goes into a barber shop." - Clarabelle Mortinson

The county of Mayberry is dry. Ben Weaver sells spirits in his store, but other than that, the only other source of spirits in Mayberry is moon shiners. Otis Campbell is a regular customer for most of the makers of moon in Mayberry. Ben Silby and Rafe Hollister often provide Otis with his usual liquid refreshment. However, the Mortinson sisters also provide the drinkers of Mayberry with beverages. But they sell elixir, and it is only to be used for celebrating special events such as National Potato Week and Bastille Day.

The prohibition era in our country was a difficult time for law enforcement workers. We all have images of bootleggers and the police during those days when liquor was outlawed in our country. For some reason, the county of Mayberry continues to enforce the laws against making or selling intoxicating beverages. This means that Sheriff Taylor and Deputy Fife spend a great deal of their time tracking down moon shiners. Because of his drinking problem, Otis Campbell is the most frequent visitor to the Mayberry jail. He appears once a week, pays his fine, and then locks himself in jail.

Barney always tries to get him to reveal his source of liquor, but Otis refuses to talk. Town drunks have a code they live by, and Otis honors that code.

The use of alcohol in Mayberry is portrayed in a very light and humorous fashion. We laugh when we see Otis Campbell come staggering into the courthouse and locking himself up for the weekend. We laugh when we see him riding a cow or talking to his invisible dog. But alcohol abuse is not funny. We never see Otis' wife sitting at home wondering where he is. We don't see the bad effects of alcohol use in Mayberry because so few people drink. But we love Otis just the same. He adds a great deal of hilarity to Mayberry, and after all, that is what Mayberry is all about. We can still enjoy the antics of Otis when he has a snootful, and we can laugh at the moon shiners in Mayberry as they try to outwit Andy and Barney.

The Mortinson sisters decide to help end moon shining in Mayberry. They tell Andy they have seen two stills because they take walks and see things. Andy and Barney decide to investigate the sightings and sure enough, Miss Jennifer and Miss Clarabelle are right. Andy and Barney arrest both Ben Sewell and Rube Sloan, and Barney busts their stills to smithereens. Andy and Barney congratulate themselves for putting an end to moon shining in Mayberry for good. Their celebration does not last very long, however, for just as they shake hands, Otis comes staggering in with a snootful.

Opie helps Andy find the source of Otis's liquor when he brings in flowers that reek of alcohol. Opie tells Andy and Barney that the Mortinson flowers are so pretty because they have a flower-making machine that has a long coil with a fire under it. So ends the elixir business of Jennifer and Clarabelle Mortinson. And so ends Otis' supply of liquor.

The debate on the evils of drinking will go on forever. For some people, it is a way of life, and they handle it responsibly. For others it is a disease, and they are unable to handle it at all. It comes down to be a matter of personal choice for each of us.

"Oh my no, but you see we had all the berries and the jars, and well, we decided to put up preserves." - Clarabelle Mortinson

Episode 18
"Andy - the Marriage Counselor"

"Sheriff, have you ever tried to get along with a rattlesnake?" - Fred Boone

The people of Mayberry are portrayed as kind, friendly, and loving people. At least most of them are portrayed as such. But every so often we meet someone in Mayberry who is a bit different. Such is the case with Fred and Jenny Boone. Fred and Jenny are very friendly to all their neighbors and friends in Mayberry. But they just cannot be kind or loving to one another

Domestic violence is a very serious problem today. Police often say that one of the most dangerous things they encounter is entering a home to settle a domestic dispute. They never know what they are going to face, and being inside the perpetrator's own home makes it even more dangerous.

Andy and Barney make visits to the Boones on a regular basis. It seems the Boone's neighbors call Andy whenever Fred and Jenny's arguments become too loud. The shouting can be heard several doors away. When Andy and Barney arrive to investigate the latest complaint, they find Jenny and Fred in a full fledged battle. They are both yelling at the top of their voices, name calling is ramped, and dishes are flying all over. Things finally settle down, and Andy and Barney leave. But first thing the next morning Barney brings the Boones in. He heard them fighting while driving by. Andy finally gets fed up with the entire situation and places the Boones on probation, meaning they must report to the court house every day for lessons on how to get along.

Dating agencies in our modern world strive to match people who have similar interests and who are totally compatible in many areas. They say that only when one finds total compatibility will one find true happiness in marriage. However, the Boones are the exception. They really do care for one another, but they can only show their love through their bickering and name calling. Deep down they do love one another, and once Andy discovers that the bickering and name calling is what really makes the Boone's happy, he comes up with the solution to the entire problem.

Andy's solution involves teaching the Boone's to speak to one another with respect. He believes if he can make it a habit for them, they will soon begin to treat each other kindly. Each morning the Boones come to the courthouse, and Andy has them practicing how to say "good morning, thank you, and please." He even has the audacity of expecting them to use such words of endearment as "dear" and "honey". Fred finds it almost impossible to say such things to Jenny, so Barney suggests he make it easier by holding his gun to Fred's head. Andy's determination and patience pays off, for before too long, both Jenny and Fred are saying things to each other that Barney never thought possible. Andy decides his plan is a success, and he sends the Boones merrily on their way. However, little does Andy know that a whole new problem will soon arise.

It is hard to understand people like the Boones. They love one another, yet they fight and argue in order to show that love. Once they get home they treat each other kindly. But they transfer that bickering with each other to their friends. No longer are they friendly to their neighbors and friends. Rather than fight with each other, they now argue and scream at others, and Andy has a new problem to deal with. He is back to square one and needs to find a way to get the Boones to treat others without hostility.

"Golly, you look as pretty as a picture in those pajamas." - Andy

Episode 19
"Mayberry on Record"

"Hey Andy, the buffalo on this nickel is facing the same way." - Barney

*B*arney is very upset when he receives his paycheck. He feels all the taxes and deductions are taking away too much of his money. He decides it is time to find some kind of investment so he can build himself a little nest egg. However, Andy cautions Barney and tells him he is just ripe for the picking. To prove his point, Andy tricks Barney into buying a nickel that is supposed to be very rare and quite valuable. Barney learns he has been duped by his best friend, but doesn't heed Andy's warning about investing money carefully.

31

Barney and the boys at the barber shop soon find an investment opportunity when Mr. Maxwell from New York comes to Mayberry hoping to make a musical album using local talent. Andy and a number of other talented musicians play for Mr. Maxwell, and it is soon apparent that a great record is in the making. When Mr. Maxwell suggests that it might be possible to sell a million records, everyone suddenly wants to buy into the venture so they can share in the profits. Everyone that is, except for Andy. Even though Andy is willing to perform for the record project, he feels it is a risky venture, and he believes Mr. Maxwell might just take their money and run.

Finding safe and honest investments is not such an easy task anymore. There are many con artists and unscrupulous people just waiting to prey on unsuspecting investors. If we are smart investors we study the prospectus given to us and investigate extensively before investing money. It is the smart way of doing business in our day and age. Gone forever are the days when agreements are sealed with a handshake.

Barney and his friends readily give money to a complete stranger in hopes of making money in return. They are given no guarantee that they would make any money. It is purely a speculative investment. Mr. Maxwell doesn't give them receipts for their money, and the boys never check into his background. For all they know he might be a swindler who is going from town to town using the same scheme.

Andy, on the other hand, does not trust the stranger at all even though he allows himself to be recorded for the record album. He is not about to part with any hard earned cash. His mistrust, however, is not based on any sound reason. He simply does not think the stranger is honest and he is quick to make his feelings known to the others.

Investments must be made carefully and intelligently. Unfortunately many people in the real world are not like the wonderful folks we meet in Mayberry. Andy is cautious and does not invest in the record business. He is critical of Barney and the boys for having placed unfounded trust in Mr. Maxwell, yet he places an unfounded mistrust in Mr. Maxwell. There needs to be a happy medium between trust and mistrust when dealing in matters that involve money. I have trusted people in my life without checking them out, and I have lost money as a result. But I have also lost out on excellent opportunities because I failed to trust people without good cause. Sometimes we need to be risk takers if we want to be successful, but the key is not to be a foolish risk taker. There is a difference. Just ask Andy; I am sure he can tell us.

"Now gentlemen, I'm going up to New York to get our album rolling, and you owe it all here to your sheriff." - Mr. Maxwell

Episode 20
"Andy Saves Barney's Morale"

"I had them Andy. I had them all dead to right. You can check the manual. Every one of them was as guilty as sin." - Barney

When Barney Fife becomes Sheriff Taylor's one and only deputy, he decides he wants to do the best job possible. Because of that desire, Barney sometimes gets over zealous in carrying out his duties. He knows the sheriff's manual inside and out, and he can name every violation by number and word. He believes in following every regulation right to the letter. He wears a complete, well groomed uniform whenever he is on duty. He keeps his gun properly maintained, and he routinely polishes his bullet. He does not tolerate jay walking, littering, or any other sort of violation. If there is a law or ordinance about something, then it is his duty to see that it is enforced.

Andy is very different from Barney. He is very laid back and informal in all of his duties as sheriff. He doesn't wear a tie or police cap. His gun is kept at the courthouse except for real emergencies. He doesn't follow all the proper procedures and regulations. He realizes that in a small community like Mayberry, he is working among his friends and relatives. He also knows that policing a small town is much different from policing a large city. While the laws on the books might be the same in both places, enforcement of those laws takes on a total different meaning in the quiet, peaceful town of Mayberry.

In his quiet common sense approach to law enforcement, Andy realizes that when you deal with people, sometimes the very laws that are meant to protect you can often get in the way of actually helping people. So Andy isn't afraid to bend the laws at times and even in some circumstances he might just plain overlook them.

During my years of teaching young children, I too learned that rules are very important. But sometimes they can be overly restrictive. You can not just see black and white while enforcing rules and handing out consequences. Every individual incident or person has to be looked at very carefully. Each person involved is unique, and the circumstances involved are unique. So one hard fast rule and one set consequence for every infraction is not always the best solution.

When Andy leaves Barney in charge of Mayberry for eight measly little hours, he is relatively sure that Barney will be able to handle the responsibility. He returns to find the streets of Mayberry quiet, and everything seems to be in order. When he opens the courthouse door, he discovers why the streets are quiet. Just about everyone in Mayberry is behind bars, including the mayor, the bank president, Aunt Bee, and even Opie. Barney does not show favoritism to anyone when he is in charge of Mayberry.

Barney informs Andy that because he was not sworn in as acting justice of the peace, he has no authority to try anyone. Andy takes on the difficult job of hearing each case. As it turns out everyone is let go, and the cells are once again empty. Barney is certain they are all guilty because he went by the book, and according to the book they had all done wrong.

It is early in Barney's police career, and Andy spends a lot of time teaching Barney. Here he tries to teach Barney that rules and regulations are put in place to help, protect, and guide people in their daily lives. They are not there just for the purpose of punishing people.

"Oh I do, but not so much for Barney Fife the man as for Barney Fife, the law and order fellow." - Barney

Episode 21
"Andy and the Gentleman Crook"

"That's my business Sheriff; making friends." - Gentleman Dan Caldwell

Scams, con artists, and identity thefts seem to be the newest things we need to be aware of in our day and age. We are warned constantly about being on the lookout for unscrupulous offers and phone calls. We read about people who have lost life savings because they trusted someone with their hard earned money. It seems as if we get unsolicited phone calls almost every night from people who want donations. Fliers are placed on our doors advertising all sorts of services. There is no end to the offers that come in the mail for money-making opportunities and great chances of winning wonderful prizes. We even have to scrutinize our emails for unlawful offers and deals.

Mayberry is not immune from these sorts of dangers. When Gentleman Dan Cadwell is brought to Mayberry as a prisoner, it doesn't take long for him to win over all the people he meets. He woos Aunt Bee with flattery. He tells her that he has never met such a charming woman before. Soon she is going through her recipe books looking for special dishes to cook for him. She puts on her best clothes so she looks nice when she takes him his meals. He wins over Opie's admiration with stories of gunfights and prison escapes. No longer is Opie satisfied to hear his "Jack tales" from Andy. They are much too dull after hearing stories about crime. Barney is engrossed with "Uncle Dan" because of his celebrity status in the criminal world. Even before his arrival, Barney makes sure his cell will be suitable for a man of his reputation. The only person not to be taken in by Gentleman Dan's charm is the ever-cautious Sheriff Taylor.

We all love to be flattered. I enjoy it when someone says something nice to me. When we are told flattering things about ourselves, our egos are tweaked and we feel good. So it isn't so unnatural for Aunt Bee and Opie to be charmed by Gentleman Dan. Aunt Bee is a middle aged single woman, and Gentleman Dan certainly is charming. Opie is just a little boy, and we all know how impressionable little boys can be. What young boy would not be captivated by the kinds of exciting stories Gentleman Dan was telling? But what about Barney? He is a trained officer of the law. He really should know better. Gentleman Dan is a professional confidence man, and it is Barney's responsibility to guard him.

When we flatter someone, or if flattery is used on us, we need to seriously consider the purpose behind the flattery. Are we using flattery as a way of conning someone into doing something we want, or are we genuine in our use of flattery? If we use it indiscriminately, it doesn't take long for others to recognize our deceit. But if we use it honestly with good intentions, others will recognize the truth and sincerity behind it.

Barney is so in awe of Dan Caldwell that he completely forgets who he is. Instead of seeing the professional criminal who uses people, Barney sees a famous man with charm treating him like a friend. This makes Barney feel important, and he loses all his sense of good judgment. Because he is taken in by Gentleman Dan, Barney places the entire Taylor family in great danger. In the future Barney will need to learn the difference between real charm and superficial charm. They certainly are different.

"Swindler, embezzler, confidence man, can be dangerous. I sure have to admit you were right about him. I sure fell for his line." - Barney

Episode 22
"Cyrano Andy"

"Thelma Lou. I like you Thelma Lou. I like you a lot. You're the cats. I've never said those three words to a girl before, Thelma Lou. But I mean it. You're the cats." - Barney

*B*arney Fife is one who is never lost for words. He usually has no difficulty telling people what he thinks. He believes he knows a lot about everything, and in most cases it is that overconfidence that gets him into trouble. He likes to give advice to others, and he enjoys telling others what they should do. However, when it comes to girls, Barney just can't find the words.

We meet Thelma Lou for the first time in "Cyrano Andy." She appears as Barney's new girlfriend. She is an attractive, sweet girl, and she likes Barney a lot. Barney is crazy about her too, but he just has a hard time telling her. He can think of a lot of other things to talk about, but he just cannot bring himself to "sweet talk" her. Girls like to be told nice things, and Barney knows what to say, but the words just won't come out.

For most of us, it is relatively easy to tell strangers or acquaintances how we feel or what we think. They won't judge us or challenge our words. We can talk about impersonal things. We can discuss sports, our families, our hobbies, or our jobs. Intimate personal feelings usually don't come up in discussions with these people. We can keep our inner most thoughts to ourselves. However, once we begin to get close to someone in a relationship, we need to become more personal. If a relationship is going to grow and blossom, one needs to share feelings, hopes, and dreams

Barney is not able to tell Thelma Lou how he feels, and she is getting tired of waiting. Hoping to help matters, Andy pays a visit to Thelma Lou and tells her how Barney really feels. Thelma Lou is delighted to hear what Andy says, but still, it is not the same as hearing them from Barney's own thin lips. Thelma Lou decides to make Barney jealous in hopes of getting him to tell her his true feelings. She calls Barney and tells him that Andy has just called on her. Little does she know the hornet's nest she has stirred up.

Ever since they were little boys, Andy and Barney have been best friends. Very few things have ever caused a rift between them. But if anything will, wouldn't you know it would have to involve girls. When Barney hears that Andy has been to see Thelma Lou, his wild imagination goes to work. He immediately assumes Andy is out to steal Thelma Lou. He doesn't accept Andy's explanation that he was only there on his behalf. Barney decides that two can play that game, so he decides if Andy can steal his girl, he can steal Andy's. After getting "the works" at Floyd's, Barney is off to Walker's Drug store to turn on the charm and steal Ellie away from Andy.

Real friendship is based on honesty and trust. Barney should realize that Andy is not trying to steal Thelma Lou. Why would he take Thelma Lou away when he has a perfectly wonderful girl in Ellie? Andy realizes Barney is not about to listen to his explanation.

When Barney makes up his mind about something it is almost impossible to get him to listen to reason. Andy and Ellie decide on a plan to get Thelma Lou and Barney back together. They manage to pull it off without either Barney or Thelma Lou realizing that they were both maneuvered right back into each other's arms.

"Ellie, it looks like we did it. Yah, Romeo and Juliet just walked off arm in arm". – Andy

Episode 23
"Andy and Opie, Housekeepers"

Taylor Home Inn Living Room

"Yah is she going to be happy when she finds out we can get along pretty good without her." - Opie

*E*veryone needs to feel needed. It is one of the basic instincts of humans. We want to be useful and we want others to need us. It gives us a sense of fulfillment and worthiness. "Andy and Opie, Housekeepers" gives us a first hand glimpse as to what it is like when one doesn't feel needed.

Aunt Bee comes to live with Andy and Opie because she is needed. They are living alone after their housekeeper Rose gets married. And now Aunt Bee has a place to live, things to do, and people to care for. Once again her life has meaning and will be fulfilling. While some people might enjoy a life of leisure, living alone somewhere, Aunt Bee does not. She is the kind of person who needs to be kept busy doing something that is rewarding and useful. She also takes a great deal of pride in her housekeeping abilities. Some people might consider housework to be menial work, and something that is done only because it must be done. But Aunt Bee enjoys keeping house, and to her, cleanliness is next to godliness.

Aunt Bee is leaving for a few days to care for an ailing cousin. She is reluctant to go because she fears the house will be in total chaos when she returns. She has to keep reminding Opie and Andy to pick things up so she can only imagine what will happen while she is gone. Andy and Opie take on all the housekeeping responsibilities, and as Aunt Bee expected, their housekeeping skills leave much to be desired. It soon becomes evident that they are not housekeepers, and the entire household becomes a shamble. Dirty dishes are everywhere, junk is strewn all over the floors, beds are unmade, and dust is found throughout the entire house.

Aunt Bee phones Andy and says that she will be coming home shortly. Andy and Opie have a decision to make. What should they do about the house? If they leave it the way it is, Aunt Bee will come home and realize that they can not get along without her. But she will also have to work very hard to get her home back in its usual spic and span order. Or, they can work hard and clean the entire house so when Aunt Bee gets home, she won't have to work. She will be able to sit down, relax, and think about how well Andy and Opie got along without her. What should they do?

They decide to do the logical thing. Clean the house. Opie and Andy get busy and go from room to room picking up junk, washing dishes, sweeping, making beds, and wiping away the dust. Before they know it the house looks as if Aunt Bee had never been gone. Then Opie's words hit Andy. What have they done? Aunt Bee will be devastated if she thinks she is not needed. Andy and Opie get back to work, and they undo all the cleaning so they can spare Aunt Bee some very hurt feelings.

Andy and Opie teach us a very important lesson about family relationships. They teach us that we need to remind those within our family that they are important to us. Every family member is important and is needed, and it is up to each of us to not only tell them but also show them. Even though Aunt Bee complains about how messy the house is when she returns, deep down within, she has to be happy knowing that her two boys just cannot get along without her.

"Why, it looks fine, just fine. It's wonderful the way you managed. Why the house looks as good, better than I could have done myself." - Aunt Bee

Episode 24
"The New Doctor"

"Tomorrow, tomorrow. Let me tell you something. One of these tomorrows is going to be too late. Barney's right. One of these days you'll call on Ellie and her husband will greet you at the door." - Aunt Bee

When we hear Aunt Bee speaking these words, she is rather upset with Andy for taking Ellie for granted. Andy has a way of just assuming he and Ellie will be going to the dances and other events in Mayberry. He doesn't need to ask her. She knows they will be going together. Then a new, single, handsome young doctor comes to Mayberry, and because of their professions, Ellie and the doctor are spending a lot of time together. Of course easy going Andy doesn't seem to mind – at least not until Barney starts putting ideas into his head.

It is very easy for all of us to take for granted the people we care about. We get used to the relationships, and we often fail to show our appreciation or voice our true feelings towards these very people. This is especially true if we are in a romantic relationship. When the relationship first begins, we are always on our best behavior, we bring little tokens of love, we use our best manners, and we make sure we always look our best. Then as time starts to pass, we may get a little careless in our appearance and behaviors. By now we feel that our relationship is secure, so we no longer need to spend so much time on the niceties that we once did.

Andy is taking Ellie for granted. He assumes that they are a couple, and that she will always be there for him. So he doesn't bother asking her to go dancing or to the movies. He simply assumes she will be going with him. However, when the new doctor starts to pay attention to Ellie, Andy and Barney begin to show their concern, and they start to watch Ellie very closely. Could Ellie really be interested in this new young doctor?

No one likes to be taken for granted. We all want to be appreciated. We want and need people to make us feel important and special. Sometimes all it takes is a little token of our love or a few kind words. Rather than speaking to Ellie about how he feels, Andy gets Barney to watch her. Barney even tries to warn the doctor about Andy's jealous nature when he goes for a physical. Andy is finally forced into action when Barney tells him that he has heard Ellie and the doctor make wedding plans, and they want Andy to perform the ceremony. Little does Barney know that they are talking about the doctor and his fiancée who will soon be coming to Mayberry.

It is only when Andy thinks he is about to lose Ellie to another that he speaks his mind. He proposes to her, and he once again takes it for granted that Ellie wants to marry him. He assumes the answer will be yes, when in reality, Ellie has no intentions of tying the knot with Andy. Sometimes we men just don't get it, do we?

We learn a very important lesson in this delightful episode about our relationships with others. Andy shows us how important it is not to take people for granted, and he helps us to understand the importance of sharing our feelings with those we care about. Both he and Barney also show us how wrong it can be to jump to premature conclusions.

"Ellie Walker we got to have us a talk and we got to have it right now too. Now I've been knowing you ever since you come to Mayberry, ain't that right?" - Andy

Episode 25
"A Plaque for Mayberry"

"How about it sheriff? My twenty four hours is up" - Otis Campbell

The people of Mayberry learn that a direct descendant of the Revolutionary War hero, Nathan Tibbs, is living right in the midst of Mayberry. Nathan Tibbs was responsible for saving the entire town of Mayberry when he set the bridge on fire at the Incident at Mayberry Bridge. The only problem is finding out who the direct descendant is. Of course Barney immediately decides he is the descendent, and he prepares his acceptance speech. However, it is soon learned that the direct descendant is none other than Mayberry's town drunk, Otis Campbell.

There is probably not a small town anywhere that cannot claim a town drunk as one of its citizens. Because the person is the "town drunk", he often brings about embarrassment and disappointment to his family and friends. Otis has the distinction of being Mayberry's "town drunk", and he often is the brunt of ridicule. The people of Mayberry are used to seeing him staggering into the courthouse. But Otis is basically a decent man. He holds down a steady job, he is always willing to help a neighbor; he sings in the choir, and he attends church whenever possible. The only reason he is locked up in jail every weekend is so he doesn't hurt himself.

Otis has a wife whose name we never learn. It is difficult for Mrs. Campbell having Otis for a husband. Otis admits that he has given her some very hard times, and when she kisses him on the head he tells Andy that the kiss is the lightest thing she has ever planted on his head. Mrs. Campbell is so proud when she finds out that Otis will be receiving the award. There have been few times when Otis has given her something to be proud of. Nothing is going to stop Otis from receiving his wonderful award.

We don't use the term "town drunk" much anymore. We have replaced it with the word alcoholic to describe the illness that so many people have in our society. The important message in this episode is to point out that even people who have serious social problems still deserve to be treated with respect and dignity. The people in Mayberry know that Otis has a problem. Many have tried to help him, but with little success. Yet they do not look down upon him and treat him as a second class citizen. At least most of the people of Mayberry do not.

Mayor Pike and Mrs. Jeffries from the Women's Historical Society both want to deny Otis the recognition that is rightfully his. The mayor orders Andy to get Otis out of town for a few days and find a replacement to accept the award. When Andy sees how important the award is to Otis and his wife, he decides to take a risk and allow Otis to attend the ceremony. Otis is late for the presentation, and when Mayor Pike asks

Andy who he got to replace Otis, Andy confesses that they are going to get the real Otis Campbell. The mayor tries to hurry up the ceremony before Otis comes staggering in, but he is too late. A crash is heard in the hallway, and when Andy investigates, he finds Mrs. Campbell and a totally sober Otis. Otis is presented the award and is asked to give a speech. Surprising everyone in attendance, Otis makes a very gracious speech and presents the award to Mayor Pike to be presented to the town of Mayberry.

"Being a descendant from a hero don't make you one. Shucks, a man can't take credit just for being born." - Otis Campbell

Episode 26
"The Inspector"

"I don't care. It's still an inspection and I think we should be ready." - Barney

*P*olka dot necktie, lace doilies, flowers in the cell, and a birthday cake with candles. These are just a few of the things that the new state inspector finds when he makes his first inspection of the Mayberry jail. Andy is expecting his old friend, Sam Allan, to do the inspection, so he is all ready to do some fishing and frog gigging. After all, when Sam comes to Mayberry, it is more like a social call rather than an inspection. Little does he know the trouble that awaits him when the unexpected inspector arrives. Andy finds out in short order that he is in no way at all like his friend Sam Allan.

Inspections are a normal part of our lives. Some time or another we all go through them. Even when we were children we had inspections. Our parents inspected our rooms to make sure they were clean. Our mothers probably inspected our ears to make sure we washed them properly. Teachers often inspected our desks and lockers to make sure they were orderly and didn't contain unnecessary treasures. Restaurants are under close scrutiny, and places of business are frequently inspected to make sure they are safe and meet all the latest codes. Even our vehicles are often inspected to make sure they are safe to be on the road.

In Mayberry, the courthouse inspections are not taken very seriously. But when Barney finds out an inspector is coming, he takes it very seriously. He tries to make everything ship shape for the inspection. He wants everything to be just right. He even goes out and gets a prisoner so the jail will be occupied. Otis gets to be Barney's prisoner. When Barney brings Otis in, Otis tells them it's his birthday. Andy decides to get a cake and have a little party when Sam Allan arrives. After all, Otis and Sam are practically buddies.

Barney also thinks Andy should be in full uniform, so he tells Opie to bring him a cap and tie. Not knowing what Barney means, Opie brings Andy a polka dotted tie and an old fishing hat. Just as Andy puts it on and models it for Barney, the new inspector arrives and all the trouble begins. By the time the inspector finishes at the courthouse and goes out on a case with Andy, it looks like Andy may not be sheriff much longer.

Inspections are an important part of maintaining order and safety. However, too often they are sometimes unrealistic, and they overlook the practical side of things. Andy runs his jail almost like a hotel because most of his prisoners are friends who fall on hard times. The inspector, on the other hand, inspects all his jails and courthouses the same. He goes by the book, and if you aren't following the guidelines, you are in trouble. Somewhere there needs to be some middle ground. The inspector is new. Hopefully his visit to Mayberry will teach him some important things about doing his job. He calls in the State Police when Andy is asked to bring in a local man who is taking pot shots at people. Andy proves he knows his job well, as he walks directly into the gunfire, knowing full well he is in no real danger. Andy knows the people of Mayberry better than anyone else, so who better is there to be sheriff other than Andy Taylor? He may not always go by the book, but he gets results and respect just the same.

"But I like you. You're both my good friends and I'm glad to be with you. Today is my birthday." - Otis Campbell

Episode 27
"Ellie Saves a Female"

"Now Ellie you ain't been living here very long and we just don't go messing around in other folks' stew unless we're asked." - Andy

We don't know where Ellie Walker came from when she moved to Mayberry, but there are often little hints in her words and behaviors that might indicate she came from a fairly large town. She sometimes has a difficult time understanding the ways of small town life in Mayberry. Ellie is a very attractive girl. She enjoys dances and movies and being in the company of young men like Andy. She most likely grew up having many friends. She enjoyed the normal activities of a teenager. She went on dates, had sleep overs with her friends, and enjoyed getting dressed up with fancy clothes and make up. It would be difficult for her to understand how life could be any different for other girls.

Frankie Flint comes into the drug store one day to buy some chewing tobacco for her father. She is the only child of Old Man Flint, a hard working farmer near Mayberry. Frankie is the complete antithesis of Ellie. She wears bib overalls, no makeup, and her hands are rough from farm work. When Ellie sees Frankie looking at the make up and perfume, her heart goes out for this poor girl who looks and dresses so differently.

When Ellie decides to help Frankie Flint by giving her all kinds of female doodads, Andy steps in and warns her about interfering in other people's lives when one is not asked. Andy explains that Flint does not want Frankie to have such things, and he tells her not to get involved. But Ellie enlists the help of Barney, and between the two of them they bring Frankie back to Mayberry and transform her from Frankie the farmer into Francis the beautiful young girl.

One very basic rule in life is that each parent has the right to raise children as they best see fit. When people interfere in how people raise their children quite often hurt feelings and broken friendships can be the result. Old Flint needs his daughter to work on the farm because he has no sons. As a result, Frankie has never experienced many of the fun things like most young single girls. She cannot wear makeup, she does not wear feminine clothes, and she most likely has never been on a date or gone to a dance.

While Ellie's intentions are of the best and the results of her interfering turn out good for everyone, we need to be very careful when we interfere in another person's life. Giving advice and offering criticism when we are not asked can bring unexpected trouble. On the other hand we should not pass up opportunities to help others when we see situations where help is needed. The difficulty is in knowing when to interfere and when not to.

Flint thinks he is doing the right thing with Frankie. The farm is all they have, and it takes both of them to make it profitable. Given a choice, under different circumstances, he probably would have encouraged Frankie to dress up nice and make herself pretty. I am sure it must have bothered him a lot knowing that Frankie could not have the kind of life other young women had. Frankie does not challenge her father's beliefs either. She sacrifices her own happiness in order to help her father maintain his life on the farm which is very important to him.

"Andy, Barney, are you ready for the unveiling?" - Ellie Walker

Episode 28
"Andy Forecloses"

"According to this mortgage contract, if Scoby misses a payment, the entire balance falls due." - Ben Weaver

*B*en Weaver holds the mortgage on the Lester Scoby house. But the Scobys have fallen on hard times and are unable to make their monthly payment. Old miserly Ben demands that Andy serve the foreclosure notice on the Scobys. Andy is a friend of the Scoby family, so he pays them a visit to hear Lester's side of the story. Lester tells Andy that he cannot come up with the monthly mortgage payment of $52.50. Andy and Barney take it upon themselves to make the payment for the Scobys, but Ben will not accept it. Because of the mortgage contract language, he demands that the entire mortgage balance of $780 be paid immediately or else the Scoby family must go.

Losing one's home has to be one of the most difficult and painful experiences in life. Yet many people do lose their homes due to difficult times or just plain overextending their monetary resources. We live in times when people are encouraged to spend money. We are given countless opportunities to get credit cards, and banks will quite often loan money for people to buy homes they simply cannot afford. Bankruptcies are at an all time high in our country, and many families just have no place to go.

This is not the case with the Scobys. Their home is not a fancy expensive home. They are not overextended with credit card debts, and they do not spend money on unnecessary things. Lester has lost his job through no fault of his own, and because of this, he just can not make the payment. His wife is taking in ironing, and Lester is doing odd jobs, but it just is not enough. It is hard to believe that Ben is so heartless that he cannot give the Scobys a little more time to raise the money. And why is he so insistent that the entire mortgage be paid at once? Ben knows it is impossible for the Scobys to raise that kind of money.

One of the advantages of living in a small town is that when a member of the community faces hardships, quite often the entire town becomes involved with fundraising activities in order to help the person in need. Rummage sales, pancake breakfasts, raffles, and car washes are often held to help raise money for the needy.

In this heartwarming episode, we experience first hand what happens when friends and neighbors come to the aid of one of their own who is in trouble. Barney gets the ball rolling when he hands over all his extra money to Andy and announces that he is going to start a "Save the Scoby Campaign". Andy thinks it is an outstanding idea, and soon he has Aunt Bee and the entire town working to raise the money for the Scoby family. When Andy realizes that all their efforts are not going to be enough, due to Ben's unreasonable demands, he decides to try a different tactic.

Telling Ben he understands his position, Andy and Ben go to the Scobys, where Andy tells the distraught family that they need to vacate the premises immediately. He begins to order them around, and he even insinuates that the Scobys will steal some of the fixtures that rightfully belong to Ben. Ben is beginning to see how unfair his actions are, and when Mrs. Scoby breaks down in tears, Ben brings the proceedings to an abrupt halt. Not knowing what has gotten into Andy, the Scobys realize that he was showing Ben just how mean and unfair he really is.

"If you gotta know, I can't spare him, he's too busy down at the store." - Ben Weaver

Episode 29
"Quiet Sam"

"The busiest man in the world has five minutes to pass the time of day." - Barney

Sam Becker is the quietest man in Mayberry. At least it seems that way to Barney. Sam comes to town and does his marketing, but doesn't take time to stop and visit with folks. Barney becomes suspicious of Sam and decides that he is some kind of sinister character who is hiding something from the law. He cases Ellie Walker's sales slips at the drug store and discovers that Sam Becker has bought large amounts of absorbent cotton, antiseptics, vitamins, tranquilizers, and swab sticks. Barney's conclusion is that Sam is hiding a man with a bullet in him.

Isn't it strange how we often become curious or suspicious of people who are unusually quiet? We might think the person is very unfriendly, or that they might even be trying to hide something. Why can't a person just be himself, and if one chooses to live his life quietly and out of the limelight, why can't we let him do it?

Sam Becker has his reasons for not talking to people when he comes to town. There is nothing sinister about it. He is in a hurry to get home. It isn't because he is unfriendly or that he is secretive. He is needed at home for a very important reason. His wife is about to give birth, and he wants to be there when he is needed. He is stocking up on medical supplies for when the time comes. It is not uncommon for rural people in and around Mayberry to choose to give birth to their children in their homes.

Jumping to conclusions about other people often creates many problems. We have seen how it can lead to untrue gossip being spread throughout a community. It can cause people to avoid or shun a person simply because the person is different. Barney has a rather wild imagination to begin with. Add to that a quiet man who purchases medical supplies, and then quickly leaves town, and it has all the makings for a wild adventure in Mayberry.

Barney persuades Andy to take a drive out to the Becker farm on a stormy night. As they watch Sam disking his field after dark, the lights in the house begin to flash off and on, and then Sam jumps off the tractor and runs into the house. This strange behavior adds fuel to Barney's imagination, and he is more convinced than ever that Sam Becker is up to no good. The only problem is he cannot convince Andy.

I know quite a few quiet people. Most are ordinary hard working people who just prefer to be good listeners rather than talkers. There is nothing strange or unfriendly about them. They are not hiding anything or planning any sinister deeds. Quietness is just part of their nature and they are happy with the way they are.

Barney's anxieties with Sam Becker come to a climax when he receives a call at the courthouse. The storm is raging, and it is difficult to hear on the phone. Andy tells Barney that he is at the Becker farm and there is some trouble. Then the phone line goes dead, and Barney's imagination once again jumps into full speed. He is convinced Andy has been overpowered, and he is in great danger. He organizes a citizen's posse and heads to the Becker farm. Upon arriving, he discovers the truth behind Sam's quiet ways. He also discovers something else. Andy is about to deliver the soon to be born baby, and it is something he has never done before.

"Gun, I haven't got a gun. Melba's got a pretty heavy walking stick. She uses it to prop open the cellar door when she brings up the preserves." - Floyd Lawson

Episode 30
"Barney Gets His Man"

"I'll get you for this deputy." - Eddie Brooks

*B*arney unexpectedly captures an escaped convict on Mayberry's Main Street while giving him a ticket for littering.   Actually Barney's feet become entangled with the escapee's, and they both fall to the ground where the entanglement continues until two state policeman capture Eddie Brook.   Several people witness Barney's encounter with Brooks, and they begin to tell what happened.   Like any important event that is witnessed by more than one person, the various accounts of Brooks' capture vary greatly.   But one thing everyone agrees on; Barney is a hero, and he did a very brave thing when he captured Brooks.   Hearing all the accounts, Barney suddenly believes all the accounts himself.   Just as the police are about to take Brooks away, he snarls at Barney and lets him know that he will get even with him.

Living in fear is not a pleasant experience.   Of course we all have fears.   My particular fear is that of heights.   Others may fear storms or dogs or speaking in public.   But we can often deal with these fears by avoiding situations that bring us face to face with them.   However, eventually a time will come when we will have to face our fears, and we will be unable to walk away from them.   Having the fear that someone is out to physically harm us would have to be particularly difficult fear to deal with; as Barney well knows.

Barney soon faces the reality of Eddie Brooks' threat when Brooks escapes once again.   Barney remembers those words, "I'll get you for this deputy," and now he has to face the fact that Brooks just might come looking for him.   And to make matters worse, only Barney knows the true circumstances of his capture of Brooks.   He knows that he is not the brave hero that everyone makes him out to be.   He knows it was just plain luck that enabled him to capture Brooks.   So what does he do now, knowing what he knows?

Barney has to make a difficult decision.   He must decide whether or not to run away from his fear or face it head on.   Living in fear of something is a terrible way to live.   It can eat away at one's self respect a little bit at a time. Add to that the shame that is felt by being afraid, and the feeling of guilt and inadequacy is compounded.

When dealing with frightening situations, sometimes we have no choice but to face them. To avoid them or to run away from them only postpones that moment when we will have to face them again. Andy senses the fear that his best friend Barney has. He helps Barney to face that fear, and together they are able to recapture Eddie Brooks. Andy knows that without his help Barney would never have faced up to the danger. But being the friend that he is, he keeps that knowledge to himself for the sake of his friend.

All of us are living in fearful times. The threat of terrorism is all around us every minute of the day. Experts predict terrorists will strike again, and that it is just a matter of time. But we continue to live our normal lives despite the fears we have. Once we succumb to our fears, we have lost. Barney will never be the brave policeman that he wants to be. He will always be afraid. But Andy helped put his fear of Brooks behind him this time. Once one fear is overcome and defeated, it makes facing the next one just a bit easier. Perhaps that is why Andy keeps Barney as his deputy. He knows that Barney needs his presence as a friend and as a mentor to help him win the battles against his fears.

"Oh that's all right Andy. Did you see the look on Brook's face when those two troopers took him away the second time?" - Barney

Episode 31
"The Guitar Player Returns"

"You make it, you spend it." - Jim Lindsey

*J*im Lindsey returns to Mayberry after having spent time playing his guitar with Bobby Fleet's band. Jim left Mayberry with barely a penny to his name, but he returns to Mayberry driving a flashy sports car. He is wearing the latest threads and an expensive watch. He is the owner of numerous expensive guitars. It is obvious that Jim has made it to the top. Yet, as time passes on his visit, people are beginning to wonder about Jim. He is not paying for anything. He is charging his stay at the hotel, he doesn't pay Floyd for his haircut, and he charges things at the drugstore. He seems to have changed. If he is the big star that he claims to be, where is his money? When the bank reposes his car, Jim says that he had to send it to a special garage to have it serviced.

Returning to a hometown is not always an easy thing to do. You want people to believe you are a success, and that you have made something of your life. I know I have experienced this when I see old friends back in my hometown. It seems like everyone is talking about their work and their successes and all the great things that have happened in their lives. No one talks about their failures and disappointments. It is rather like people who go to casinos and gamble. They only tell you about their winnings. They never mention the losses. Of course I do the same thing. It is only natural. No one wants to admit that one's dreams have not come to fruition.

Jim Lindsey is no different. Even though he returns to Mayberry in debt and no longer a part of Bobby Fleet's band, he leads his friends in Mayberry to believe that he is a big success and has money to burn. It is only when he fails to pay his bills in Mayberry that Andy and the rest of Jim's former friends learn the truth about Jim's life.

Isn't it sad that we are quite often the most dishonest with those who care about us the most? Why does it have to be so difficult for us to admit failure? If people are truly our friends, they will accept us for what we are. True friends will stand by us and support us as we go through the trials of life, just as they do when we go through the good times.

Jim cannot bring himself to tell his friends the truth. He does not want them to know that he left Bobby Fleet because he believes he is the main attraction for the band. Jim's success went to his head in a hurry. He went from being a nobody to being a somebody so fast that he could not handle the change. From having no money to spend to having lots of money to spend, Jim again could not handle the change, and before he knows it he is out of a job and deeply in debt.

There are people in the world like Jim. We read about them all the time. Young super athletes are given multimillion-dollar contracts before they play one professional game. A young singer or actor becomes a celebrity over night after having a successful music or movie, and before they know it, the money is rolling in, and they have money to burn.

Jim Lindsey was fortunate to have a friend like Andy. Andy reminds him that his friends treated him good before he became a star, and they will treat him the same no matter what the circumstances. Once Jim realizes Bobby will take him back, his humility returns, and he is given a second chance to fulfill his dream.

"Say, why don't I join in on the next number, huh? What'll it be? I'm Just a Vagabond Lover, Roll out the Barrel, Tiptoe Through the Tulips?" - Barney

Episode 32
"Bringing up Opie"

"Young man, what kind of language is that? – Aunt Bee

One of the great things I loved about growing up in a small town back in the 1950's was the freedom and safety that I felt when I roamed around town and discovered all the interesting places there were to be found. I often found myself playing among the giant rocks at our local stone quarry. Going to the town dump on Saturday morning always meant bringing home a wagon full of treasures. And the fun I had after dark playing all sorts of games with my friends is a special memory that I shall keep forever.

The children in Mayberry had the freedom to run and play almost anywhere they desired. We often see Opie or Leon walking the streets of Mayberry wearing their cowboy outfits. They have nothing to fear. Mayberry is a safe place where everyone knows one another. There are no child predators lurking behind closed doors. Amber alerts and safe houses do not exist. Childhood is the way it is meant to be – fun, safe, and exciting. But that doesn't mean Opie can't get himself in some serious trouble from time to time. After all, he is a small boy, and small boys have a way of finding trouble.

As a child I didn't have a father around to spend time with like most of my friends did. Most of my free time was spent with friends my own age. I had two older brothers, but they had their own friends, so

I was left on my own to make my own fun. I had many friends who enjoyed doing the same things I did, so I was never bored. Like Opie, I spent many hours wandering around town with my friends.

Opie is a lucky boy, despite not having a mother; he is able to spend many hours with his father. They go fishing together, and they sit on the front porch and just talk. But the one thing that Opie enjoys the most is spending time with Andy at the courthouse.

In "Bringing up Opie," Aunt Bee decides that the jail is not a proper environment for Opie. When he is there, he hears stories about criminals, practices drawing his gun, and sees Otis stagger into his cell with a snootful. Aunt Bee convinces Andy that he should bar Opie from the jail. Without being able to visit his paw at the courthouse, Opie soon becomes bored. He gets in trouble when he goes off on his own and explores an old mine that almost caves in. He eventually ends up taking a ride in the back of a truck, and he winds up miles from Mayberry.

Raising a young child is a very difficult challenge. There are all kinds of temptations and dangers that a child can encounter. Children cannot be watched twenty four hours a day. Yet unsupervised time can be an especially dangerous time for a vulnerable child. Aunt Bee came to realize that even though the time Opie spent at the courthouse may not be the most desirable environment for him, it was where he should be. She understands that Opie needs to spend time with his father.

Many people today say it isn't the amount of time a father spends with a child that is important, but it is the quality of the time that matters. I don't think I totally agree with this concept. Somehow I think sitting on a porch with one's father, or sitting along a shoreline holding a fishing pole are more important. Better yet, I don't think anything could be better for a child than having breakfast and dinner with a father every day.

"You know, I think I know why he got in trouble today. He hasn't been seeing enough of his paw." - Aunt Bee

Season Number Two

Episode 33
"Opie and the Bully"

"It was as plain as the nose on your face. It couldn't been nothing else. It's just plain extortion is what it is." - Barney

Season two begins with a beautifully told story of how a father must at times allow his son to experience painful lessons in life in order to grow up to be an independent and self confident man. Parents cannot and should not fight all their children's battles. Childhood is a time for learning many things. Many lessons are wonderful, exciting, and beautiful. But some lessons of childhood are painful and ugly. But life is full of both beautiful things and ugly things, and it is vital that children learn to deal with both.

One morning just as he is leaving for school, Opie asks Aunt Bee for a nickel for his milk money. He then goes into the living room and asks Andy if he can have a nickel for milk. While talking with Aunt Bee, Andy learns that Opie has asked for milk money twice; something he has never done before. Later at the office, Andy tells Barney about the nickel issue. Barney tries to explain why Opie may want two nickels, but then tells Andy that Opie also asked him if he had a nickel he wasn't using.

Opie is being threatened by a bully every morning as he walks to school. If he doesn't hand over his milk money each day, Sheldon threatens to beat Opie up. To make matters worse, if Opie tells anyone, Sheldon will pulverize and stomp on him. So Opie gives Sheldon his nickel each morning, and he goes on to school feeling lower than low and mighty ashamed. But what can Opie do? Sheldon is a bigger and tougher boy.

Barney follows Opie to school one morning and discovers the truth behind Opie's asking everyone for money. He shares his discovery with Andy, which puts Andy in a very precarious position. Should he

55

go to Sheldon's parents and tell them about the extortion, or should he let Opie take care of his own problem?

Parents are often faced with the same decision as Andy. A child has gotten into trouble. It may be at school or it may be a fight with a friend while playing. However, a parent cannot always run to a child's aid. There comes a time when every child must learn to stand on his own two feet. A parent cannot always step in and make things okay. But bullying should never be taken lightly. It is a very serious problem for kids.

Andy does a very difficult thing when he allows Opie to face Sheldon. He knows that Opie will most likely get hurt. What parent wants to see a child get hurt? But Andy also knows that there is a much more important lesson for Opie to learn. Opie is feeling ashamed of himself because he will not stand up to Sheldon. After all, Opie has a right to walk to school without fear of being bullied. If Andy steps in and takes care of Sheldon, what will happen the next time Opie is faced with a bully? He will meet many Sheldons in his life and he won't be able to run away from them all.

It is important for children to learn that fighting seldom is the answer to problems. Violence normally leads to more violence and can escalate things. But children also need to learn that there are times when one must stand up for what is right, and sometimes it might mean defending yourself. It is one of the sad realities of life.

"Do you want to know something Paw? A sandwich sure tastes better with milk." - Opie

Episode 34
"Barney's Replacement"

"Well now I've heard everything. So that's all I am, just a figure on a chart. You completely ignore the fact that I'm a human being." - Barney

*H*ave you ever been at your job and then one day you discover that you are about to be replaced? It is not a very good feeling, yet it is a reality in the workplace, and it happens to thousands of people every year. It is one thing to be replaced because it is one's choice, but it is an entirely different matter when it is not a choice. We all like to think we are irreplaceable when it comes to our job. We are hired because we are good at what we do, so therefore we are kept at our job because no one of our quality can be found to replace us. At least that is what we like to think.

I have been very fortunate in my life to have never been fired or laid off from a job. I like to think it is because I am a hard worker and I am good at what I do. But I have resigned from several positions over the years. I recall being at my farewell parties where speeches were made about my work. I was told it was going to be impossible to replace me. No one would be able to come in and fill my shoes. Yet within a few weeks, after screening hundreds of applicants, I found out my replacement was already hired. It certainly seemed quick considering I was going to be "impossible to replace".

One day, without any advanced notice, Bob Rogers appears at the courthouse and informs Andy and Barney that he has been assigned to be a new deputy in Mayberry. He proves to be a highly efficient eager person. Barney has the idea that Andy is grooming Bob to replace him, and he thinks that Andy cannot find the words to fire him. Barney decides to make it easy for Andy by leaving the force. He takes a job selling vacuum cleaners door to door. The selling business does not go well at all for Barney, but his pride will not let him admit this to Andy. He convinces Andy that he is making more money than he ever could as a deputy. But when Andy looks as his sales book, he discovers Barney has made no sales at all. Naturally, being Barney's best friend, Andy must find a way to persuade Barney to come back to work as a deputy.

Losing one's job can create some very destructive feelings within a person. It can bring about feelings of inadequacy and worthlessness. Too often our work often defines who we are. Barney loves being a lawman, yet he is also Andy's best friend. He believes Andy does not know how to fire him, so he resigns in order to save Andy from being the bad guy. Little does Barney know that Andy never has any intention of replacing him with Bob Rogers. Despite all his bumbling and mistakes, Andy understands that no one can ever really replace Barney Fife.

Andy knows Barney well enough to realize that all the talking in the world will not get Barney to change his mind. Barney is very proud. So the only other option Andy has is to come up with a way to get

Barney to come back on his own. When Bob Rogers tells Andy that Barney is selling his vacuum cleaners without a permit, he orders Bob to arrest Barney and bring him in. This is all it takes to get Barney back to work. When he finds out he is just another statistic to Bob, Barney decides to fight for his job. In the end, it is Bob Rogers who learns a lesson from Barney Fife about how a police officer should do his job. People are not statistics, and they are not to be treated as such.

"And you'd better gird your loins buster. You've got a fight on your hands." - Barney

Episode 35
"Andy and the Woman Speeder"

A Gathering of Mayberry Squad Cars

"I guess it's a case of too much bullheadedness." - Elizabeth Crowley

Small towns are often accused of having "speed traps" which target out of state drivers. When Elizabeth Crowley speeds past Andy, Barney, Floyd, and Opie when they are out fishing, this is exactly what happens. She is brought before Justice Taylor for sentencing. Andy sets a rather nominal fine; and although she is guilty, Miss Crowley cannot let matters rest; she accuses Andy of running up her fine. Andy has finally heard enough, and he fines her for insulting the dignity of his robes, so she decides to spend the night in jail while awaiting Mayor's Court the following day.

When a person is cited for a traffic violation, the normal procedure is to just pay the fine. If a person believes he has been wrongly cited, there is always the option of going to court. This is an important right that we all have as citizens. Miss Crowley decides to dispute the charges and fine, so rather than paying the fine, she chooses to spend the night in the Mayberry jail. This presents a problem for Andy because they are not exactly equipped to handle female prisoners. Andy sends Barney out to buy some pink towels, and Aunt Bee takes on the responsibility of being a matron. When Miss Crowley tells Andy he is being very kind by having Aunt Bee help, he reminds her that the law requires a matron for female prisoners. She is not getting any preferential treatment.

How one conducts oneself when challenging a citation can vary greatly. Miss Crowley decides to use unscrupulous methods to avoid paying a fine that she rightly deserves. There is no doubt of her guilt. Andy has three witnesses other than himself. Barney, Floyd, and Opie were all in the car as they gave chase to Miss Crowley. But she is determined to have the charges dropped. She flatters Floyd, butters up Barney, and gains Opie's affections by giving him a new baseball. As a result of her methods, no one will testify against her and the charges against her are dropped.

Andy is very disappointed in the outcome. He is certain Barney will testify against Miss Crowley. He is a trained police officer and he should never allow flattery and flirtations to cloud his judgment. Floyd is an honest businessman and a friend of Andy's, so he certainly thinks he can count on him to give an accurate testimony. Although he is disappointed in Opie, he understands how a little boy can be swayed by a new baseball.

Hopefully most people have a conscience, and their conscience will guide them to doing the right thing. Fighting for what is right is important. But winning a fight through the use of dishonest or unethical practices is never right. Fortunately Miss Crowley comes to regret her methods, and she devises a plan where she can pay her original fine. She not only restores Andy's faith in her, she also restores Andy's faith in the justice system.

Knowing what the right thing to do is one thing, but doing the right thing is quite another matter. Thankfully the good folks of Mayberry seem to always come through for us by both knowing what the right thing is and doing the right thing. Of course Barney may not learn it as fast as others. But that is what makes Barney the great character he is.

> *"That's a fine day's work. You outsmarted justice and you made a mockery of this court. And you turned three people against me that I would'a sworn would never leave my side." -*
> *Andy*

Episode 36
"Mayberry Goes Bankrupt"

"Oh he's going to have to be evicted. Why fight it Andy? You're just wasting your sympathy." - Mayor Pike

*M*ayberry Goes Bankrupt" is the second episode where Sheriff Taylor is ordered to serve an eviction notice. The first occasion for the eviction was because the Scobys could not pay their mortgage payment to Ben Weaver. In this second episode, Frank Myers owes the town of Mayberry a considerable sum in back taxes.

Frank Myers is a kind, gentle, likable, elderly man who has a run down house just on the edge of Mayberry. It is the first place seen when entering town. His home is an embarrassment to the city fathers, and they have decided it is time for Frank to be evicted. If they can get rid of Frank, they can then get rid of that eye sore of a house.

Taxes are an evil necessity of life. In many states they are the primary source of income for public schools. Taxes help pay for parks, police, fire departments, and many other public services. Everyone benefits from the service provided by our various taxes. Frank Myers has not paid his taxes for quite some time because his business is not doing very well. He is self employed; he makes dried berries for ladies' hats. Poor Frank does not realize there isn't much demand for his berries, but he hopes styles will change. If berries were to come back, he will have it made. But until then, he is going to have to leave his home and find somewhere else to live.

Like the Lester Scoby family, Frank is about to lose his home. Unlike the Scobys, easy going Frank takes it in stride. He doesn't have a wife and child to worry about, like Lester did. Fortunately for Frank, Opie gives Andy and Aunt Bee the idea that Frank should come live with them. Opie figures as long as it is his father who tells Frank he has to move out, his father should be the one to give him a place to live. Sometimes a child's simplistic way of looking at things far surpasses that of an adult.

When Frank Myers owes the town of Mayberry back taxes, no one has any sympathy. But suddenly Frank Myers becomes a wealthy man, and Mayor Pike and everyone else starts to see things differently. While looking through Frank's strong box, Andy and Frank find an old $100 bond that was issued to Frank's great granddaddy back in 1861. When Andy has the bank compute its value, they discover the town of Mayberry owes Frank Myers $349,119.27. Naturally Mayberry is not able to pay Frank, so Andy is delegated to tell Frank the bad news. So will this still mean that Frank still has to move?

Mayor Pike and the councilmen decide to fix up Frank's house as payment for what they owe him. They all work together, and Frank's house is transformed into a beautiful little house. Everyone is feeling wonderful because of the fine thing they did. The town of Mayberry is free from its debt, and Frank has a house of which he can be proud.

Unfortunately for Frank, it is discovered the bond has no value at all because it was issued when Mayberry was part of the Confederacy. So everything is back to square one, and once again Frank is asked to leave his home. Andy reminds everyone that they have done a good thing for a neighbor. He convinces the bank to give Frank a loan to pay his taxes, and Frank Myers gets to stay in his lovely home.

"Not more than five minutes ago you was all willing to help out a neighbor, now you're turning on him like a pack of wolves." - Andy

Episode 37
"Barney on the Rebound"

"Andy, you're kind of cute in your old fashioned ways, you know that?" - Barney

*A*nyone who knows Barney Fife quite well knows that he is seldom really true to Thelma Lou. He often dates Juanita from the diner, and it is well known that he also has stepped out with other Mayberry girls. But Thelma Lou seems to always forgive and forget when it comes to Barney's shenanigans. However, when beautiful young Melissa Stevens moves to Mayberry with her father, George, Barney goes a bit overboard welcoming her to town. He gives her a police escort with siren blasting all the way to the post office, which happens to be just across the street. Being a police officer, he feels it is his duty to escort her inside to show her all the difficult things there are to find; like the stamp machine, the parcel post window, and the outgoing airmail slot. He learns that her daddy owned a cotton gin and also had some shipping interests. Melissa and George are going to live at the Pearson Place on old Post Road. Barney makes the big mistake of telling all this to Thelma Lou and then accuses her of suffering from jealousy.

Most young single men get "smitten" over a pretty young girl at one time or another. I know I have. I recall several times when a pretty young girl may have innocently given me a little attention. That was all it took for me to overreact to that attention. Looking back, I now realize I must have looked very foolish pursuing someone who really had no interest in me at all. She was just being kind and maybe even feeling a bit sorry for me. But unlike Barney I did not already have a steady girl, so the only person who was going to get hurt was me.

Thelma Lou is a lovely girl who really cares for Barney. But Barney takes Thelma Lou for granted. This gets him into hot water quite often with her. Barney likes to think of himself as a ladies' man to begin with, so whenever a young girl gives him attention, he immediately thinks she is in love with him. This is rather an immature way for a thirty something man to behave, but Barney does it anyway. Melissa bats her eyes and uses her cute little southern drawl when asking Barney for directions, and he immediately starts acting like a silly little school boy with puppy love.

Developing and maintaining a lasting relationship is not an easy thing to do in our society. We live in a culture where "open relationships" seem to be the norm rather than the exception. Commitments are also seen less frequently. Many people today stay with a relationship only until they get bored or until someone better comes along.

Thelma Lou is always willing to forgive Barney. She loves Barney so much that she overlooks his roaming eyes. Barney just seems never to learn from his mistakes. This time he really gets himself in a bind when he somehow and unknowingly proposes to Melissa while sitting with her in the dimly lit parlor. George is all for the marriage and it looks as if there may be a wedding in Barney's future. Of course Barney has no intention to get married, so he goes to Melissa and quickly ends the relationship. When George threatens Barney with a breach of promise suit, Andy cleverly exposes Melissa and George for what they really are – man and wife. Barney is very grateful to Andy for saving him, but only until Andy tells him what made him decide it was a put up job.

"But that really wasn't the thing that clinched it. Well, I just got to studying. Why would a girl who looked as pretty and flashy and big city as she did, why would a girl like that want to get involved with a squirt." - Andy

Episode 38
"Opie's Hobo Friend"

"The most perfect day to start any job – tomorrow. The most marvelous day ever invented. There is absolutely nothing a man can't do, tomorrow." - Mr. Dave

*O*ne day while fishing, Andy and Opie meet an interesting stranger. He is a friendly, easygoing soul, and Opie immediately takes a liking to him. He can talk fish talk, he makes money disappear behind your ears, he can make a gollywobbler, and he can get free gum from a gumball machine. Then Barney brings him into the courthouse that same afternoon on a charge of vagrancy. Andy lets him go with a friendly reminder that the Mayberry police are always on duty. Later when Barney brings him in again for loitering,

Andy decides he will give the man a job at his house trimming his hedges.

Raising a child is not an easy task – especially for a single parent such as Andy. Opie is very impressionable, and when he sees Mr. Dave get free gumballs by using magic talk, he is very much in awe. Mr. Dave also tells him that tomorrow is the best time to do anything. He shares lunch with Mr. Dave, who somehow magically manages to get a whole chicken and an apple pie without money.

Many kids are like Opie. They are impressionable and are very easily swayed by others. This can be especially true if they are with an older person who seems to be able to do anything he wants, and get anything he needs without much work or effort.

Parents need to protect their children from all sorts of things. Strangers today are much different from the strangers who come to Mayberry. Most of the strangers who frequent Mayberry are harmless people who just happen to be passing through town.

Children are trusting, so we need to teach them to be cautious of strangers and other adults without instilling in them a fear of everyone they meet. Opie often takes little gifts from people he does not know, and Andy seldom disapproves. But in the real world of today, this kind of behavior should never be taken lightly.

Andy decides to end the friendship between Opie and Mr. Dave. Opie is picking up some bad habits from Mr. Dave. Andy realizes something must be done when Barney catches Opie sneaking into the courthouse back door in search of a fishing pole. Opie is playing hooky from school; something he has never done before. It doesn't take Andy long to figure out where he got that idea. It is not going to be easy dealing with Mr. Dave, because Opie idolizes him. Fortunately for Andy, Mr. Dave takes it upon himself to find a way to sever the friendship without making Andy take the blame.

Mr. Dave is not a bad person. He simply chooses to live a different style of life than most people would choose. He prefers to live by his wits. He is not above bending the law if it means getting a meal or having a place to live. Mr. Dave comes to realize that he needs to change Opie's opinion of him, so he steals Aunt Bee's handbag. Opie is in the courthouse when Barney brings Mr. Dave in, and he learns that he stole from Aunt Bee. Opie returns his gollywobbler and leaves the courthouse a very dejected little boy. The one thing he does not know, however, is that the stolen purse is one that Aunt Bee has thrown in the trash. There is no law in Mayberry against trash collecting, so Andy releases Mr. Dave. He leaves Mayberry never to return, and Andy's problem is solved.

"There seems to be something wrong with his thinking. He's gotten a little twisted on things lately; like being able to tell the difference between right and wrong." - Andy

Episode 39
"Crime Free Mayberry"

"I guess to sum it up I guess you could say there are three reasons there's so little crime in Mayberry. There's Andy and there's me, and baby makes three." - Barney

One of the benefits of living in a small rural community is that there usually isn't much crime. This is especially true in Mayberry, and as a result Mayberry is being honored for having the lowest crime rate in the entire country for a town of its size. The entire town is excited, and Mayor Pike decides that both Andy and Barney will be presented medals. Andy is totally against the idea, but humble Barney looks forward to receiving his medal. He doesn't want anything gaudy though; just plain simple solid gold. He definitely does not want diamonds, but something containing his birth stone, rubies, will be fine.

The town of Mayberry even organizes a new association; The Greater Mayberry Historical and Tourist Bureau, LTD. Plans are in the making for souvenir booklets featuring the life stories of Andy and Barney, complete with pictures. Floyd is giving tours of the courthouse to people on the bus, and he only charges two bits apiece. A representative from the F.B.I. has arrived, as well as a reporter from *Intercontinental News*. A big celebration will be in the town hall, and everyone will be there. There is just one slight problem. The entire event is one big scam. The F.B.I. agent and reporter are really thieves who plan to open the bank vault during the award ceremony.

Just who should get the credit when a community is a safe crime free place to live? Should the credit go to the police who enforce the laws, or should it go to the people who obey the laws? Andy believes the credit lies with the law abiding citizens of Mayberry, while humble Barney believes the credit show go to him and Andy. After all, Andy has just as much to do with it as he does. In reality, it is a combination of both efforts.

In order for a community to be safe and relatively crime free there needs to be direct cooperation between the police and the citizens. They need to work together in harmony to not only solve crimes, but more importantly to prevent crimes. The people of Mayberry respect Andy, and in return Andy respects the people of Mayberry. Add to this the fact that the citizens of Mayberry respect one another, and you have all the ingredients to make Mayberry a crime free place to live.

Barney is so wrapped up in all the excitement, he doesn't suspect a thing. He is thinking about his medal and picture that will be in the paper. Andy, on the other hand, is leery of the entire proceeding. He just wants to do his job and doesn't believe there is any need for all the attention. He becomes suspicious of the two men when the F.B.I. special agent allows his picture to be taken with him. Andy knows they do not allow themselves to be photographed for publicity.

Publicity and special attention can often cause a person to lose sight of good judgment. Barney was so engrossed with all the attention he was receiving; he completely forgot his duties as a police officer. We see quite clearly in this episode the two different personalities of Andy and Barney. While Barney enjoys being in the limelight and loves recognition, Andy prefers to take a back seat without any recognition at all.

"In these cells ladies and gentlemen we keep our most incorrigible criminals. They were captured only last night after one of the most brilliant pieces of detective work in the history of crime detecting." - Barney

Episode 40
"The Perfect Female"

"Ma'am, I don't know if you realize it or not but you have hooked a mighty big fish." - Barney

When it comes to Andy being single, Barney usually has a one track mind. Andy needs to get married. Barney is always asking him when he is going to get married, and he often attempts to find him a prospective wife. When Thelma Lou's pretty cousin, Karen, comes for a visit, Barney once again cannot resist being the matchmaker. He convinces Thelma Lou that they should get her a date with Andy. But Andy has been burned one time too often by Barney's blind dates, so Barney and Thelma Lou concoct a plan to get the two of them together.

Barney knows Andy will not agree to go on a blind date, so he decides he will get Andy over to the coffee shop at exactly the same time Thelma Lou brings Karen. They will act as if it is a coincidence that they meet. But Barney is not very adept at being subtle, so when Andy baulks at the idea of going for coffee, Barney comes right out and tells him about Karen and Thelma Lou. Taking Barney completely by surprise, Andy agrees to go to the coffee shop to meet Karen. Good old Barney is really excited now.

Blind dates can be very interesting. I went on a few of them in my younger day. I sometimes wonder who was more disappointed – me or my dates. Blind dates can also be a lot of fun. I am sure there are many happily married couples who can say they met their spouse on a blind date; but most blind dates are usually meant for just one evening out with a new person. They aren't expected to lead to marriage. When one is on a blind date, often there are few expectations. One can be relaxed and unpretentious knowing the date is only for one night. Neither party thinks the one date will lead to another. Perhaps this is exactly the reason Andy so easily agrees to meet Karen.

However, good old Barney always seems to get overly excited with his schemes. This certainly is true when Andy and Karen discover they really do like one another and decide to make a second date. Andy decides to take Karen crow shooting, as he already has plans to go, but both Barney and Thelma Lou think it is not much of a date. Hitting it off on their afternoon at Finnegan Flats, Andy invites Karen to the house for supper so she can meet Aunt Bee and Opie. Barney's plan is working perfectly.

Barney and Thelma Lou have the best intentions when trying to get Andy and Karen together. But one needs to be very careful when trying to manipulate another's life. Too often good intentions only lead to problems. Barney learns the hard way that he cannot push Andy and Karen together. They need to make their own decisions. It is okay for Barney to introduce Andy and Karen; but he should leave it at that. After all, with all the problems Barney has with women, he certainly is no expert when it comes to love. Even though Andy and Karen's relationship appears to be going in the right direction, for some reason it comes to an end. Karen leaves Mayberry never to be seen again.

"Who's your favorite American author? Oh, and please tell me just one thing. Do you think you could ever make a living doing anything beside sheriffin'?" - Karen Moore

Episode 41
"Aunt Bee's Brief Encounter"

"My aunt overlooked one little detail. How much are you charging us to save our roses?" - Andy

*A*unt Bee has a fulfilling life taking care of Opie and Andy. She loves them dearly. Her many social activities give her many hours of enjoyment. Could a possible romance add more happiness to her life? The love bug seems to bite Aunt Bee one day when a traveling handy man by the name of Henry Wheeler arrives in Mayberry. He stops at the Taylor house to spray some roses, and Aunt Bee takes an immediate liking to him.

Mr. Wheeler appears to be a kind and gentle man. He has no family, and he sleeps and eats in the back of his truck. His love for flowers appeals to Aunt Bee, as she too appreciates their lovely beauty. When Mr. Wheeler asks to borrow an onion for his stew, Aunt Bee invites him to stay for dinner. He accepts, and the next thing he knows, he is sleeping under the Taylor roof. No one seems to want him to leave.

A common goal for many of us is to some day find that perfect someone, get married, and settle down. We want to put down our roots. When we settle down in one place, we become a member of a community, and we develop friendships and purpose in our lives. We may become a part of a church family, and together we work and play. Our lives take on a deeper and more fulfilling meaning.

There are always some people who just can't settle down. We often see folks of all kinds come into Mayberry, and then for some reason we never see them again. Perhaps they are just passing through because of their job. Or perhaps, like Mr. Wheeler, they are just plain restless. They don't want to stay in one place for very long.

When a person settles down, it means there will be responsibilities. Once you have put down your roots, you will become responsible to your family, your employer, and your community. Perhaps this is why drifters continue to drift from one place to another. They either cannot or will not accept the responsibility that comes with settling down in one place. But on the other hand, they also miss out on all the joys that come along with being a part of a family and community. They never develop lasting relationships.

Andy can see that Aunt Bee enjoys being with Mr. Wheeler. He treats her with kindness and affection. They enjoy walking around Mayberry, going to the movies, and stopping for an ice cream soda. Perhaps Aunt Bee is going to finally find a man with whom she wants to spend the rest of her life. It would make her very happy, and Andy wants only the best for his special aunt. Then Andy learns the truth about Mr. Wheeler.

Upon learning Mr. Wheeler is a loafer who travels around sponging off unsuspecting women, Andy has a decision to make. He does not want Aunt Bee to get hurt, yet he knows she will be if she learns the truth about Mr. Wheeler. Andy decides to beat Mr. Wheeler at his own game. If Mr. Wheeler can con his way into the Taylor house, perhaps Andy can con Mr. Wheeler into leaving. Andy's plan works, and Aunt Bee is sad to see Mr. Wheeler go. Although Andy's plan brings sadness to Aunt Bee for a while, he is able to prevent a real heartbreak if she were to learn the truth about Mr. Wheeler. And the last thing Andy wants is for Aunt Bee to be hurt badly.

"Well, I guess that's how it is with these drifters. They just get the urge and they go. Pity they're so restless, unable to stay in one place for long. They miss so much." - Aunt Bee

Episode 42
"The Clubmen"

"Well, it's just… Andy, we just felt he wouldn't fit in. I guess he's a nice enough fellow, and I'm sure he's a very competent deputy." - Roger Courtney

*A*ndy Taylor and Barney Fife are the best of friends. They are also cousins. Where you find Andy, you will usually find Barney. Whether it is at the office, at church, or on a date, you generally will not find one without the other. As children they went to school together and had stayed over night at each other's houses. They went to Mayberry Union High together and were in the same class. Barney is Opie's godfather. You won't find two friends any closer than Barney Fife and Andy Taylor. So what will happen when one of them is invited to join a prestigious club while the other is not?

When I was in high school there were quite a number of cliques. There were the "jocks" that were the stars of the football and basketball teams. There were those who came from affluent families. They wore the latest style of clothes, and they had their own cars. We also had a wide variety of school clubs, and after joining, you automatically became a part of a group with like interests. Usually good friends joined the same clubs so they could be together for all the activities. Our clubs were open to all.

Somehow there seems to be an unwritten rule that certain clubs need to be exclusive. Sometimes the rules are even written down very specifically as to who can join and who can't. One doesn't have to look too far back in history to find evidence of this. There were segregated clubs found everywhere where membership was determined by one's wealth, race, religion, or gender. There had to be certain requirements in order for one to join. Often times one had to be voted in before actually becoming a member.

"The Clubmen" begins with Andy returning from a day of fishing with Roger Courtney. Roger is a classy guy who lives up at the state capital. Roger wants to return some of Mayberry's hospitality, so he invites Andy to visit his Esquire Club. Andy tells Roger that whenever he goes somewhere, he usually takes Barney along. Roger invites Barney as well, and informs Andy that he will put them both up for membership. Barney is just beside himself when he hears that they might become members. He begins to think about it and decides that he and Andy need to act like they have stocks and bonds and stuff. Needless to say, Barney makes a big mess of things when he tries so hard to be somebody that he isn't. The members see through Barney's façade in a hurry, and they decide he will not fit in. They do accept Andy, but Andy decides that he doesn't fit in either, and he declines the membership invitation. But now, what does he tell Barney?

Segregated clubs and organizations are becoming a thing of the past, yet some still exist. More often than not their exclusivity is based on financial and social status. Andy tells Barney that only one of them has been accepted into the Esquires. Barney assumes it is he that was accepted. He is livid that Andy has been turned down, and being the good friend that he is, he sends his letter of resignation. If Andy isn't good enough, then he isn't either. Andy, being the good friend he is, never tells Barney any different. It sure would be interesting to find out how Andy explains Barney's letter to Roger Courtney the next time they are fishing. But knowing Andy, he will think of something to save Barney any embarrassment. That's the kind of friend he is.

"You ain't one to pry? You're always asking me when I'm gonna get married and how much I send my mother every month." - Barney

Episode 43
"The Pickle Story"

"Barney, that poor soul just lives for that contest and if she got nosed out by a store bought pickle I'd never forgive myself." - Andy

*A*unt Bee is a marvelous cook. Her pork chops, apple pies, and Sunday dinners are just about the best thing you could ever ask for. But when it comes to making pickles, poor Aunt Bee just doesn't have the knack. She has just made eight quarts for Opie, Barney, and Andy, and she brings them to the courthouse for Barney and Andy's lunch. Even though they are awful and taste like kerosene, no one can hurt Aunt Bee's feelings by telling her that they just aren't any good; and that's where the deception begins.

Deception and lying are learned behaviors. It is learned very early in life. If a child is confronted with doing something wrong, he will just about always try to lie his way out of it. Children really don't understand the consequences of lying. They just see it as a quick and easy way to avoid trouble. They don't understand that it might just be postponing the inevitable punishment that awaits them. All they know is the lie keeps them out of trouble for the time being.

There are various kinds of deception and lying. We often engage in "protective lying" where we lie in order to protect one's feelings from being hurt. But we need to ask ourselves when we engage in this kind of deceit. Whose feelings are we trying to protect, ours or someone else's? Most of us justify this form of lying.

Deceptions quite often begin with good intentions. However, those innocent beginnings usually lead to more deceptions and then more lies. Before we know what has happened, we have broken trust between people. Once a lie is told, it doesn't take long for another lie to come along to cover up the first one. The cycle continues, and soon so many lies are told it isn't possible to keep them all straight.

Before engaging in any kind of deception or lie, we need to seriously consider the probable consequences of our actions. Andy, Barney, and Opie engage in many lies and deceptions for a very good reason. They want to protect Aunt Bee's feelings, and they are willing to do almost anything to do so. But like us, when they practice their deceptions, they become so entangled in their lies that it is difficult to know what to do next. In the end, all their lying and deceit results in only more deceit and lies.

When Andy and Barney decide they just cannot face eight quarts of Aunt Bee's pickles, they come up with a plan. They buy eight quarts of store bought pickles and go into "Operation Pickle Switch." They even get Opie involved. Andy reminds Opie that the only reason they are doing it is so they don't hurt Aunt Bee's feelings. When Aunt Bee tastes the store bought pickles, she is so delighted; she decides to enter them in a contest at the fair. Realizing they cannot let Aunt Bee enter pickles she did not make, Andy, Barney, and Opie eat all the store bought pickles as fast as possible so Aunt Bee must make a new batch of her own. Their plan works to perfection; Aunt Bee makes more pickles, and she enters them in the contest. Of course she loses, but as Aunt Bee points out; the boys are the real winners. She made sixteen quarts, and they will have them everyday. Now they have but one option; they must learn to love them.

"You know, when Mr. Johnson was alive, he just loved them so much. He always used to say to me, 'Clara, when my time comes and I go to heaven, I'll just bet they don't put down a pickle that can compare with yours'." - Clara Johnson

Episode 44
"Sheriff Barney"

"Oh, I'm sure we couldn't get Taylor, but how about this deputy, this, ah, Fife fellow? Gentlemen, I recommend we make him an offer." - Mayor Purdy

What would you do if you saw a very good friend about to do something that you believed was not the best thing to do? Would you try to prevent your friend from doing it even though you knew it was something he really wanted to do? Or would you allow your friend to forge ahead knowing full well he would probably fail?

This is the dilemma that Andy faces when Barney is offered a sheriff's job in the neighboring small town of Greendale. Barney is very flattered that Mayor Purdy wants him as sheriff, and he is eager to take the job. Andy, on the other hand, believes Barney needs more experience, and he tries to persuade him to stay in Mayberry as his deputy. But Barney always has to play second fiddle to Andy. Now he has the opportunity to become Andy's equal, and he wants to go for it.

Most people work hard hoping that some day they will be promoted to a new position with more responsibility and compensation.

However taking on a new job that is beyond one's capabilities may be very risky. If one fails, another opportunity of future advancement may not come along. Yet if one does not take the risk of trying something new, one may never find out what one's real potentials are. Barney believes he can handle the job as Greendale's sheriff. He doesn't seem to remember all the times Andy has stepped in to help him get out of some very serious problems.

Andy does something that is very difficult for many people. When Barney asks him if he thinks he should take the job, Andy's answer is a definite "no". He does not give Barney the answer he wants to hear. Instead he tells him the truth. Sometimes people will give friends favorable recommendations hoping it will help them get a job. Too often the things said are not accurate. This is neither fair to the job seeker nor to the prospective employer. Andy is so concerned with his best friend's welfare that he risks some hurt feelings in order to prevent failure. Andy, more than anyone else, knows Barney's limitations.

Opie tells Andy that the kids are really going to miss Barney as a crossing guard. He asks why he and Barney can't take turns being sheriff. This gives Andy a great idea. He makes Barney sheriff for one day in the hopes that he will discover for himself just how difficult a job being sheriff really is. As expected, Barney has a bad time. Otis makes a joke out of Barney's methods of trying to locate a still. After failing miserably while trying to settle a fencing dispute between two farmers, Andy steps in and settles the entire conflict in a matter of minutes. Andy's plan is working, but it is working too well. Barney becomes very dejected over his failings, turns the sheriff badge back over to Andy, and leaves the courthouse sulking.

It isn't easy admitting our limitations. I once had aspirations of being an elementary school principal. I had the opportunity to try it for two years on a part time basis. It didn't take me long to realize I was not cut out for that job. Not everyone can be a leader.

Barney is fortunate to have a friend like Andy; a friend who will be honest and direct. It is often said that relatives or good friends should never work together, but in the case of Andy and Barney, I would say it was the perfect combination; especially for Barney.

"Well, you see the truth is Mayor, Mayberry needs me." - Barney

Episode 45
"The Farmer Takes a Wife"

"I figure I'll stick around town a couple days and look over the available stock, pick one out, take her back to the farm." - Jeff Pruitt

When big Jeff Pruitt comes into Mayberry looking for a wife, it sounds as if he is going to buy a new head of cattle for his farm. He plans to look over all the available girls, pick the one he likes the best, and then he will take her back to his farm as his wife. Jeff is so confident about his qualities that he just assumes any girl he finds will jump at the chance to be his bride. He figures the entire process will only take a few days.

When I was courting my wife, I did not think at all like Jeff Pruitt. I was afraid if I asked her to marry me, she would turn me down. Unlike Jeff, I had very little to offer. I was only in my third year of teaching. I didn't own a house, and I didn't have any money in the bank. Why would she want to marry me? But I was wrong. When I finally had enough courage to pop the question, she accepted my proposal, and we were married eight months later. That was thirty-six years ago.

Jeff Pruitt is like many men in one aspect. He truly believes he is "God's gift to women," and as a result he doesn't have to go through the trouble of "courting" a young lady. But courtship is an important step before marriage. During courtship both parties get to know their prospective mate. It takes more than beauty and passion for a relationship to last. But Jeff doesn't seem to think courtship should last very long. I sometimes get the impression his wife just might end up being an unpaid hired hand.

Barney apparently has not learned anything about matchmaking from when he tried to get Andy and Karen Moore together. He tells Jeff that he and Andy will help him find a wife. Jeff has some rather unusual criteria when he is checking out the girls on Mayberry's busy Main Street. He even teaches Opie a few things about picking up girls. You stand on the street corner, and when one comes along, you pick her up, set her back down, and say, "Excuse me ma'am, just checking your weight."

When Barney finds out Thelma Lou is having a "hen party" at her house, he takes Jeff to the party so he can screen all the girls. Barney's plan works a little better than he plans. Jeff finds the perfect bride, but it turns out to be Thelma Lou. Jeff wastes no time courting Thelma Lou, and he soon asks Thelma Lou to be his wife. Andy knows once Jeff has his mind set on Thelma Lou, nothing is going to change it, so again Andy must come up with some kind of scheme to get Jeff to forget about Thelma Lou. He and Thelma Lou go to work on Jeff, and they get the results they are hoping for. After dressing Jeff in a new suit and teaching him some manners, Andy sends him over to Thelma Lou's. Jeff finds out that his meals are not going to be what he thought they were. Also, Andy has found a house in town for him, and a new job selling shoes awaits him. Jeff quickly goes home to his farm. He decides if he wants a wife, he will settle for his neighbor, Bertha. After all, she likes him just the way he is.

Most married men I know didn't start out like Jeff. They did not decide one day that it was time to get married. Marriage sort of sneaked up on them without much warning. Most say they weren't even thinking about marriage when they met their present wives. Their relationship began slowly and over time they decided that they had finally met the person with whom they want to share their life. At least that is how it happened to me.

"Imagine, caring how much a girl weighs." - Opie

Episode 46
"Keeper of the Flame"

"Aunt Bee, that boy's been playing with matches and he's got to get a whippin'." - Andy

Whenever I hear Andy Taylor speak these words I feel very troubled. I just cannot envision Andy ever whippin' little Opie. I cannot believe for one moment that Opie could ever do something so terrible that Andy would actually whip him. Because this bothers me so much, I contacted a number of people who live in the southern part of the United States, and I asked them what the phrase "get a whippin' means. Being a 'Northerner" I did not hear that phrase ever used when I was a child. None of my friends had ever gotten a whippin' from their parents, and my siblings and I certainly never did. To me a whippin' meant getting hit with a strap or a stick or some other such object.

My mind was set at ease when every one of the people I contacted answered my inquiry the same. They all said whippin' means a good old-fashioned spanking. Most of the people who responded told me they had gotten a "whippin" and it was nothing like I had imagined. Now I can watch this episode knowing that the worst that will happen to Opie will be a spanking. I have gotten a few of those in my day as well.

Forming secret clubs is a common childhood activity. It is always fun to find a place to meet, think up a good name, and then do all kinds of neat things. Having a secret password adds to the excitement of it, and then if one has to pay dues, it really seems like the real thing. Opie is delighted when he joins a secret club with his best friends.

Opie gets himself into some serious trouble with his new secret club. Not only do he and his friends trespass and go into another person's building without permission, he also plays with matches and candles. I can understand Andy's anger when Aunt Bee discovers the spent matches and candle under Opie's pillow. Andy has told Opie that he is not allowed to play with fire. He knows the dangers involved, and he wants to spare Opie any chance of getting burned. Children and matches quite often lead to injuries.

When I was about ten years old, a friend and I were playing in their old barn. We had a kerosene lantern. Somehow the kerosene spilled on me and became ignited. I received third degree burns over my face, hands, and chest. I spent more than a week in a hospital, and even though it is fifty years later, I still have the scars to remind me of that terrible day. The barn we were in was very similar to Jubell Foster's barn. It was old and dry, and it could have caught fire easily. Luckily for me, my brother happened to come by, and he rolled me on the floor and put the fire out. I was one fortunate boy.

Opie and Andy learn an important lesson in this episode. Opie learns the dangers of fire and respect for other's private property. Andy learns the importance of not believing someone is guilty without having all the facts. Andy once told Opie that he should always keep promises. Opie is in a bind when it comes to telling Andy about his secret club. He took an oath when he joined the club, and an oath is a promise, so he can not even tell his father about the club. When Opie learns that Andy has to pay for the damage, he admits he was at Jubell Foster's farm. But Opie knows that he did not start any fire. The only thing that matters now is that Andy believes him. In an ironic twist of fate, it is good old Barney who finds the evidence to prove Opie's innocence. And he has a little fun while finding it too.

"You're looking at the man who's going to have to pay for that barn. I just want you to know that." - Andy

Episode 47
"Bailey's Bad Boy"

"Sheriff, maybe I had better straighten you out. Like it says right there on the license, my name is Bailey. My father is John Justin Bailey. You have heard of him?" - Ron Bailey

*T*he old biblical proverb states, "Spare the rod, spoil the child." The writer of these ancient words of wisdom may well have written them for this story. Many people believe young people who are pampered and spoiled as children will live their adult lives the same way.

When young, rich Ron Bailey causes an accident in Mayberry, he thinks because he is the son of John Judson Bailey, an important man in the state, he should be allowed to just go on his way with no consequences at all. He tries to buy his way out of the accident, but Andy has no part of that. Then Ron informs Andy that his father can have just about anything he wants in the state, including Andy's "junior G-man badge." Andy and Barney have a different idea. No one is above the law in Mayberry, so they arrest Ron and place him in jail. Ron calls his father's attorney and just can't wait for his father to show up in Mayberry to set Andy straight. But Ron doesn't know who he is dealing with when Sheriff Andy Taylor arrests him. He is in for one big surprise.

Prisoners in Mayberry are not treated like prisoners in other jails. The Mayberry jail closes for Sunday, and the prisoners go to the Taylor house for dinner. When no one is available to guard the prisoner when Andy and Opie want to go fishing, the solution is rather easy. They take the prisoner fishing with them. Young Ron Bailey seems to be having a good time when he is fishing with Andy and Opie. When he catches a big fish, Andy and Opie praise him, but Ron thinks they are just buttering him up, so he throws the fish back. Ron doesn't know that people can be kind without ulterior motives. Like many rich, spoiled, young men, Ron Bailey truly believes he is above the law. He has a pocket full of money, a fancy convertible, and lots of idle time on his hands. Whenever he gets in some kind of trouble, good old Dad is always there to bail him out. So you can imagine the shock he gets when he finds out things are much different in Mayberry.

Ron sees some new things while in the custody of Sheriff Taylor. He watches as Andy makes Opie use his own allowance money to pay for a broken window. And at the same time he sees the love and wonderful relationship that exists between Andy and Opie. He sees a loving family making ice cream after church on a lazy summer day. He sees new things that he most likely has never experienced in his entire life.

I have given a rather simple survey in my classroom. I would ask one very simple question of my students. The question was, "If you had a choice, which would you choose; a brand new expensive bike, or one afternoon alone with your father fishing? In all the years I asked this question, there were probably not more than a handful that chose the bike. Almost everyone wanted some time for fishing with Dad.

In the end Ron does something that everyone needs to do. He takes the responsibility for his own mistakes. Although he knows his father will not understand what he is doing, Ron decides that it is time for him to stand on his own two feet. Ron's father does him no favors by always bailing him out. His father substitutes money and fancy cars for a much more valuable commodity – time.

"Well….I'll say I hope Fletch enjoys his new truck because I gotta feeling he's gonna be driving one." - Andy

Episode 48
"The Manicurist"

"You know what I think? I think this isn't a very friendly town after all and I think you got a nerve putting up a sign saying that it is." - Ellen Brown

What man alive doesn't enjoy looking at a pretty girl from time to time? And what man wouldn't enjoy sitting back and having a pretty girl give him a manicure? Well, that's exactly what happens when pretty Ellen Brown gets off the bus at Mayberry one day. She walks right into Floyd's Barber Shop and announces that she is a manicurist, and she would like to work for Floyd. Floyd gets tongue tied and stutters a bit, and before he knows it, Ellen is setting up a table for her customers. Floyd is now offering a new service to his friends and customers. But how will the people of Mayberry react to this?

I have to admit that I would feel a bit intimidated and rather shy if I ever had a manicure given to me by a pretty girl. I have a difficult enough time having young females cut my hair. It did take me a while to get used to it. Ever since I was a small child, I have always had my hair cut by a male barber. It was rather different for me the first time a young lady cut my hair. But I soon adjusted to the change, and I must admit that the older I get, the more I seem to be enjoying haircuts.

The men in Mayberry are very reluctant to get manicures. It is a new and very radical thing in Mayberry. And besides that, what will their wives think? So no one is getting their nails done. Ellen gets off the bus at Mayberry because the sign outside of town says Mayberry is a friendly town. But she doesn't think it is friendly at all, especially after she overhears Andy saying she won't last twenty-four hours. Andy feels terrible for hurting young Ellen, so he becomes her first customer and gets his nails done. In an effort to prove Mayberry is a friendly town, he convinces all the men folk that it is a real pleasure having his nails done by a pretty girl like Ellen. She wears the prettiest perfume, and he says it is a pleasure to just sit next to her and breathe.

Andy's little scheme to get all the men to have manicures is done with the best intentions. He feels badly that he has hurt Ellen's feelings, but even more so he feels badly that she thinks Mayberry is not a very friendly town. So he has the men get manicures as a way to convince Ellen that Mayberry is indeed a friendly town. Little does he know that the wives of Mayberry will become very jealous, and they will forbid their husbands to have any more manicures. That is one problem that he didn't anticipate. And how will Ellen feel now when all her customers suddenly stay away?

Friendliness is an important virtue for everyone to have. But one must be careful that one's friendliness isn't misconstrued as something else. Andy decides he needs to sit Ellen down and explain to her why the wives resent her. When he tells Ellen how good nature has been to her, and how it would be better if she was not unattached, Ellen thinks Andy is proposing to her. Luckily for Andy, Helen has already decided to go back to her fiancé, Pierre. Of course all the men are devastated that there will no longer be a manicurist in town, so Floyd decides to hire a new girl. When Mayor Pike and Andy see her sign in the window, the mayor decides he will get the first manicure. He is in for a big disappointment though when he discovers the manicurist is none other than old Emma Watson. Floyd wants to make sure there are no more jealous wives in Mayberry.

"Well, I don't know whether you know this or not, but nature has been good to you. I mean real, real, real good. I can't remember when I've seen nature spend so much time on any one person." - Andy

Episode 49
"The Jinx"

"There are atmospheric rays which control bodily motions. Now if a person containing negative or hexin qualities gets between you and them rays he creates a static that jars any successful motion into an unsuccessful motion." - Barney

Superstitions have been around for a long time. From quiga boards, tarot cards, and chain letters, people try to tell fortunes, bring good luck, or ward off all kinds of evils. Superstitions are also found in Mayberry. The Darlings use all sorts of potions and incantations to cure illnesses or ward off evil. Excitable Barney Fife has the habit of dabbling in magic and superstition at times. For the most part it is just some innocent fun, but when it almost causes one of Mayberry's citizens to leave town, then it is time for Andy to step in and stop it.

Henry Bennett is one of Mayberry's longtime citizens. He is a quiet man who causes no problems, and he minds his own business. He comes into Floyd's Barber Shop one day while Barney and Floyd are playing a game of checkers. He enters quietly and stands watching the game over Barney's left shoulder. When Barney loses the game, he conveniently blames Henry for being a jinx. Soon everyone in the shop starts to tell tales about times when bad things happened in the presence of Henry Bennett.

Fortune cookies and crystal balls can be used for innocent entertainment. It is when superstitious beliefs are used to interfere in people's lives that they can become harmful. Poor Henry Bennett is accused of being a jinx simply because Barney's superstitious nature gets totally out of control. What starts out as a little innocent teasing turns into vicious suspicions which almost cause Henry to leave the town he loves and the people he considers to be his friends. Now he is not so sure about either.

Barney does not listen to reason. He thinks he is an expert on the topic of jinxes. To prove Barney wrong, Andy asks Henry to share his boat at an upcoming fishing contest. Andy and Barney always win, so Andy figures when they win with Henry in the boat, Barney will have to admit that Henry being a jinx is nothing but a bunch of nonsense. Of course Barney is totally against the idea, and when they are in the boat fishing, he rubs his rabbit foot and recites good luck incants. Despite all his precautions, the boat sinks, and Barney believes more than ever that Henry Bennett is indeed a jinx.

It is often said that if you keep telling a person that he is bad, pretty soon the person will begin to believe it. After the fishing fiasco, Henry begins to wonder if perhaps he is a jinx. Now Andy's problem is twofold. He must convince both Barney and Henry that there just isn't such a thing as a jinx. Andy decides to fix an upcoming raffle drawing so Henry will win. When Andy calls out the winning number, which should be Henry's, Henry once again loses because he pulls out the hat size tag rather than a raffle number. Now more than ever, Henry believes himself to be a jinx. He can't even win a raffle that was rigged so no one else could be the winner.

Henry finds out that he really does have friends in Mayberry when everyone decides that he should keep the TV that he won. Henry's belief that he is a jinx is finally put to rest, but the same thing can not be said for Barney. He gets to drive Henry home.

"Huh, bad luck Barney, you've done it again." - Andy

Episode 50
"Jailbreak"

"Anyway I suppose you have plenty of other things to keep you busy, chicken thieves and whatnot." - Morton, State Bureau of Investigation

*L*oss of respect is something no one likes to experience. Whether it is from one's family, friends, or coworkers, when one loses respect, a very important part of that relationship is gone. A person can survive the loss of many things, but not one's own respect.

Law enforcement workers are very dependent upon people's respect. How can a police officer be an effective servant of the people if he doesn't have their respect? When the state police request that Andy and Barney stay out of the search for a criminal, Opie and the town's people begin to ask Andy why he isn't helping. After realizing that he is responsible to the citizens of Mayberry, Andy and Barney join in on the manhunt.

When it comes to comparing police, it isn't too difficult to see that the State Police are better equipped to handle serious crime. They have more men, superior equipment, and better training. Yet it isn't very professional for the State Police to tell Andy and Barney to stay out of the investigation. After all, it is their town, and who else but Andy and Barney know the people and the terrain better? Besides, the Mayberry Sheriff's office has handled more serious things than just "chicken thieves and whatnot."

The State Police manage to capture Doc Malloy, and they put him in the Mayberry jail. His partner is still on the loose, so Andy decides he has an obligation to the people of Mayberry to go after him. Barney is put in charge of guarding Malloy. As usual, Barney takes it upon himself to try to help out. He dresses in a black suit and quietly locks himself in the cell with Malloy. His pretends to be a big time crook and offers to help Malloy escape if he shares his loot. Unknown to Barney, Malloy spots a picture of Barney in his uniform, so Barney's real identity comes to light. Malloy manages to escape, but Barney is left behind in the cell all tied up.

One would think that Andy would be extremely upset with Barney for allowing Malloy to escape. Barney is totally dejected over his blunder, but Andy allows him to fill his gun with bullets after they spot Malloy's car parked on Main Street. They see a trailer hitch on the car, and they realize Malloy is holding up out at the trailer park.

A story theme that occurs time and time again is how Andy repeatedly stands behind Barney despite his bumbling police work. It gives us a true appreciation of the friendship that Andy has for Barney. He keeps his faith in Barney and continues to give him responsibility as a deputy. When they find Malloy's car at the trailer park, Andy allows Barney to look for him. Not only does Barney find Malloy and his female partner, he also finds Norton tied up inside the trailer. Knowing he must act quickly, Barney jumps in Malloy's car and erratically drives the car and trailer to the courthouse steps, with Andy chasing close behind. Chalk one up for the Mayberry Sheriff's Office.

Norton comes to appreciate the help given by Andy and Barney. Perhaps the next time he is after someone, he won't be so quick to refuse help from the locals. Norton shows that he is not so bad after all when he gives Opie a detective disguise kit. However, it is Barney who finds an immediate use for a disguise, and not Opie.

"Three weeks on a job and everything's bungled up by a rube sheriff who can't even keep a cell door locked." - Morton, State Bureau of Investigation

Episode 51
"A Medal for Opie"

"It's nice to win something. It's real nice to win something. But it's more important to know how not to win something." - Andy

We are living in a society where there is tremendous pressure on our young people to play sports. Playing sports can be an excellent learning tool for children, but it can turn into a negative tool if there is over emphasis on winning. Children today are often participating in competitive team sports as early as five or six years old. They are dressed in full uniform, while parents and neighbors yell out orders and encouragement. Trophies are awarded to the winners, while the losers learn early that they get nothing. It is not uncommon for young children to be spending their Sundays participating in such events, rather than having a relaxing day at their church and home.

Growing up in the '50's I did not participate in organized sporting activities. There were not any. If I wanted to play a game of football or baseball, I would get together a group of friends and organize a game on any available empty lot or field. There were no sports facilities. No adults were around to settle our disputes or critique our play. If there were disputes, we settled them on our own, and the game moved on. In most cases, the score did not matter. It was the fun of playing that was important.

When I was older I did play on a school basketball team. We were terrible, but we had fun. I still remember very vividly one particular game. We lost by a score of 88-0, and the game was stopped at the end of the third quarter. I remember our coach laughing with us on our way home. It was a tremendous learning experience for all of us. Our coach and parents kept sports in the right perspective.

In this episode Opie is a very poor loser when it comes to sports. It is one of the few times when we see a negative side of his behavior. He wants to win a medal so badly. He is so sure he will win because he has worked hard with Barney, and Barney keeps telling him he will win a medal for sure. But when Opie not only loses, but comes in dead last, he cannot deal with the humiliation. He is not only angry with himself, he is angry at his friends. They won his medal and they now are no longer his friends.

Barney blames himself for much of Opie's attitude. Perhaps he does play a role in it. After all he is the one who works with Opie and convinces him that he will win the medal. But Opie is responsible for his own behavior. He just cannot accept the fact that someone else won his medal. Nothing Andy can say will change his mind – nothing that is until Andy tells him how disappointed he is. When Opie finds out that his father is disappointed in him because of how he acts, and not because he lost, that is when he accepts his defeat. Opie learns there are more important things than a medal; such as his father's opinion of him. It hurts to hear that he has disappointed his own father.

One of the wonderful things about this story is the attitude that Andy takes toward Opie's entering the contest. Andy never puts any pressure on Opie to win. He is just happy that Opie is entering the event, and is pleased to see him compete. Whether he wins a medal is secondary to Andy. When he gets home and finds Opie pouting on the couch, he does not tell him he is disappointed because he lost. He is disappointed in how he is acting about losing. There is a big difference, and Andy wants to be sure Opie understands it. After all, Opie is going to have a lot more disappointments coming up in his life. If he doesn't believe Andy, maybe he should talk to Barney. He knows.

"Paw, I don't want you to be disappointed in me." - Opie

Episode 52
"Barney and the Choir"

"But Barney can't sing. He's a warm wonderful person and I love him dearly, but he can't sing." - Thelma Lou

*J*ohn Masters has a real problem. Just weeks before a contest, he finds himself without a tenor. Hearing about John's dilemma, Barney hints that he has a trained voice, and that he sings tenor. Without even hearing Barney sing one single note, John welcomes Barney aboard. Andy is aghast at John's move. He attempts to get

John to wait, but John is so excited to hear that Barney can sing tenor, he ignores Andy. But Barney can't sing. Barney practices his singing in the courthouse, so Andy knows about Barney's "trained voice." Andy also knows that when Barney shows up for his first practice, everyone in the choir will discover the truth. Barney cannot sing one note on key.

I am sure we all think we are better at doing something than we probably really are. No one likes to be told that he is not good enough to be a member of a sports team, a musical group, or some other such activity. Usually auditions or try outs are held, a person demonstrates his skills, and then the leader chooses who will become a part of the group. It is a normal procedure, and for most people, they realize there is always a risk of not being chosen. This is a chance one takes when auditioning for something.

After hearing Barney sing at the first practice, John Masters wants to tell him that he is out of the choir, but being Barney's best friend, Andy tells John that he cannot kick Barney out of the choir on the very same day he invites him to join. No one wants to be the one to tell Barney the bad news, including Andy. So Andy comes up with a scheme in which they can trick Barney into believing he is really doing a solo part, when in reality, another member of the choir is singing. Isn't it amazing how all the people in Mayberry go to so much trouble not to have to hurt feelings? But I guess that is what makes the people of Mayberry such wonderful, loveable people.

Being truthful and honest is always the simplest way to tell people bad news. It may hurt one's feelings for a while, but if we do it in a kind and sincere way, it will be in everyone's best interest. Allowing a person to wrongfully believe that he is really good at something is not doing the best thing for the person. Eventually the truth will be known, and wouldn't it be best to find out from a true friend?

Andy tries very hard to protect Barney's feelings. He convinces the entire choir to allow Barney to sing a solo using a dead microphone. While Barney is mouthing the words, Glen Cripe will be backstage singing into the live microphone. At the next practice Barney practices with a microphone. Andy tells Barney to sing softer and softer until finally he is only moving his mouth. Andy convinces Barney that when the microphone is turned on, his voice will reverberate through the entire auditorium. And on the night of the concert, it does; except it is Glen Cripe's deep mellow voice filling the auditorium.

There is one more bit of deception up Andy's sleeve. How is he going to prevent Barney from singing again after he thinks he had a wonderful performance? Andy informs Barney that he can no longer be in the choir because of the ten dollar merchandise certificate he won for being the outstanding performer. Barney is now a professional. But do you really think this will stop Barney from singing? I doubt it.

> *"They gave you remuneration for your talent, and that makes you a professional singer, and you're no longer eligible to sing in the amateur ranks." - Andy*

Episode 53
"Guest of Honor"

> *"I think it's an amazing coincidence. That's exactly the same idea I had." - Barney*

Founder's Day is an important event in Mayberry. It is an annual event, and the people of Mayberry look forward to it with great anticipation. Some years they have a historical pageant. One year there was a beauty contest. This year the town council is trying to come up with a new idea that is different and rather unique. They want to find a way to attract outsiders to come to Mayberry. After all, Mayberry calls itself "The Friendly Town". So this year it is decided that the first person not from Mayberry who drives into town will be honored as Mayberry's guest for the day. He will be showered with gifts, and he will be presented the key to the city. Speeches will be made, and he will be honored at a town gathering. The only question remaining is who will the guest of honor be? On Founder's Day the town leaders and the Mayberry Drum and Bugle Corp anxiously await at the entry to Mayberry for their guest of honor to arrive.

Small town celebrations are an important part of Americana. Every summer thousands of towns of all sizes celebrate their community's heritage. Coming from the Midwest, I have attended such important celebrations as Cheese Days, Dairy Days, Corn Festivals, and even

Cucumber Days. School bands, queens, and food stands line the streets and everyone is in a festive mood. There are carnivals, beer gardens, food stands, and all sorts of fun things to do. Many hours of planning and hard work go into making sure these festivities come off without a hitch. Things are no different at all in Mayberry.

When Andy discovers that the person they chose for Mayberry's guest for the day, Thomas A. Mooney, a.k.a. Sheldon, is nothing more than a common pickpocket, he decides to keep this a secret, and he allows Mooney to fulfill the honor which has been bestowed upon him. He decides that his special deputies for the day will keep a close watch on their guest. Wherever he goes, someone will watch him. Everything is going according to plan, and there are no problems until Barney takes over watching Mooney.

Barney knows about Mooney, so of course he needs to do something. He decides to have a little talk with him, so he explains to him that people usually steal because they are either rotten or else they don't feel trusted. Barney wants Mooney to think he trusts him, so he takes off his expensive jeweled watch, and places it on the table. He turns his back, and when he turns around, the pickpocket is gone; but the watch is still there. Thinking he has reformed Mooney, Barney returns to the courthouse, only to discover that all the keys to the stores in Mayberry are missing from his key ring.

Andy and Barney begin a search for Mooney, and they find him sneaking out the back door of the jewelry store. Mooney is feeling quite smug with his latest heist, so he takes out a cigarette, only to have Andy light it. Once again Barney survives another major bungling, and Mooney is arrested. The only thing left for Andy to do is to tell the townspeople about their honored guest. Unfortunately, we never do find out just how Andy explains it. But knowing Andy, he will tell the truth, and hopefully they all learn a valuable lesson about trust. Perhaps Barney has learned a little about security too.

"Oh what a tangled web we weave, when first we practice to deceive." - Andy

Episode 54
"The Merchant of Mayberry"

"I hope you're gonna like the way I do my job. I can sell, but I just don't push myself on anybody." - Bert Miller

*B*en Weaver owns the largest store in Mayberry, Weaver's Department Store. He has the most customers and makes the most money. He has little competition in Mayberry, so he can set his prices a bit higher because he knows the people need to shop at his store. He is a very shrewd businessman. We have seen Ben before when he was set upon evicting The Scoby family. He appeared as a cantankerous man who was only interested in money. He appeared again in "The Christmas Story" and we saw a somewhat gentler side of Ben. Ben appears for a third time, and this time he goes after the "little guy" because he feels he is a threat to his business.

When door to door peddler, Bert Miller, arrives in Mayberry, he stops at the courthouse to visit his good friends Andy and Barney. Aunt Bee joins in, and Bert ends up making three quick sales. Ben Weaver sees Bert selling the merchandise out of his suitcase, and he isn't at all happy about it. He approaches Andy and Barney and demands that Bert not be allowed to peddle his goods on the street. Seeing it's a slow day in Mayberry, Andy and Barney decide to needle Ben a bit, so they set up Bert in a little business on the empty lot next to the courthouse. Andy's joke on Ben is just beginning.

The small family owned store was once the backbone of every small town. Many of the "mom and pop" stores of yesterday are now gone because large discount chain stores have emerged. They can increase their buying volume and thus offer lower prices than the smaller stores. Ben has sort of a monopoly in Mayberry, and he has every intention of keeping it that way. He can not stand the thought of Bert selling a few handkerchiefs and socks. The people buy from Bert because of his easy manner. He doesn't push people into buying things they do not need.

A hard sale is a fact of our times. Quite often we buy our products from total strangers. We no longer are buying things from our friends and neighbors. Salespeople feel freer to use hard sale tactics. If they do not personally know a customer, then they probably don't feel obligated to be as fair to them. Unfortunately, as more and more small businesses go by the wayside, this will be even more common in the future.

Old Ben resents Andy and Barney's helping Bert Miller. Every time Ben complains and threatens Andy and Barney, they raise the bar a little higher, and help Bert more. Ben says Bert needs a roof over his head; Andy puts a roof over his head. When Ben says that a store has to be a proper structure, Andy and Barney build Bert a proper structure. Andy even gets Bert more merchandise from Mt. Pilot. By the time Andy is done, Bert has a steady stream of customers, and Ben Weaver is very angry.

Andy and Barney are playing a joke on Ben Weaver. Sometimes jokes can get carried away and people can be hurt. Unfortunately, Andy's joke hurts Bert Miller. Just when Bert is thinking he will no longer have to carry that heavy suitcase, and listen to those ringing doorbells, Ben lowers his prices, and gives away free balloons and gum. All Ben's customers go back to him, and Bert is stuck with unsold merchandise. Andy feels bad about this, so through a little salesmanship of his own, he persuades Ben to give Bert a sales job in his store. In the end everyone gains. Ben gets himself a very good salesman, and Bert no longer has to travel door to door in order to sell.

"I'll tell you one thing. You're getting the best salesman in Mayberry." - Barney

Episode 55
"Aunt Bee the Warden"

"Andy, you've got to get me out of this. She's about to work me to death." - Otis

*O*tis Campbell is a regular visitor to the Mayberry jail. Every weekend he staggers into the courthouse, takes the cell key off the wall peg, unlocks the cell door, and then locks himself up. This has been a regular ritual for quite some time, and Otis considers the jail his home away from home. But one Friday night Otis finds himself locked out of his cell because Andy has arrested a family of moon shiners, and he needs the cell space. There is no way Andy can put Otis in the cell with them, as it is already crowded. The back room is out of the question, as that will be used by whoever spends the night with the prisoners. Andy decides the only option left is to take Otis to his house and let him sleep it off. His home is about to become a jail annex with Aunt Bee serving as warden.

Our penal system is set up basically as a system of punishment. Hardened or dangerous criminals are rarely if ever rehabilitated. They are locked up in prisons as a means of punishment and also as a means of protecting citizens. The rate at which criminals return to jails after being released certainly isn't something our penal system can be proud of. In many cases, the men and women who are incarcerated for long periods of time only become more hardened during their prison terms. From what we see in Mayberry, this is not the approach used by Sheriff Taylor and Deputy Fife.

When Otis is taken to the Taylor home to serve out his weekend sentence, Aunt Bee is aghast at the thought. Her home is not a jail, and besides, the ladies are in the kitchen baking cakes for the church bazaar. But when Andy explains his predicament, she reluctantly agrees to his plan. When Aunt Bee brings Otis his breakfast in the morning, he decides he wants to sleep a little later, and he mistakenly tells Aunt Bee that he expects to be treated like a prisoner. Aunt Bee takes Otis at his word, and she immediately puts him to work doing all kinds of chores around the house.

There is often much debate as to how prisoners should be treated. Taxpayers everywhere get enraged when they see their hard earned dollars being used to house criminals in modern detention centers with many comforts. Seeing prisoners sitting idol and watching televisions or working on computers doesn't seem like much of a punishment to some. Many feel prisoners should be working rather than spending their time in idleness. It is an attitude that is completely shared by Warden Bee Taylor.

A hospital where I volunteer recently undertook a major landscaping project at the Regional Cancer Center. Since the work was going to be done by volunteers, it was decided to utilize the help of inmates at our country jail. They were brought to the hospital each day, and they worked hard on the project. They were treated with respect and dignity, and it proved to be a positive experience for everyone involved.

Andy Taylor always treats Otis Campbell with dignity. He is often accused of being too soft with him. He even tells Otis bedtime stories when he can't sleep, and he serves him breakfast in bed. Otis gets a little lesson in reality when Aunt Bee becomes his warden at "The Rock". He even gives her the nickname "Bloody Mary". Some would say more of the "Bloody Mary" philosophy is what prisoners need for their rehabilitation. But somehow, I don't think Otis will agree.

"Oh what a mess I've made of my life." - Otis Campbell

Episode 56
"The County Nurse"

"When I was born I had my mama and when I die I'll have the undertaker. I don't see no sense in cluttering things up in between." - Rafe Hollister

*R*afe Hollister is one of Mayberry's less prominent citizens. He is sort of a backward farmer who has little education, and he is frequently arrested for making illegal moonshine. He is also someone whom the other farmers in his region respect. People sort of look to Rafe as their leader, and he has a lot of influence over them. If Rafe says something is right, they will follow him, and if Rafe says something is wrong, they will listen to him. He sets the pace for others to follow.

When the new nurse in Mayberry discovers that Rafe hasn't had his tetanus shot, she decides to visit him and make sure he is inoculated. She realizes that if she does not get Rafe to take his shot, then she has little if any chance to get the other farmers to take theirs. Andy takes Mary to the Hollister farm, and he instructs Mary to take it very slow when talking to Rafe. Mary and Andy show Rafe all the latest medical tools, but when it comes to giving him his shot, Rafe quickly sends them back to Mayberry.

Barney listens to Mary's woeful tale about not getting Rafe to take his shot. She says that if she can't get Rafe to have the shot, she won't get any of the farmers up his way to have theirs. Barney tells Mary that Andy was too soft on Rafe and that he would take Mary back to the Hollister farm, and he will tell Rafe he is getting his shot.

He insists that Rafe will only listen if he is treated like a child. Barney's orders fall on deaf ears, and Rafe sends Barney back to town by firing a few shots at him.

Trying to change people who have done things the same way for many years can be an almost impossible task. Barney found that out when he tried to help Ellie with Frankie Flint. One needs to be patient and understanding, even if it is in the person's best interest. Trying to bring about change too quickly can often be counter productive.

Rafe Hollister holds on to some age old beliefs. Going to a doctor is one of them. Andy knows if Mary is going to get Rafe to take his shot, she will have to be very careful in her approach. Rafe does not readily accept change in his beliefs. Telling Rafe he is wrong will be telling Rafe that his entire family before him has been wrong, and that will accomplish nothing. It is a wonderful thing to try to help people when we see that they are in jeopardy of harming themselves. But interfering in someone's life without being asked can be very risky as Barney and Mary discover.

Andy brings Rafe to jail for shooting at Barney and Mary. Once again he uses his knowledge of the simple folk of Mayberry to show Rafe how important it is for him to get his shot. At no time does Andy tell Rafe what to do. He uses simple psychology with Rafe to show him how important the shot is, even though Rafe doesn't understand what Andy is doing. Andy tells Rafe that he is smart for not taking the shot. He explains to him that by not taking the shot he will become a hero. He will some day step on a rusty nail or cut himself and then he will die. By dying, Rafe will become a folk hero to the people who live around him. They will learn through Rafe's death the importance of the tetanus shot, and they will all get theirs. But Rafe decides he doesn't want to be a hero, and he agrees to get the shot, and he promises to get the other farmers to have theirs.

"You otta feel a little ashamed too, a big grown up making a big tadoo over a little thing like a shot. Sometimes it's the big ones that make the worst babies." - Barney

Episode 57
"Andy and Barney in the Big City"

Raleigh, North Carolina

"There's worse things than being a plain hick; like being a hungry one." - Andy

I grew up in a small Midwestern village of about 400 people. When I was a senior in high school our school choir took a trip to New York City, where we performed at the 1964 New York World's Fair in Flushing Meadows, New York. As I walked around New York City with my friends, I am sure I stuck out like a sore thumb. My mouth was probably agape, as I stared at the skyscrapers, strangely dressed people, and the rush hour traffic. As I recall, I also had a camera hanging around my neck. I am sure I was an embarrassment to those with me. I indeed looked like "a country hick in the city for the first time" - which is exactly what I was, "a country hick in the city for the first time."

When Andy and Barney travel to Raleigh, they are certainly out of their element. But right from the very beginning, Barney is out to impress everyone with his sophisticated ways. He signs the hotel register, Bernard P. Fife, M.D. Naturally, the registration clerk assumes Barney is a doctor, when in reality the M.D. stands for Mayberry Detective.

Everything is so different in Raleigh – even the menus. They aren't even written in English. Rather than risk looking like a hick by asking for help, Barney decides to point out several choices. After all, they are in the hotel restaurant, and if it is on the menu, it is bound to be good. Besides, it will be a good way to learn some new words. Andy, on the other hand, believes that good old plain talk is the best way to handle the problem of ignorance. So he asks for a steak, baked potato, and green beans. Once again Andy is proven right. He ends up with his steak, baked potato, and green beans while Barney gets brains and snails.

None of us likes to admit that we don't know something. Few of us enjoy looking like "hicks" around other people. But pretending to be something that we are not usually is not the best approach. In the end we are still who we are, and we probably need to ask ourselves an important question. Do I really need to try to impress someone so much that I cannot be who I really am?

Barney doesn't learn much from his dinner experience. He has decided to nab himself a jewel thief while in Raleigh. If he can get their names in the paper, it would help get more money to buy equipment back in Mayberry. When they first check into the hotel, Barney spots a suspicious man eyeing up some jewels that a guest is wearing. He immediately thinks the man is a jewel thief, and he decides to capture him in the act. While Andy is visiting the Raleigh Police Department, Barney continues on his case by teaming up with a man he thinks owns a newspaper company. Together they follow the suspicious man. They end up locking him in a closet, and while Barney goes to call Andy, the newspaper man hopes to slip away with the jewels in his pocket.

Each of us has a certain place in life. The important thing is to find our place. Not everyone can be the person at the top. For every important hospital brain surgeon, there must be a small town family practitioner. This does not mean one is more important than the other. Barney needs to accept that he is a deputy sheriff in a small town. He is not a big city detective. I imagine once Barney finds out who he really has in the closet; he just might be a little closer to reality. But with Barney, one just never does know. For tomorrow there will be another crime, and Barney will be there too.

"Right over there, eating mints. He's had eight so far." - Barney

Episode 58
"Wedding Bells for Aunt Bee"

Living Room at the Taylor Home Inn

"You can love a whole lot of people – the more the better. You see, that's the regular kind of love. And it's a fine, fine thing." - Andy

The Taylor house is undeniably a household full of love. The love between Andy and Opie is woven throughout every episode. The love that Aunt Bee has for Andy and Opie is evident by the way she cares for their every need. Opie and Andy's love for Aunt Bee is also easy to see as they go about their closely knit lives in Mayberry. Much has changed since the very first episode when Opie does not want Rose to leave, and he can not accept Aunt Bee's presence in his life. She now has a special place in his heart, and it will be there for a long, long time.

A real dilemma arises in the Taylor home when Aunt Bee's best friend, Clara, convinces her that she is standing in the way of Andy's true happiness. Clara gives Aunt Bee the idea that Andy doesn't have time for romance in his life as long as she is living in the house. Her being there does not allow Andy the freedom he needs to get a wife for himself and a mother for Opie. So Aunt Bee decides to invite Fred Goss, owner of Goss' Cleaners, to supper. Fred was asking Aunt Bee to go to a dance that very day. Aunt Bee doesn't particularly like Fred, but Clara reminds her that at their ages, they can't be too choosy. Thus a very unlikely romance begins between Aunt Bee and Fred.

Aunt Bee is a truly unselfish person in this wonderful episode. She is very happy living with Andy and Opie; but she is willing to sacrifice her own happiness in order to assure that Andy can find a wife. She is even willing to go so far as marrying a man she does not love. Fred continues to court Aunt Bee, and it looks as if it will only be a matter of time before they set a date. Everything seems to be moving along perfectly until Andy tells Opie that Aunt Bee is getting married because she has that special deep down kind of love for Fred Goss. When Andy sees the tears in Aunt Bee's eyes, he realizes something is wrong. How many of us would ever consider making the sacrifice that Aunt Bee is willing to make for Andy's happiness? In the end Aunt Bee finds out that Andy's love for her is equally as great as hers is for him. Andy would no more turn Aunt Bee out of his home than he would Opie, and he makes sure Aunt Bee understands that fact.

Families are bound together by blood and love. The Taylor family may be a small one, but there is enough love between them to fill many a home. When Andy discovers the real reason for Aunt Bee's romance with Fred, he quickly assures Aunt Bee of her place in his home. But now they have a problem about what to do with Fred Goss. They certainly don't want to hurt Fred's feelings. As far as he is concerned, Aunt Bee cares for him deeply, and he feels the same way about her. The thing to do is come up with a way to change Fred's feelings. Knowing that Fred is passionate about his cleaning business, and he really detests paper taffeta dresses with buttons and rhinestones, Andy describes the dress that Aunt Bee will be wearing to the big dance, and he suggests once all the women see it, they will all want one. Fred falls for the fabricated story and decides to take Clara to the dance instead. She is wearing a plain cotton dress with no rhinestones. It sounds to me like this could be a match made in heaven.

"Now the rule around here has got to be no marrying off unless it's of the absolutely overwhelming nature." - Andy

Episode 59
"Three's A Crowd

"Thelma Lou, Barn. Listen, we can't make it over to Mary's tonight. Ah, Andy and I want to spend some time alone. Now you call Mary." - Barney

We have all heard the old saying, "Two's company, three's a crowd." Well, apparently Barney Fife has never heard it. Although Barney is Andy's dearest and oldest friend, and although Andy enjoys spending a lot of time with Barney, there is a limit to what a friend must have to endure. All during their long friendship Barney and Andy have been double dating. Now they are even triple dating; it's Andy, Mary, and Barney.

Andy enjoys a developing relationship with Mary, the new nurse in Mayberry. But the only time he gets to spend time with her is when he and Mary and Barney and Thelma Lou are out together. One night Andy finally decides something needs to change. Andy, Mary, Barney, and Thelma Lou are spending the evening together at Mary's house. It is getting late, so Thelma Lou asks Barney to take her home. Andy is delighted with this bit of news, for he now thinks he will have some time alone with Mary. Andy and Mary are about to have some pizza and some precious time alone when Barney suddenly returns. He has decided it is too early for him to go home, so he might as well come back and spend some more time with Andy and Mary.

Andy has hinted and hinted to Barney that he wants to spend some time alone with Mary, so he can talk to her. Even when he comes straight out and tells Barney, poor old Barney just does not get it. Then when the light bulb in his brain finally lights up, he jumps to the conclusion that Andy wants to be alone with Mary so he can "pop the question". Barney organizes a big party, and the plan is to go to Mary's house later that night, after Andy has had a chance to propose to Mary. But when they barge in to surprise the happy couple, they find an empty house.

Courtships in Mayberry are far different from what we know today. A date in Mayberry probably means going to the movies and then stopping off at the diner for a hamburger followed by a leisurely walk home. As the romance progresses, perhaps there will be a drive out in the country to Meyer's Lake or even the duck pond. Quite often young couples attend the church socials or the Harvest Balls which are held in Mayberry every fall. In any event, the courtships move at a slow pace, and quite often last for years before the big step into marriage finally takes place.

After Barney and his friends find Mary's house empty, Barney decides they must have taken a drive. He takes the entire crowd out to Myer's Lake where they find Andy and Mary sitting in Mary's car with the top down listening to soft music. So much for time alone. But everyone takes the news about Barney's big mistake in good spirit, as all join in with singing and eating while Andy asks Mary if it is all right for him to kiss her.

Unfortunately, the romance between Andy and Mary ends here, for we never see Mary again. Perhaps Barney's constant tagging along with Andy was too much for Mary to take, and she decides to just leave Mayberry for good. Or perhaps she thinks Andy really is going to propose to her, so she decides to end the relationship on her own. Like so many other girls in Andy's life, Mary just quietly disappears from Mayberry. Will Andy ever find that special someone who will become a permanent part of his life?

"Everybody got enough potato salad? Come on speak up now, let's finish everything. We're only going to have to throw it out, you know." - Barney

Episode 60
"The Bookie Barber"

"Look out now, a two chair shop. Now there's something you've always wanted Floyd." - Andy

Floyd Lawson has a dream of owning a two-chair shop. But he has never taken the risk of adding an additional chair to his business. Change doesn't come easily for Floyd. He tried having a female manicurist in the shop, but that did not work out the way he had hoped, so the chances of his adding another chair are probably quite slim.

One day Mr. Medwin enters Floyd's Barber Shop and makes Floyd an offer. Mr. Medwin tells Floyd that he is a semi-retired barber who wants to settle down in a small town. He offers Floyd his services as a second barber. He will bring in another chair, and he even offers to provide his own customers.

Floyd is one of those people we all know who is quite gullible and naïve. He spends all his time in his barber shop cutting hair and visiting with the friendly folks in town. He isn't very worldly, and he has probably spent his entire life in Mayberry. So what will he do about this possible change in business? Andy is present when Mr. Medwin makes his offer, and he seems to think it is just great, so Mr. Medwin and Floyd settle everything with a handshake, and Floyd's Barber Shop becomes a two chair shop.

Soon some very suspicious and strange looking customers start arriving to get haircuts, shampoos, and facials from Mr. Medwin, and old trusting Floyd just takes it in stride thinking about all the money he is making. Even when these same men come back day after day, Floyd suspects nothing is wrong. Andy seems to think that something might be amiss when he sees the same three men return the very next day for haircuts. But Barney has an explanation. He says they all have a haircut "compellsion". That is something like a hand washing "compellsion."

As it turns out, Mr. Medwin has no intentions of supplementing his retirement income by cutting hair. He is a bookie, and he is using Floyd's Barber Shop as his collection place. Now quite often we read about criminals who are caught because of their stupidity and carelessness. I think I would have to categorize Mr. Medwin as one of these types. There are several strange things about his entire bookie business. Why does Mr. Medwin set up his bookie organization on Main Street right next to the sheriff's office? Why do he and his men exchange their takings right out in the open where everyone can look through the large picture window and witness the entire thing? Certainly he can find a more private and secluded place to do his illegal activities.

I imagine Mr. Medwin thinks that the sleepy little town of Mayberry, with the sheriff without a gun, is the perfect place to operate his organization. But he underestimates Andy and Barney and the good people of Mayberry. Little does he realize that Sarah, the telephone operator, routinely listens in on conversations and then passes this information along. Andy soon learns the truth behind Mr. Medwin, and when he shares this information with Barney, Mayberry's Main Street once again becomes the scene of another exciting capture by Deputy Sheriff Barney Fife. But this time he becomes entangled with three crooks, and not just one.

"Those phone calls were from girlfriends. Yeh, I just had a message that Apple Dumpling is coming in at ten to one." - Floyd

Episode 61
"Andy on Trial"

"Maybe I will take one for my deputy. He likes to smoke one of these when he's feeling especially sporty." - Andy

*A*ndy on Trial" is an episode where we see a very different side of Deputy Barney Fife. Although we do see Barney bragging and elevating himself while having a soda with a pretty young girl, we also see a very humble side of Barney when he defends Andy's sheriff abilities with a true passion that only a best friend can do.

Andy arrests J. Howard Jackson, a big city newspaper publisher, for failing to return to Mayberry to face a traffic charge. He brings him back to Mayberry to face the charges. The publisher is outraged at Andy's actions, but he reluctantly returns to Mayberry with Andy, because that is all he can do. When Andy fines Mr. Jackson $15.00, he is further outraged for having to come all the way to Mayberry for that pittance. Mr. Jackson orchestrates a personal vendetta against Andy to punish him for having the audacity to arrest him and waste his time.

Important people sometimes think they are above the law. Some think that because they have a position of importance or influence, special consideration will be taken when they are caught doing something wrong. Mr. Jackson thinks briefly about bribery, until Andy sets him straight on that prospect. Andy believes that no one is above the law, and he has no qualms about arresting the important newspaper publisher. He may overlook some minor offenses by the people of Mayberry, but when it comes to flaunting the law by refusing to attend a trial, that is an entirely different matter.

Mr. Jackson puts his vendetta into action when he sends Jean Boswell, a pretty young reporter, to Mayberry posing as a college student. She meets Barney, and tells him she is researching small town government for a class. Barney takes it upon himself to give her a tour of the town. Not knowing who the young girl really is, Barney tells her that if he were sheriff, he would do things a lot differently in Mayberry. He tells her of Andy's many weaknesses and the crimes that go unpunished in Mayberry, not knowing that his statements will be used to get Andy suspended as sheriff.

Jean Boswell returns to her newspaper, and a scathing article about Andy's poor performance as sheriff appears in Mr. Jackson's newspaper. A hearing is ordered to decide whether Andy should remain as sheriff of Mayberry. Barney's true loyalty to Andy comes through as he testifies at the hearing against Andy. Barney admits that he sometimes brags and says things he shouldn't. He insists that he be allowed to speak on Andy's behalf, and we witness Barney's deep respect for Andy.

Friendship is a very valuable and special thing. A true test of friendship is how friends react during times of adversity. Barney does not let Andy down. Because of his passionate praise of Andy and his abilities, Andy is restored as sheriff of Mayberry. Unfortunately, Barney does not learn much from this experience. No sooner is the hearing over, and Barney is once again bragging to Thelma Lou how he got Andy off the hook. But that's the true Barney, and I wouldn't want him any other way.

"Why Andy's the best friend I got in the whole world. As far as I'm concerned he's the best sheriff too." - Barney

Episode 62
"Cousin Virgil"

"Yeh, it's all here. We just have to get it back on the plates." - Andy

*f*or the first and only time ever we meet a member of Barney's family. We did get a glimpse of Barney's mother when Barney frisks her back in Episode 2, "The Manhunt," but now we actually meet Barney's Cousin Virgil, and it shouldn't come as a surprise that he is an awkward, uncoordinated, bumbling person. Now if Barney and Andy are cousins, doesn't that make Virgil part of Andy's family too? Andy and Virgil never call each other cousin, so apparently they are not related. Most likely it is much to Andy's delight; for having one Fife in his family is enough, but two just might be more than Andy could handle.

Barney decides that Cousin Virgil will help out around the sheriff's office while visiting in Mayberry. Virgil, however, does not make a very good first impression with Andy. After having to look for Virgil because he misses his bus, and after having him at his house for dinner, Andy decides he does not want Virgil working anywhere near the courthouse. While eating dinner, Virgil knocks over glasses of water on the table, and then the meat lands in Andy's lap. To make matters even worse, he crashes the squad car into the garage while getting it for Barney. The next day Barney allows Virgil to do a few simple jobs around the courthouse, but everything goes wrong, and Virgil ends up breaking a glass cabinet and ruining the cell keys. To make matters worse, Otis is in jail and it appears he will be late for a job interview because the cell doors can't be opened.

In some ways I can identify with Cousin Virgil. When it comes to a mechanical aptitude, I am sure I would score somewhere near the bottom of the scale. I just do not have the fine motor skills to do carpentry work or any kind of craft activities. It seems whenever I try to fix something around our house, I end up having to hire someone to repair what I have only made worse. I am also rather self conscious if there is someone watching me while I work, so I tend to do things better when I work by myself.

Cousin Virgil has always been rather awkward and clumsy. He tells Andy that it makes him very nervous when someone stands over him while he works. When Andy sees the beautiful hand carved toys that Virgil makes for Opie, he finds it almost impossible to believe that Virgil made them. Virgil explains that he made them when no one was watching. Andy begins to get a new appreciation for the problems that face young Virgil.

Virgil is like many people. He has no confidence in himself. Perhaps he grew up in a household where he was criticized for everything he did. Perhaps school was difficult for him, and his teachers never took the time to praise Virgil when he did things right.

In any event, Virgil believes he is clumsy and awkward, and so he is clumsy and awkward. Only when Andy gives Virgil an opportunity to do something difficult by himself, does Virgil discover that he can actually do something right. Even though they are cousins and alike in many ways, Barney and Virgil are vastly different in one important aspect. While Virgil has no self confidence and believes he is not good at anything, Cousin Barney is full of confidence, and he believes he knows everything. Too bad a little of Virgil can't rub off on Barney, and a little of Barney can't rub off on Virgil.

"Every once in a while he'd give me a job to do and I'm kind of awkward, you know. Well I'd start to do a job and with him watching me I'd get all jumpy and fumbly and so he had to take over." - Cousin Virgil

Episode 63
"Deputy Otis"

"I know I done wrong Andy but I figured what's the harm. I didn't know they were coming here. See, I was always the black sheep in my family and it just felt good changing colors." - Otis Campbell

*O*tis Campbell is Mayberry's town drunk. Everyone in Mayberry knows this and they accept Otis for who he is. Otis isn't a bad sort of fellow. Five days a week he is a hard working man. He works as a glue dipper at the Mayberry Furniture Company. But come the weekend, everyone knows Otis will be spending his time in the Mayberry jail. It isn't because Otis is being mean or dangerous; it is so he will not hurt himself. Andy tries numerous times to get Otis to stop drinking, but it never works. So Andy now takes Otis as he is, and in fact, he is one of Otis' best friends. Only in Mayberry can the county sheriff be good friends with the town drunk.

Attitudes toward alcohol abuse have changed dramatically since the days of Mayberry. People who abuse alcohol were once thought to be people who just liked to drink. The same thing is true in Mayberry. The people of Mayberry laugh at Otis' antics, and we laugh right along with them. In today's world, Otis would not be so readily accepted. He would not be laughed at; he would be pitied. We have come to realize that alcoholism is a disease, and it needs to be treated as such. With Otis, we need to look beyond his drinking problem. When we do, we find a wonderful, warm, caring person, who has a very tender heart, despite his problem. It is that Otis who we have come to love. And it is that Otis that Andy tries so hard to help in this touching episode.

Andy is always one to think about a person's feelings. He knows Otis will be very embarrassed if his family finds out about Otis' drinking. To make matters even worse, Otis has told his brother that he is working for the sheriff. Otis has written letters to him using the courthouse stationary. To help Otis out, Andy comes up with a plan to make Otis a temporary deputy while his family is visiting. If he is able to help Otis avoid some embarrassment, then he is going to do whatever he can. After all, Otis is his friend.

There are those who might say Andy does wrong by passing off Otis as a deputy. How can he justify making a common drunk a deputy? By hiding the truth from Otis' family isn't Andy condoning Otis' drinking? Andy thinks not. Andy believes that by giving Otis a chance to avoid embarrassment, perhaps some good will come of it. After all, doesn't everyone deserve a chance?

Otis makes a very unexpected and shocking discovery while under the guise as a deputy. He becomes worried when he can not find Ralph late in the day. He is certain Ralph is asking questions around Mayberry, and he will discover the truth. But it is Otis who discovers the truth about Ralph when he comes staggering into the jail and locks himself up. You see, Ralph is the town drunk back home. But he vows to Otis that he is going to stop drinking and become respectable. After all, if Otis can do it, so can he. Andy hopes his little deception will end up helping Otis. He has no idea that in the end, it will be Ralph who will benefit the most. Perhaps we all need to take a closer look at those around us who suffer from alcohol abuse. A lot can be learned from how Andy treats his friend Otis.

"Ralph Campbell, I'm ashamed of you." - Otis Campbell

Season Number Three

Episode 64
"Mr. McBeevee"

"No, Mr. McBeevee is easy to see; especially his hat. He wears a great big shiny silver hat." - Opie

*O*pie has a lot of fun in his back yard playing with his horse Blackie. One morning at breakfast Opie tells Barney all about Blackie. Excitable Barney immediately goes to the back yard hoping to see Blackie. When Blackie fails to appear after Barney calls and whistles to him, Andy tells Barney that Blackie is a bit on the invisible side. Barney becomes rather upset because Andy keeps leading him on about Blackie when all the time he is just an imaginary horse. Apparently Barney never had any invisible pets or friends when he was a child. Or maybe he has just forgotten how much fun they can be.

Most children have invisible make-believe friends or pets sometime in their childhood. Pretending is a normal, healthy part of childhood. What would childhood be without fairies, elves, ghosts, witches, or make-believe horses? It is when children start to really believe in such things and can't distinguish between the real world and the world of make-believe, when there is a possibility of problems arising. Opie knows his horse is just pretend, yet having Blackie is almost as much fun as having a real horse.

Andy sees no problem with Opie having an invisible horse. But when Opie shows Andy a new hatchet, which he says he got from a Mr. McBeevee, Andy begins to wonder. Opie describes Mr. McBeevee as a man with a silver hat and many hands. He jingles when he walks in the trees, and he can make smoke come out of his ears. He learned that from the cannibals. But it is when Opie finally shows Andy a shiny new quarter that Mr. McBeevee gives him that Andy decides some action on his part must be taken. It is time for Opie to learn the difference between real and make believe.

107

As we might expect, Barney has to involve himself in Andy's problem. He tells Andy that he thinks Opie really believes in Mr. McBeevee. Barney decides to practice his identification techniques to get at the truth, so he asks Opie to describe Mr. McBeevee. When Opie gives Barney his description of his strange friend, Barney ends his experiment in frustration. Andy, however, is determined to get to the truth.

Parents want to believe their children when they are told things. Andy wants to believe there is a Mr. McBeevee. But the description and story Opie tells him are just too unbelievable for Andy. When he puts his foot down and insists that Opie admit there is no Mr. McBeevee, Opie just cannot do it. He refuses to deny Mr. McBeevee, and with tear filled eyes he asks Andy if he believes him. Hesitantly, Andy says he does.

Like so many parents, Andy is faced with a real dilemma. Should he force Opie to deny something he believes in and punish him if he doesn't, or should he believe in his own little boy? Andy tells Opie that, yes, he believes him. What Andy really means is that he believes in Opie, but not in Mr. McBeevee. Andy goes for a walk in the very woods where Opie claims to have seen Mr. McBeevee. He doesn't go there hoping to find Mr. McBeevee; he goes there to think. But when he says "Mr. McBeevee," out of frustration, Andy gets a big surprise. Someone is up in the trees and it is none other than Mr. McBeevee. Now Opie and Andy both know there is a real Mr. McBeevee. The only thing left to do is convince Barney. And that may take some real doing.

"No, no, no. I do believe in Opie." - Andy

Episode 65
"Andy's Rich Girlfriend"

"And she is one of the rich and they are different. From the minute they're born with that silver spoon in their hand life is different." - Barney

ndy has had a number of girlfriends come and go throughout the past few years. Andy's first sweetheart, Ellie Walker, suddenly disappears from Andy's life. Then Andy courts Mary for a short time, and she too leaves Mayberry. Now Peggy McMillan enters Andy's life, and once again romance seems to be in the air. We know that Barney always seems to get involved in Andy's relationships with young women. He just can not let Andy manage his own affairs. He always has to tell Andy what to do or what not to do, but one thing is certain. He is always encouraging Andy to stay involved with his girlfriends. He is eager for Andy to get married. So why does Barney actually try to persuade Andy not to court Peggy when she comes to Mayberry? It seems so out of character for Barney. There must be something terribly wrong with Peggy.

Andy and Peggy enjoy being together a great deal. The simple lifestyle in Mayberry seems to be just what Peggy is looking for. She enjoys going out to Myer's Lake with Andy, Barney and Thelma Lou. Everything seems to be going along just great until her father suddenly sends her a brand new expensive convertible. It is then that Andy discovers that Peggy comes from a very wealthy family. Her father owns a large feed and grain company, and Peggy has had every advantage during the years she was growing up. Once Andy shares this information with Barney, Barney decides Andy must break up with Peggy. He gives a very convincing argument for it, but will Andy listen?

It is usually not a very good idea to get involved in another's romantic lives. We should not offer advice unless we are asked, and even then we should give it sparingly. We have seen many times that Barney is not shy when it comes to telling others what to do. He tells Andy in no uncertain terms that Peggy is not the girl for him. After Andy experiences a miserable evening out with her at an expensive restaurant in Raleigh, Andy decides to take Barney's advice and he begins avoiding Mary with no explanation.

How important is it in a relationship that both people have the same economic status? Is it possible for a wealthy person to find happiness with a person who has few material assets? Will these economic differences cause jealousy and hard feelings at some point, or can two people overlook these differences and have a meaningful and lasting relationship? In some cultures, people of different classes can never consider marriage. One just does not marry beneath, or above, one's station in life. It is not acceptable, and in some societies, it is not legally allowed.

When Peggy finds out the reason Andy is avoiding her, she confronts Andy and calls him a snob? He is snubbing her because he can not believe that she enjoys doing the simple things Andy and his friends enjoy. In the end, it is Andy who learns a valuable lesson about the importance money should or should not have in a relationship. He also is reminded, once again, that he maybe does not need to listen to Barney's advice when it comes to his courtships. Perhaps it is true that "Father Knows Best", but whether "Barney Knows Best" is an entirely different matter.

"You know, one night Thelma Lou, the next night, somebody else. You know, keep them guessing; it's lighter." - Barney

Episode 66
"Andy and the New Mayor"

"Well Mayor, if there is somebody I have to shoot at I'll get a gun and shoot at 'em. I'll give Barney some bullets and he'll shoot at 'em too."- Andy

*A*nyone who lives in a small town knows that small town politics can be rather interesting. Mayberry's form of government is a town council which is led by a mayor. In "Andy and the New Mayor," we say farewell to Mayberry's fat little Mayor Pike, and we meet Mayberry's newly elected Mayor Stoner. Being new to the office, Mayor Stoner arrives at his office early on his first day, and he decides to meet with all the important departments of Mayberry's government to discuss impending improvements and changes. There is no way for Andy to get out of the meeting with Mayor Stoner, as the mayor's office is directly above the jail. But Andy is late to the meeting because he and Opie have been fishing, and by the time he gets to the mayor's office, all the other town officials are gone. To say Andy's first meeting with the new mayor gets off to a rather rocky start, is an understatement, to say the least.

From the very onset of Mayor Stoner being elected mayor, he becomes a thorn in Andy's side. He and Andy just do not see eye to eye on how things should be done. On his very first day in office, he questions why Andy does not wear a gun. He has a rather lengthy list of things he wants to see improved. When he visits Andy's office a little later, he orders Andy to not release Jess Morgan for three days so he can get his crops harvested. No sooner does the mayor leave when Andy releases Jess, which sets up a major confrontation with the mayor. Of course Barney is a nervous wreck over the entire ordeal. He thinks Andy is just asking for trouble, so he goes about trying to protect him.

Mayor Stoner's attitude is not unusual for elected officials. His position of leadership goes to his head, and he likes to use the power that the voters have bestowed upon him. However, he does not always use his power in constructive ways. Rather than working with Andy, he chooses to give orders without really knowing how the sheriff's office is run. The mayor does not concern himself with Jess' personal problems. The law says he is to be locked up, and locked up is what he is going to be. It is apparent that Mayor Stoner does not agree with Andy's "human equation" philosophy.

Andy always looks at a prisoner as a person first. Most of the people he arrests are friends and neighbors. Most of the offenses are for traffic violations or moon shining. Moon shining is a way of life for some folks around Mayberry, and even though it is a crime, Andy knows the people involved are not bad people. None of his usual prisoners are a danger to anyone. Most of them have simply fallen on hard times or have made poor choices. So Andy gives them the benefit of the doubt and treats them accordingly.

The thing that makes Andy such a successful sheriff is that he always shows compassion and respect for everyone. He does not look down upon those who are being held in his jail. They are not second class citizens. He always believes that treating everyone with dignity and respect is very important – even if they are prisoners.

"You see mayor, if you'd let me run my own office, Jess wouldn't be up in that tree, and you wouldn't be up there beside him with your clothes all torn up, and we wouldn't be down here with a bear in our back seat. You beat everything, you know that." - Andy

Episode 67
"Andy and Opie Bachelors"

"We could chew tar. Johnny Paul Jason says chewing tar is real good for the teeth." - Opie

*A*ndy and Opie very seldom need to care for themselves. Aunt Bee is always there to provide their every need. So what happens when Aunt Bee suddenly has to leave town for a few days? Will Andy and Opie be able to cope as bachelors? Aunt Bee is convinced that she should not go. All the way to the bus stop she continues fretting about how the boys will get along without her. She is reminding Andy about the cooking and his underwear when Peggy McMillan joins their little group at the bus stop. Aunt Bee asks Peggy if she will check in on the boys, and Peggy assures her that she will.

Most of the men who live in Mayberry are rather inept at household duties. Mayberry families are traditional families, with the woman of the house staying home to keep house, do the marketing, and prepare the meals. The men are the breadwinners, and as a result have little time to learn and develop their domestic skills. They are totally dependent upon their women folk to tend to their basic needs in life. And in Mayberry, the women seem to be quite content with their appointed roles.

After Aunt Bee leaves Andy and Opie, things do not go too well for the two bachelors. Andy is not a very good cook, and making the meals proves to be far more difficult than he expected. Peggy happens to come over just as Andy is preparing dinner. The roast in the oven is burnt to a crisp, and the kettle on the stove is in flames. Peggy offers to cook supper for Andy and Opie, and after a few protests, Andy reluctantly accepts her offer. It proves to be a very wise decision, as Peggy is an excellent cook, and she enjoys helping out the two helpless bachelors. She prepares a wonderful meal, and the table is set to perfection, with candles and a flower centerpiece. Their dinner is perfect.

When Floyd Lawson hears that Peggy is cooking for Andy and Opie, he wastes no time in informing Andy that it won't be long before Andy will be changing the name on his mailbox to read Mr. and Mrs. Andrew Taylor. Andy doesn't take Floyd too seriously until Peggy insists that she continue to drop in to help the boys. Floyd's words of warning suddenly come back to Andy so he decides that he needs to put a stop to Peggy's help.

Peggy wants to help Andy and Opie because she truly enjoys it. She has no ulterior motive despite what Floyd thinks. Andy does not understand that Peggy just wants to help him when he needs it for the simple pleasure of it. He allows Floyd's wild imagination to cloud his opinion of Peggy. Before Floyd comes into the picture, Andy is enjoying having Peggy around, and Opie is thrilled to be with her. But once Floyd puts ideas in Andy's head, things change in a hurry. Andy tells Peggy that she needs to stop going to so much trouble, and he doesn't seem to notice that Peggy looks hurt.

There are many kind and helpful people in the world just like Peggy. They enjoy helping people in need. They expect nothing in return. They do it for the pure satisfaction in knowing they are being of use. Fortunately Andy realizes his mistake, and once again he allows Peggy to join Opie and him at their family table. They find supper is much more enjoyable. Andy feels like singing again, and Opie wants to talk. They both discover something very important. A home is just not a home without the presence of a woman. And if that woman isn't Aunt Bee, why not let it be Peggy?

"You're not troubling me and bothering me at all. I'll just fix you up something you'll just love." - Miss Peggy

Episode 68
"The Cow Thief"

"A moulage? Yah, that's right. We decided not to make a moulage. Oh we told a few people, but we decided it didn't make sense to upset folks running around blabbing, making a big moulage out of it." - Barney

*M*ayberry is a relatively crime free town. On occasion, however, a crime is committed that tests the crime solving abilities of Sheriff Taylor and Deputy Fife. This time someone is stealing some of the local farmers' prize cows, and Andy and Barney are not making much headway in their investigation. Mayor Stoner once again takes it upon himself to criticize Andy, and he decides to call in an expert to help solve the case. In the past Andy and Barney have not had much luck when working with outsiders. The State Police have always asked them to stay out of the cases. They always thought Andy had other things to do, like tracking down chicken thieves and whatnot.

How will Andy and Barney react when an outsider comes to Mayberry to help them do their job? Will they resent the person who is coming to take charge of the case? Or will they welcome him as a person who might possibly help them solve a real mystery? It might just depend upon what kind of person this outsider turns out to be.

When Mr. Upchurch, the outsider, does arrive, Barney has decided he will be an interloper so he is going to give him the big freeze. Andy, on the other hand, decides he will welcome the assistance and feels it might be of help in solving the case. So Mr. Upchurch arrives on the scene. Even Barney welcomes Mr. Upchurch, and eagerly sets out to help him. Of course Barney had to change his tune when Upchurch praises his recent report on country road safety that he has submitted. He especially likes Barney's little jingle, "Walk on the left side after dark, and you'll end up playing a harp."

How should we treat outsiders who are assigned to work with us at our jobs? An important consideration is that in many cases these outsiders do not ask to help us. In fact they may resent coming to us as much as we resent their coming. How we treat these outsiders, and how we work with them can greatly determine if their help will be successful. It is easy to feel threatened when an outsider is assigned to work with us. We might feel they will be critical of our techniques and efforts. It just might be that we all harbor some insecurity within, and the presence of an outsider on our home turf may well cause some of that insecurity to surface.

Mr. Upchurch is only doing his job. He doesn't come to Mayberry to belittle Andy's crime solving techniques. He comes with the intention of offering his expertise and experience. Andy understands this, and he accepts his help without feeling threatened. As it turns out, it is Andy who is able to teach Mr. Upchurch a few things about solving crimes. Andy always seems to have a sixth sense when it comes to knowing the people in Mayberry. He can notice things that other people do not see. While Mr. Upchurch and Barney are busy making their footprint moulage, Andy is also thinking about footprints. But he is not thinking about the footprints that they found; he is thinking about the footprints that they did not find. And that proves to be the decisive clue. Chalk one up for the Mayberry Sheriff's Department and good old common sense.

"Some bad fellow's been stealing cows. Know anything about that, do you? Seems three fellows been doing it. Two of them pretty good size." - Luke Jensen

Episode 69
"Barney Mends a Broken Heart"

"Yah, an old college pal of hers. Guess what his name was? Don. Wouldn't you know his name would be Don?" - Andy

$\mathcal{J}$ealousy is a normal emotion. We all experience it from time to time. Yet jealousy can be one of the most destructive emotions if we do not keep it under control. It is easy to be jealous of others when we live in a very materialistic society. We see our neighbors get a new car, and a little bit of jealousy surfaces in us. Our coworker gets a big promotion, which means a raise in salary and more perks, and jealousy creeps its way into our soul. We may feel it just isn't fair when the other guys seem to have it all.

There is another jealousy that can be more destructive; it can destroy relationships. It comes when the one we love receives attention by another. With men and women working so closely together these days, people sometimes form many close friendships. Innocent flirtations and close proximity with others can bring about jealousy; even when there is no reason for it. All of us have friends of the opposite sex. Many are friends that we have had for a long time. When we enter into a serious relationship with one person, it is difficult for us if we need to let go of these old friendships we cherish. Yet, sometimes they can cause hard feelings and insecurities to our spouse or significant other. When we decide to have a serious relationship with just one person, we may find ourselves having to spend much less time with our previous close friends.

When Andy arrives at Peggy's house for a date, a strange man answers the door. He is an old friend of Peggy's, and he unexpectedly shows up at her house. Because he is an old friend, Peggy feels she can not just leave him and go on her date with Andy. Rather than be understanding of the predicament that Peggy is facing, Andy allows jealousy to take over. He gets upset with Peggy for not going with him, and he leaves in a jealous huff, resulting in a serious rift which proves to be difficult to mend.

Who is at fault for the misunderstanding between Andy and Peggy? Should Peggy tell her friend Don that she can not entertain him because she has a previous engagement? Or should Andy be more understanding, and simply tell Peggy to enjoy her time with her friend, and that they will go out the next night? Either action will prevent the problem between them, but neither one is taken, which means Barney will have to intervene.

The problem probably isn't so much that Peggy does not go out with Andy. The problem is more that Andy is jealous of Don. I doubt if Andy would have reacted the way he did if Peggy's visitor would have been an old girlfriend. Andy does not like the idea of a good looking male friend of Peggy's spending the evening alone with her. Is it that Andy really thinks he might lose Peggy to Don, or is it simply that his ego is damaged a little by what he thinks might be competition for Peggy's affection? Or perhaps it is just difficult for Andy to admit Peggy may have had other boyfriends before he came along.

Unfortunately for Andy, Barney once again decides to get involved. Believing things are over between Andy and Peggy, Barney arranges for Andy to go out with other girls. Of course Andy has no interest in any of them, but unknown to Andy, Barney's interfering ways will actually bring him back together with Peggy. But it certainly doesn't happen the way Andy would have chosen. But at least Peggy and Andy make up and are back together. And despite his bumbling efforts, Barney takes credit for the whole thing.

"That's a fine plan, Barn. You win your girl, and you lose your eye." - Barney

Episode 70
"Lawman Barney"

"I wish you hadn't done that. Now he's gonna play that ugly game he always plays. I just hate it when he does that." - Andy

*D*eputy Barney Fife does not fit the stereotype of a police officer. He is short, skinny, and very high strung. I doubt if too many people feel threatened or intimidated when Barney makes an arrest or issues a traffic ticket. Most policemen I know are just the opposite of Barney. They are fairly tall, rather well built, and rather stoic by nature. Barney would most likely never be accepted as a police officer with today's standards. He certainly would not be allowed to carry a gun once it is learned he has a greasy finger. He might even be assigned to desk duty where he could fill out reports all day.

Barney quite often gets himself into trouble. He is his own worst enemy. One of the main reasons is that he has the habit of ordering people about, acting very important. But it usually doesn't take long for people to see through this façade. That's when the trouble begins. They just don't take him seriously. Some may even call him a clown.

When coming out of the Snack Bar, Barney notices two farmers selling produce on the streets of Mayberry. This is not allowed in Mayberry, as it takes away business from the local merchants. When Barney confronts the two farmers he starts waving his arms around, and giving orders. Rather than explaining the reasons why they must leave and calmly telling them to go, he gets on his high horse. The farmers see through Barney very quickly, and before long it is Barney who is running away in fear. The farmers threaten Barney, and when they stomp their feet at him, he takes off like a scared rabbit. He returns to the courthouse, where Andy finds him feeling mighty dejected and low.

People of Barney's stature sometimes try to come across as tough guys. Perhaps they realize their size is a disadvantage, and feel they need to make up for it by talking tough. In the case of Barney and the farmers, it really backfires. Barney leaves looking like a whipped puppy. He realizes that when it comes to the two farmers, he has lost any credibility as a police officer. He is scared, and what good is

117

a lawman that is so afraid he cannot carry out his duties. Barney's self confidence has hit a new low.

The depth of Barney's and Andy's friendship once again comes through in this episode. Even though Andy is Barney's boss, he is a friend first. When Andy finds out the farmer's have frightened Barney away, he devises a plan that will get the farmers to leave town, and also restore Barney's pride. Andy returns to the farmers, and he tells them how Barney pretends to be afraid. He says Barney is just setting people up for the kill. He warns them about Barney's clearing his throat, tugging his tie, and hitting his holster. When Barney returns a few minutes later, he does what Andy predicts, and this time it is the farmers who run scared. Unfortunately, Floyd tells the farmers the truth about Barney, so they return to their spot and take up selling again.

An important lesson is illustrated when we see how Andy helps Barney. Even though his plan fails, Andy shows all of us that rather than belittling or ridiculing a person when he has met failure, it is far more constructive and helpful to build him back up. Barney realizes that if he is to be a policeman, he must earn the respect of others. He returns on his own, and through calm talk and words of wisdom, he convinces the farmers it is in their best interest to leave town. Of course Andy was close by; just in case.

"You see Barn; your badge did all your talking for you. You didn't even have to use your gun." - Andy

Episode 71
"The Mayberry Band"

"Well I will admit they sound better than they did last year, but they are still the most disgusting band I have ever heard in all my life. No trip!" - Mayor Stoner

Mayor Stoner and Andy are at it again. However, it has nothing to do with Andy's abilities as sheriff. It is a disagreement about sending the Mayberry Town Band on a trip to Raleigh. As we have seen previously, Mayor Stoner is not the easiest person to get along with. He is very set in his ways, and he enjoys having authority over other people. It doesn't help matters when Mayor Stoner has control over the town's money.

The Mayberry Town Band is a group of men who gets together to play for important functions in Mayberry. They are seen leading the various parades down Main Street. They play for the annual Founder's Day celebration, and each year they participate in the Apricot Festival. These men volunteer their time for practices and performances, and each year the town council sends them to Raleigh as a way of saying thank you for their work. However, this year Mayor Stoner decides that he will not send the band because he believes they are the most disgusting band he has ever heard.

Andy Taylor is well known for his scheming ways. If there is a need to resolve a difficult problem, he will not hesitate to use some rather unusual methods. He doesn't break any laws, or any hard fast rules; he just bends them a little to his advantage. So once again he must come up with a plan to get Mayor Stoner to change his mind. But how can he do it when he also realizes that the band is perhaps the most disgusting band that he has ever heard? But he truly believes the men need to be rewarded for all their work, and he is going to see to it that they get their just reward.

Mayberry is not a very sophisticated town. Most of its citizens have probably never been to an opera or symphony. Their tastes in music lean more toward bluegrass and folk songs. On occasion they hear a wonderful concert by John Masters' choir. For the most part, they spend their lives living within the boundaries of Mayberry. A trip to the state capital is a major outing in their lives. Add to that an opportunity to perform in a music contest and it becomes an even bigger event. So it is only natural for the members of the band to be very disappointed when they find out their trip is not to be.

Once again Andy is able to deceive Mayor Stoner by tricking him into thinking a group of professional musicians is really the Mayberry Town Band. Andy enlists the help of Freddy Fleet's band, as he threatens to hold his vehicle for a bug inspection unless he helps out. Andy may be using some rather underhanded methods to get the band their reward, but he justifies his actions knowing he is not doing it for any personal gain or recognition. He is doing it for the members of the band.

Rewards are an important part of life. We all like to receive recognition for our efforts. Not every person or organization can be great. Yet, there are still many people and groups who work hard at what they do. They may not achieve greatness, and some may not be very good at all. Andy knows the limitations of the Mayberry Town Band. He understands that they will not perform well when they go to the capital. He does know, however, that the members of the band deserve to be rewarded for all their efforts. And besides that, Barney has spent good money on a pair of Andre Kostalanez Marchers. By the way, those are solid brass cymbals and not shoes.

"I just want you to know that I am proud of each and every one of you. You've overcome innumerable obstacles to play well." - Mayor Stoner

Episode 72
"Floyd the Gay Deceiver"

"Floyd Lawson, I'm ashamed of you. You're nothing but a lying wretch." - Floyd

*D*eception seems to be a very common pastime in Mayberry. Andy, Barney and Opie deceive Aunt Bee with their store bought pickles. Andy deceives Otis' family when he makes Otis a temporary deputy. Mayor Stoner is deceived by Andy with the band. Now Andy is about to help Floyd pull off a deception. And it is the granddaddy of them all.

Deception is such a part of human nature. How many of us can honestly say that we never use deception to get something we want? Now if we somehow manage to combine deception with romance, we really can create problems. After all, isn't honesty one of the key elements when one is hoping to develop a romantic relationship? Just try telling that to Floyd Lawson and see what he says.

Floyd is a lonely widower. He is not the most articulate person in the world. He has a habit of mumbling and stuttering whenever he gets into situations where he has to communicate verbally. Knowing his limitations, Floyd joins a lonely-hearts club, and begins exchanging letters with Madeline Grayson, a rich widow. Mrs. Grayson tells Floyd about her wonderful homes, and she sends him a beautiful picture of herself.

Floyd enjoys his correspondence with Mrs. Grayson, but he is not honest in his letters. He deceives Madeline Grayson by telling her he is a rich widower. He even goes so far as doctoring up an old photo, and he includes it in a letter. All of this comes back to haunt old Floyd, when one day he receives a letter from Mrs. Grayson saying she is coming to Mayberry for a visit. It is the beginning of more deceptions when Floyd asks for Andy's help. At first Andy wants nothing to do with Floyd's scheme. Floyd's plan is to have Andy help him to pose as the man he claims to be. When Andy refuses, Floyd threatens to go to Nashville. Being the softhearted man that he is, Andy finally decides to help. He goes one step further, and decides if they are going to pass Floyd off as a rich widower, they might as well do the job right. Andy is watching Cliff Devereaux's house while he is out of town. The house is a stately mansion and will be perfect to use as Floyd's home. Andy also gets Aunt Bee to play the part of "Beatrice the Maid."

As we have seen in early episodes, one deception usually creates more deceptions, and by the time everything is said and done, the deceiving person usually ends up with more problems than can be handled. The time finally comes for Floyd to meet Madeline Grayson. Everything seems to be going along just fine until Mrs. Grayson announces to Floyd that she can stay for an entire week. Andy decides it is time for the truth, but before he can tell Mrs. Grayson about Floyd's deception, he discovers she has been deceiving Floyd as well. Not wanting to hurt Floyd's feelings, Andy never tells him the truth about her, and she leaves quietly, with Floyd thinking she is quite a sport.

Wouldn't it be wonderful if everyone could just be satisfied with whom they are? There would be no need for lies and deceptions. If only we could just say, "Here am I. Take me as I am or don't take me at all." Floyd is a nice man. Certainly by being himself, he would eventually find someone to fill the lonely gap in his life. All he needs to do is take a few lessons on speaking. Then perhaps he would be able to keep his stuttering and mumbling antics under control. This certainly would help him a great deal.

"Ha ha ha, wouldn't you know it? Wouldn't you just know it? All right sheriff, all right, but just tell me one thing. Where did I make my mistake?" - Madeline Grayson

Episode 73
"Opie's Rival"

Peaceful Myer's Lake

"In the name of Boojum Snark, spirit of fire, and Brillen Trant, spirit of the water, and Grovely Barch, spirit of the ash, I hereby declare us blood brothers never to be separated for ever and ever."- Andy

*L*ittle Opie Taylor has no mother. From what we know she most likely died when Opie was very young. Perhaps he doesn't even remember her. But Opie does have a father, and he looks up to him as much as it is humanly possible for a little boy to admire a father. They do everything together. When Opie is not at home or at school, he is usually found at the courthouse spending time with Andy. However, the absolute favorite activity for Andy and Opie to share is fishing. We are reminded of this every time we hear the song "The Fishing Hole" being whistled at the beginning of every episode.

Opie's close relationship with Andy brings him a great deal of comfort and security.   This is exactly what any little motherless boy needs.   But what if someone should come along who might be a threat to that special relationship? How will a little eight year old boy react if suddenly he were no longer the center of his father's life? How will Opie feel if that somebody turns out to be an attractive woman who Andy seems to like very much? Opie once had a very difficult time accepting Aunt Bee into his life when she came to live with them. Will those same feelings resurface again when it comes to Peggy?

Andy and Peggy McMillan are developing a very close relationship. They enjoy each other's company a great deal. They like going to picture shows and out to dinner. They spend time out at Myer's Lake. At first Opie accepts Peggy's relationship with his father for he can see it makes Andy happy, and it really doesn't interfere with the special times he and Andy have. Then one morning Andy discovers that Peggy likes to fish, so he invites her to go fishing with him and Opie the following day. Suddenly things begin to change in Opie's mind. Why does his father want Peggy to go fishing with them? After all, they are blood brothers and they have made a pact. Fishing is something he and his father do alone, or maybe sometimes with Barney? But Barney is special. He is part of the family, and Barney has always been an important part of his life.

Opie has already lost his mother. Now he fears that he may lose his father to Peggy. Who will take him fishing? Who will read to him at night? How will they spend special times together if Peggy is with Andy? These are all things that may be running through Opie's mind as he tries to go to sleep at night? When people grow up it is easy to forget how young children think. Andy doesn't even think about Opie's feelings when he asks Peggy to join them for fishing. He doesn't realize how important it is for Opie to have time alone with his father. So Andy does not foresee the problem that is looming ahead.

Fear of losing a parent is a very real fear among children. It doesn't have to be the death of a parent. It can be fear of losing a parent as the result of a divorce or a remarriage. In Opie's mind his fear is very real. When he sets out to sabotage Andy's relationship with Peggy, he is doing the only thing his young mind can think of.

Parents need to reassure children that they will always be there for them, even if they cannot live in the same house. Love and security are vital for all children, no matter what age. Andy realizes this, and he lets Opie know that he will always be his first love.

"Well, it used to be just you and me. Then Peggy came and you always want her along now and I'm left out. Someday you might not want me anymore." - Opie

Episode 74
"Convicts at Large"

"That insulting attitude of yours isn't getting us anywhere." -
Floyd

*O*ne would think that a day of fishing in Mayberry is a relatively safe pastime. For the most part it is, except when Floyd and Barney run out of gas taking a short cut. After spending time blaming one another for their misadventure, they decide to go looking for a source of gasoline. They soon come upon a cabin in the woods, which Barney says belongs to Mr. O'Malley, a rich resident of Mayberry who made his money in shoes.

When a strange voice answers Barney's call for Mr. O'Malley, Barney just assumes someone is using the cabin, and they readily enter the cabin when invited in. No sooner are they in the cabin, when they find three women all dressed in similar clothes. Barney realizes that the woman are convicts, but before he can do anything about it, the leader of the group grabs Barney's gun, and thanks to Floyd's telling Big Maud where Barney keeps his bullet, they suddenly become two rather helpless hostages.

Barney is never at a loss for words when he is around women. He usually takes charge immediately by talking about himself and bragging about his job on the police force. However, when he is held captive by the three women convicts who have his gun, he is a completely different person. Having Floyd, the meek and nervous barber along, certainly isn't much help. Floyd actually appears to be enjoying the adventure, as he sits on the couch eating bananas and listening to the phonograph. A lot of help he will be if they hope to get away from the convicts.

It is often said that whenever one faces serious trouble, the number one rule is to remain calm. Floyd certainly remembers this rule while being held captive. He sits calmly on the couch and just watches everything as if he doesn't have a care in the world. It seems to be just another day and there isn't anything to get excited about. Floyd has the perfect opportunity to get help when Big Maud sends him to town with Sally to buy groceries. While Floyd goes into the store, Sally stays in the car. This is a chance for Floyd to call Andy and tell him that they are being held captive. But Floyd doesn't say a word, and even when he talks to Andy on the street, he fails to get him to understand the serious situation he and Barney are facing.

I often wonder how I would react if I were in Floyd's place. Not being a trained lawman, perhaps like Floyd, I would be afraid to do anything. Floyd is warned that if he tries anything funny while in town, "Al", will get it. Perhaps it is concern for Barney's safety that keeps Floyd from doing anything heroic while in town. When dealing with a criminal such as Big Maud, one never can tell what might happen. Andy thinks nothing is strange about O'Malley having a party with friends at his cabin. He believes Floyd and then goes on his way. When Andy sees Mr. O'Malley in town, he suspects something is amiss.

As is the case in most situations, Andy is the one who comes to the rescue. With Mr. O'Malley's help, they are able to capture all three convicts. But much to Barney's dismay, Floyd receives front page coverage as the real hero. Poor Barney just can't win. Even when he does help to catch three convicts, he doesn't get the credit. I wonder who it was who told the newspaper that it was Floyd who made the capture. I doubt it if were Andy or Barney.

"Maud, Al, if those hamburgers are ruined, I won't be responsible." - Floyd

Episode 75
"The Bed Jacket"

"Andy, let me make something quite clear. I'm going to be very upset if you do anything foolish about my birthday."- Aunt Bee

*B*irthdays are one of those special days that come around but once a year. We all have them, yet we celebrate them in different ways. Some people enjoy a big party with family and friends, while others perhaps want just a special dinner without much fuss. Then there are those who treat birthdays like they were just another day with no celebration at all. Much perhaps depends on the age of the person with the birthday.

It is Aunt Bee's birthday and she informs Andy that she does not want any fuss made, and she doesn't want him to spend money on an expensive gift. She is trying to downplay the entire thing. But deep down, her heart is set on a beautiful rather expensive bed jacket that she sees in the window at Mrs. Luken's Style Shop. She tries to give Andy some subtle hints about it, and when this doesn't seem to work, she does the same with Mayor Stoner hoping that he will pass the information on to Andy. She isn't quite so subtle with the Mayor though, and she is quite confident he will mention it to Andy when he sees him at their meeting.

My wife and I enjoy celebrating birthdays. When they come around we usually go out to eat, and we enjoy buying gifts. Being a man I have difficulty deciding if I should get something practical or frivolous. I lean toward the practical side because my wife is a practical person. Occasionally I do buy something which I consider frivolous and despite my wife's chastising me for spending the money, I can see that she is very pleased. I do find that the older we get, the more practical we become, and birthdays don't have quite the excitement to them as they once did.

When Andy decides to give Aunt Bee two dozen canning jars, he truly believes he is getting her something she will like. Aunt Bee is a very practical person. She enjoys her housework and cooking. She doesn't wear a lot of jewelry or make-up. Her clothes are very nice, but they would not be considered flashy. So Andy thinks the canning jars are a good gift because they will be very useful to Aunt Bee.

Aunt Bee has her heart set on the bed jacket. Normally she would accept the canning jars graciously and would be happy to have them. But for some reason the bed jacket has really caught her eye. It is all she can think of. But of course it is much too extravagant, and Andy will never buy it. Then she sees Mrs. Luken remove the bed jacket from the store window, and she hands it to Andy. Aunt Bee is thrilled. Her wish is going to come true, and she is going to have the best birthday of her life.

It is not always a good idea to get our hearts set on materialistic things. If we want something so badly, we might be setting ourselves up for disappointment when we do not receive it. Andy wants Aunt Bee's birthday to be special, but then he finds out Aunt Bee saw him buying the bed jacket - the bed jacket she thinks she is getting for her birthday. But it is really the bed jacket Andy has picked up for Mayor

Stoner. This results in Andy having to make a very difficult decision about giving up something that is very important to him – Old Eagle Eyed Annie.

"I said I kept it because it gave me so much enjoyment and that I wouldn't sell it for money. And I didn't sell it for money. I just kind of swapped it for a different kind of enjoyment." - Andy

Episode 76
"The Bank Job"

"I'm so disgusted, I don't feel like eating. Come here; Andy these people are making a fool out of the word security. The bank guard is a joke; look at him. Cash drawers are left open, the vault door is open." - Barney

*D*eputy Sheriff Barney Fife takes his job very seriously. He doesn't tolerate littering or jaywalking on the streets of Mayberry. Parking in front of a fireplug will guarantee a citation. If an ordinance is enacted, then it must be enforced, and Deputy Fife is just the one to enforce it. He takes great pride in arresting people. It means he is doing his job.

Ever so often Barney gets the feeling that he is working in a "hick town". This is especially true after he watches Glen Ford movies. They always have a tendency to get Barney all worked up, and he goes around town looking for wrongs to right. On one such morning Barney walks into the Mayberry Security Bank. Seeing Asa the guard fast asleep, money drawers and the bank vault door open, Barney decides it is his duty to prove to everyone that the Mayberry Security Bank in no way lives up to its name. They need to be taught a thing or two about security.

Banks generally have very distinct safety precautions. Quite often the bank tellers are behind bullet proof windows, alarm buttons are found throughout the bank, and plans of action are developed in case of an actual robbery attempt. But no one at the Mayberry bank seems to think there is a problem. Even when Barney tells Andy about all the deficiencies in the bank security, he is told he should go have a businessman's lunch topped off with a phosphate. It is more than Barney can tolerate, and he leaves the bank in a huff, and is even more determined than ever to teach everyone a lesson.

Now in the real world of police work, if a bank has no security measures, the local police department will probably meet with the bank manager to develop a plan of action. But that is not how things are done in Mayberry. The people in Mayberry are very complacent at times, and no one thinks for a moment that the bank is in any danger of being robbed. After all, the Mayberry Bank does not have the kind of money to attract thieves. At least that is what the people at the bank believe.

What Barney does next would never be tolerated in any police department, unless of course the sheriff is a best friend and cousin. Barney dresses up as an old woman and enters the bank claiming to be a replacement cleaning woman for Mrs. Magruder. He enters the bank vault and starts to fill his cleaning pail with money. When the owner of the bank, Mr. Meldrim, learns that it is really Barney in disguise, he shouts at him, thus scaring Barney into closing the vault door. Barney is locked within the vault and it cannot be opened until the following day. While Gomer Pyle works at cutting the vault open with a torch, Barney calmly breaks his way through the back of the vault ending up in the adjacent beauty parlor. This bit of action certainly will prove that the bank is a pushover for any possible robbers.

As usual, Barney's intentions are good. He fakes a robbery in order to prove a point. But the old saying that 'the end result doesn't justify the means' certainly is true in this scenario. Many things could have gone wrong with Barney's scheme. Innocent people may have gotten hurt- which is almost what did happen. Because of Barney's poor judgment in trying to prove a point, the Mayberry Security Bank almost gets robbed.

"Yah, genuine brass. They won't rust in case the gun gets wet." - Asa

Episode 77
"One Punch Opie"

"What'd you say your name was? Opie or Dopy?" - Steve Quincy

One of the difficult problems in growing up is that there will always be kids who pick on other kids. It is one of the unwritten rules of childhood. Teasing and name-calling are two things very few children will ever escape. So if it is unavoidable, then children need to find ways to deal with it. When he was younger, Opie had to face Sheldon the bully. Now he once again faces the problem of a bigger boy who enjoys picking on him.

Steve Quincy is a new boy in Mayberry. He is bored and thinks fishing is stupid. When Opie and his friends plan a day of fishing, Steve persuades them to go along with him to do something more fun – like swiping apples. Opie decides not to go along. He does not like Steve Quincy. From the very beginning, Steve starts calling Opie names and plays the roll of tough guy. So how will Opie handle this new difficult situation?

Opie does what many boys might do when confronted with a show down with a bigger and tougher acting boy. He walks away. Opie does not like being called "Dopie", but what can he do about it? His friends seem to be joining Steve. They do not come to Opie's defense when the name-calling begins. Instead they go off with Steve to swipe apples. Opie must feel betrayed by his friends. He has been friends with them for a long time, and suddenly they leave him to go off with the new boy in town.

There is always a controversy as to whether or not kids should ever stand up for themselves by fighting. As a teacher of young children for many years, I always tried to get my students to understand that a nonviolent way of settling differences is always the best solution. But what if someone else begins a physical confrontation? What if a child is threatened by another child? Is walking away and doing nothing the only option? This is the dilemma that Opie faces. Will he remember what his father told him back when he had to face Sheldon? Will it mean another fight and another black eye for Opie?

Steve Quincy continues to pick on Opie. He has won over Opie's friends. They are stealing apples and throwing tomatoes at the store owner. Steve even talks Opie into throwing apples at the glass streetlight. When Opie purposely misses, Steve then hits the lamp and breaks it. When they see the sheriff's car coming, Steve gives Opie the apples and everyone takes off running except Opie. He alone stays to face Andy.

Opie has a decision to make. How much longer can he simply ignore Steve Quincy's troublesome ways? Before he came to town Opie and his friends enjoyed fishing and other activities that were fun. Now they are constantly getting into trouble. Then he overhears Andy telling Barney that Steve will continue to cause trouble until someone stands up to him. It was then that Opie decides it is time for him to do something.

Being a kid in today's dangerous world is not an easy thing. It is now more than forty years since the days of Mayberry, and the world seems to have many more bullies. There will always be difficult choices to make. As adults, we can give our children the tools they need to make the right ones. Luckily, Opie has Andy to help guide him.

"Well, you can say what you like. And I ain't taking anything away from the way you stood up to that new boy Opie, it was good you did that, but you know what I think had an effect on them little fellows? That little speech I give 'em." - Barney

Episode 78
"Barney and the Governor"

"You can tell the governor for me that he's gone and bought himself a traffic ticket complements of Barney Fife." - Barney

*B*arney gets himself into difficult situations many times due to his overzealousness in enforcing the laws in Mayberry. Usually Andy is around to bail Barney out and help him save face in the embarrassing situations. But is there anything that Andy can do now to help Barney's latest problem? Barney writes the governor's chauffer a ticket for illegal parking in front of the post office. Imagine that, Barney giving the governor a citation.

Most small town police officers would probably think twice about ticketing a governor's car. In fact many of them might consider it any honor that the driver chose to stop in town. But as we know, Barney Fife is not your ordinary run of the mill small town cop. He is extremely conscientious in carrying out his duties. However, in the case of ticketing the governor's car, it actually is brought about by some of the town cronies. They enjoy needling Barney when they think he may be derelict in his duties, and if they can get the better of him, they are not going to let the opportunity pass by.

When a group of townsmen discovers the governor's car illegally parked, they begin to needle Barney about not being on the ball. Not being one to overlook something, Barney quickly writes out a ticket, not knowing the car belongs to the governor. When the governor's driver is given the ticket, and Barney realizes who the car belongs to, it is too late to back down and tear up the ticket. He refuses to admit he may have made a mistake; at least not in front of those old good for nothing loafers.

Some people might say that the smart thing for Barney to do would be to tear up the ticket. After all, it is the governor's car. But in his defense, Barney makes a very good point. As a police officer, he is sworn to uphold the laws. It does not mean just the laws for the ordinary people, but also the same laws for important people. Why should the governor's chauffer be allowed to break the law just because he works for the governor of the state? Isn't he obligated to follow the same rules as everyone else?

We live in times when many politicians and celebrities seem to think that because of their status, they should be given special consideration in many matters. But should influential and wealthy people be immune from consequences simply because of their place in society? Well, Barney Fife thinks not. And in this case the governor himself agrees. He tells Andy and Mayor Stoner that he thinks what Deputy Fife did was commendable. Then he comes to Mayberry to shake Barney's hand.

Perhaps we would all be better off if we had more politicians like the Governor of North Carolina and fewer like Mayor Stoner. While Mayor Stoner likes to flaunt his power in the community, the governor is one who believes he is not above the law. His coming to Mayberry to shake Barney's hand is not a political ploy to gain votes. The governor is sincere in saying he thinks Barney did a commendable job. Too often Barney is the brunt of jokes and ridicule. Isn't it nice to see him come out on top for once? I wonder what the town cronies will say when they see the governor himself is in the car when it returns to Mayberry, and he is coming to congratulate Deputy Sheriff Barnard P. Fife.

"Imagine that. Can you just imagine that? And the mayor and Andy both in on it. Oh boy oh boy. I just can't believe it." -
Barney

Episode 79
"Man in a Hurry"

Taylor Home Inn Front Porch

"You people are living in another world. This is the twentieth century, don't you realize that? The whole world is living in a desperate space age. Men are orbiting the earth. International television has been developed and here a whole town is standing still because two old women's feet fall asleep." -
Malcolm Tucker

Sundays in small town America are very unique. People often attend church in the morning and then go home to read the Sunday paper. They have their Sunday dinner, and the rest of the day is spent either at home or perhaps out in the family car for a drive in the country. At least that is the way it was when I grew up in the small town of Dorchester, Wisconsin- population 450. If I was lucky, we went for a drive in the family car, and then stopped for an ice cream cone somewhere. Every Sunday was pretty much the same. It was quiet, and there really was very little to do.

Mayberry is a typical small rural community. There are no convenient stores or malls anywhere. The small stores in town are closed on Sundays. If one wants a bottle of pop, a walk to Wally's Gas Station is required. Everything just seems to stand still. It is a day for rest and family gatherings. It is just the way things are, and everyone likes it that way. But what will happen when a stranger from a large city happens to arrive in Mayberry on one of these lazy Sunday afternoons? And what will happen if he needs immediate work done on his car? What will he do if he can't find anyone to help him?

"Man in a Hurry" is one of the best loved episodes portraying life in Mayberry. When Malcolm Tucker arrives in Mayberry, he finds what many of today's people are searching for. He finds a town that is totally unspoiled by the hustle and bustle of big city life. He finds simple people who know how to take life easy. The merchants of Mayberry know that having a day of rest on Sunday is much more important than making a few extra dollars of profit. So they close their doors and spend the day at their homes.

Malcolm Tucker is the kind of person that most Mayberry folks are not. He has a type A personality, and his work is the most important thing in his life. He is always on the go and seldom has time to enjoy the simple pleasures of life. He does not understand how anyone can sit around on a front porch on a Sunday afternoon when there is work to be done and money to be made. It is like stepping back into a new and unfamiliar time.

Fortunately, Mr. Tucker's car breaks down in Mayberry on Sunday afternoon. If it doesn't, he will miss a very wonderful experience. He will miss meeting the people of Mayberry. He won't ever know what it is like to sit on a front porch on a warm evening. Mr. Tucker does not understand the people of Mayberry. Imagine, trying to peel an apple without breaking the skin. But after spending one Sunday with the Taylors, a change comes over Mr. Tucker. His eyes are opened, and he sees things differently for the very first time. He sees how happy and contented everyone is. He sees the friendship between Andy's family and a simple young man like Gomer Pyle. He sees how Gomer and Goober are willing to give up their Sunday to help out a stranger without charging one single cent. Yes, Mr. Tucker's eyes see things that perhaps he has never seen before, and he likes what he sees so much he decides to spend the night at the Taylor house. Isn't it too bad that everyone's car can't break down for at least one day in the wonderful town of Mayberry?

"Here you are Mr. Tucker. It's a penny that's been run over by a train. It will protect you during your travels. It's lucky." - Opie

Episode 80
"High Noon in Mayberry"

"Well maybe there's something about this guy I don't know. Maybe he's a long lost relative or a lodge brother or something. Or maybe he just misses the fun you used to have shooting him in the leg." - Barney

Sheriff Andy Taylor is frequently referred to as "the sheriff without a gun". In this rather suspenseful story, we find out that Andy has on one occasion actually shot a person. It was during a robbery and the man who was shot by Andy is Luke Comstock. We have no idea where or when the robbery took place, but we do know that Luke Comstock is sent to prison. Now, after considerable time has passed, Andy receives a letter from Comstock saying he is coming to Mayberry to set things straight between them.

Andy no sooner shares the letter with Barney when Barney's wild imagination jumps into full speed. He is certain that Comstock is coming to Mayberry to gun Andy down. He enlists the help of Gomer Pyle and Otis Campbell to help protect Andy. Between the three of them, they plan to watch Andy twenty four hours a day. Being novices to police work, Gomer and Otis remind Barney that none of them are very good at that sort of thing, and they might be in real danger themselves. But Barney immediately reminds them that Andy will be near them the whole time looking out for them.

Police officers, district attorneys, and judges always run the risk of criminals coming after them for revenge. It happens in our dangerous society. Many of these public safety workers have unlisted phone numbers and security systems installed at their homes. They take extra precautions, not necessarily because of fear, but because it just makes sense to be careful. It is a sad commentary on our society that our public servants often have to face the reality that they may someday be victims at the hands of people who they have arrested or sent to jail.

Andy is used to Barney's imagination and excitable nature. But when he gets a report that a stranger with a limp is seen getting off the bus with a gun case in hand, he begins to think perhaps Barney might be right after all. Then when Comstock calls his house, and says he is coming over, Andy takes additional precautions by sending Aunt Bee and Opie to the neighbors. He even gets his pistol and begins to load it before deciding to face Comstock as the "sheriff without a gun."

Even though Mayberry is a peaceful little town, it is not immune from dangerous people or crime. We know that if Andy has shot someone, he must not have had any other choice. Andy's use of a gun is always a last resort in any situation. After all, if Comstock is really coming to gun him down, why does he call and say he is coming? Perhaps there is another reason for his visit. Andy is very trusting, and even when Comstock comes to his door carrying a gun, Andy welcomes him into his home.

When criminals are released from jail or prison, they always have two choices. They can return to their previous life of crime, or they can turn their lives around and make something of themselves. Luke Comstock is no different. But which will it be? Andy is about to find out. Is he coming to set things straight, and if he is just what does he mean? Setting things straight between people can mean two vastly different things.

"Ah, this is our Mayberry knot tying class. It meets here every Tuesday. That's a nice one you've got there boys." - Andy

Episode 81
"The Loaded Goat"

"Wow, that's a new one. First time I ever fell off a bed onto a wall." - Otis

We meet many interesting characters in the town of Mayberry. Most of them are permanent residents, and we see them in almost every episode. We know them well – Andy, Opie, Barney, Aunt Bee, Floyd, and Otis, just to name a few.

Occasionally strangers come to Mayberry, and we see them for a short time, and then they leave, and we never see them again. They all have one distinct trait in common. They are all human. But now we meet another resident of the Mayberry area for the one and only time - Jimmy the Goat. Old Hutch brings his goat Jimmy into town, and because it is such a new experience for him, Jimmy decides to explore the town in hopes of finding something good to eat. And he certainly does find something to eat.

While exploring Mayberry, Jimmy wanders into an old shed in an alley. There he feasts upon a crateful of dynamite which is being stored. This brings up a rather interesting question. Why would a case of open dynamite be stored in an unlocked shed in an alley just behind Main Street? While the explosives are being used by a construction company building a new underpass, wouldn't it be more responsible to have it locked up somewhere close to where the work is being done? But then if they do that, Jimmy will not eat any, and we wouldn't have this hilarious episode to enjoy. We have seen before that things in Mayberry sometimes defy logic, and that's what makes living in Mayberry such a wonderful thing. It is unlike any other town anywhere.

Andy and Barney soon find Jimmy, and they also discover that he has eaten a lot of dynamite. Not knowing how to handle this unusual situation, they decide to lock Jimmy up in a cell and pad it with straw and pillows. This is not only for the safety of the people in Mayberry, but also so Jimmy does not come to any harm. He is a very special friend to Hutch, and he would be devastated if anything were to happen to Jimmy.

Once again Andy and Mayor Stoner are at odds. Rather than allowing Andy to deal with the situation, he orders Andy to destroy Jimmy by shooting him on the spot. This will allow the construction workers to resume the halted blasting, which in turn will enable the underpass to be completed on time to help Mayor Stoner's brother's gas station business. But when Andy hands Mayor Stoner a rifle to do the job, he changes his mind and decides there must be a more humane way to deal with Jimmy.

Andy struggles with his decision whether or not to sacrifice Jimmy in order to make Mayberry safe again. Isn't there a way for him to save Jimmy, while at the same time getting rid of the danger to Mayberry? Together Andy and Barney seek a way to save Jimmy's life. It turns out that Barney's skill on the harmonica saves both Jimmy and the townspeople. Andy's old fashioned common sense once again provides the solution to the problem of "The Loaded Goat." He gets Barney to play a soothing song on his harmonica while slowly leading Jimmy out to the countryside where he will be safe from all danger. Isn't it wonderful to know people like Andy and Barney who understand how important animals are to people? They went to a lot of trouble just to save the life of one old goat. But then again, Jimmy isn't just any old goat. He is Hutch's friend, and Andy isn't about to let anything happen to a friend of Hutch's.

"That's right, nothing to worry about. No sense getting into a panic. Just stay calm, cool. There he goes!" - Barney

Episode 82
"Class Reunion"

"It's kind of scary, isn't it? You know the idea of seeing how old everybody has gotten." - Barney

While moving a trunk full of Barney's belongings to the Taylor garage for storage, Andy and Barney discover an old Mayberry Union High yearbook, the Cutlass. The two former classmates enjoy paging through the book, and reminiscing about their high school days together. Andy decides that they should have a class reunion. According to him, some classes have them every year. There are a number of classmates still living in Mayberry, so Andy and Barney get the ball rolling. Like most guys will, Barney and Andy begin to think about their high school sweethearts who may come to the dance. For Barney there is Ramona Wiley, and for Andy there is the beautiful Sharon Duspaine.

The night of the big reunion finally arrives. Andy and Barney are sharing the duties of hosts, and between the two of them they use Barney's old Cutlass to match the names with faces they no longer can remember. For the most part Barney does a good job, but after angering Ralph Haines for not remembering who he is, they decide to put away the book and admit to people that they just can't recall their names.

High school class reunions are a special event for small town schools. In a small high school like Mayberry Union High, everyone knows one another. The teachers know all the students by name, and the students know the names of everyone else; even those who are not in the same class. So when small school reunions are held, a lot of familiar faces come together to relive those wonderful high school days. Sometimes old high school romances are even rekindled. And that is exactly what Barney Fife fears.

Barney claims that Ramona Wiley was crazy about him in high school. He even recalls the exact words she had written in his senior Cutlass. "Barney beloved, the tears on my pillow speak the pain that is my heart." And now Ramona is at the reunion. But she is no longer Ramona Wiley; she is now Mrs. Harry Becktoris. Barney is hoping that she will be able to control herself when they meet. After all, he doesn't want to break up a marriage. Poor Barney believes his high school sweetheart will still be in love with him.

Sharon Duspaine also returns to Mayberry to attend the reunion. She and Andy seem to be picking up where they left off. But soon they get into an argument about where one should live, and the memory of why they never got together resurfaces. Being the mature adults they have become, they are able to enjoy the reunion as good friends.

Class reunions may sometimes have a sobering effect to them. I know they do for me. When I attend my small town class reunions, I think back to all the dreams we had as young graduates going out in to the world. We were full of ambition, and we were going to do our part to make the world a better place. Then when we come together again years later, I find that for many of us our dreams just never did materialize. We have all aged, and for some, the lives once hoped for just never came to be.

Andy and Barney share this bit of melancholy as they drive home after the reunion. Their high school days are far in the past; gone forever. Life moves on for them and for their friends back in Mayberry Union High. Barney and Andy were anxious to attend their first reunion. They wanted to find out who had made it and who didn't. And that is probably just what they found. Some of them did make it, and some of them didn't.

"All together I'd say it was an emotion packed evening, wouldn't you?" - Barney

Episode 83
"Rafe Hollister Sings"

"Well I reckon seeing they're never around when I'm taking a bath; I had best go on over there." - Rafe Hollister

*J*ohn Masters is holding try outs for an upcoming concert in Mayberry. Of course Barney believes he has a wonderful voice, so he plans to audition. Rafe Hollister, our Mayberry farmer and part time moon shiner, happens to be in the courthouse delivering some beans for Aunt Bee when he hears Barney singing. Barney is not doing the song quite right, so Rafe joins in the singing and takes the wind right out of Barney's sail by singing the song perfectly with a rich deep voice. Knowing Rafe's singing is exceptional, Andy encourages him to audition for John Masters' concert. Rafe does audition, and he is selected. But Andy has a problem. He must tell Barney that he did not win the audition.

When John Masters chooses Rafe Hollister as Mayberry's representative in the upcoming musical concert, he creates another major conflict between Mayor Stoner and Andy. The mayor blames Andy for Rafe's winning the contest, and he orders Andy to tell Rafe he cannot perform. But why does the mayor object so strongly to Rafe Hollister? The answer is quite simple. Rafe's appearance is not acceptable in the eyes of the mayor. "He's seedy." Now Andy is delegated to get rid of Rafe Hollister just like he was delegated to get rid of Otis Campbell when he was to be presented a plaque. Certainly Andy will not defy another order by the mayor. Or will he?

People are very often judged by appearances. We stereotype people by the way they look. In today's world we find many different ways to show nonconformity and to express our individuality. Clothing styles are such that the more skin that is revealed the more stylish it is. Hair is cut in unusual styles and dyed in many bright colors. We see tattoos of all sorts on just about every body part visible. Body piercing is another popular form of expressing oneself. Rings and studs are pierced into ears, noses, eyebrows, lips, and even naval cavities. Whether it is fair or unfair, people who choose to change their appearance in these ways are often judged by how they look rather than by whom they are or what they can do.

Rafe Hollister's appearance isn't as radical as some of today's styles. He would perhaps be labeled as being more unkempt or dirty. But he is a farmer and he works hard. He has no need for fashionable clothing. His idea of being dressed up is wearing a plaid shirt and tie underneath his overalls. Add to that the fact that he is overweight and doesn't shave everyday, and one can almost understand the Mayor's concern.

Mayor Stoner is never a very diplomatic person. It is his attitude toward Rafe Hollister that is troublesome. He belittles Rafe and insults his appearance within earshot of Rafe's wife. He doesn't take in to consideration her feelings or Rafe's for that matter. The only thing that concerns him is that Rafe Hollister's appearance will make the town of Mayberry look bad, and more importantly it will make him look bad. This simply must not be done. But Andy does not allow the Mayor to prevent Rafe from performing. He was chosen fair and square, and he has a right to sing. So Andy finds a rather ingenious solution to make Rafe's natural appearance acceptable. Rafe performs magnificently just as he is, and everybody in attendance loves him just as he is.

"Well it means a lot to the town too; to have somebody up on that stage that we won't be ashamed of." - Mayor Stoner

Episode 84
"Opie and the Spoiled Kid"

"Now if it happens again, try to remember the following things; age of the boy, color of his hair, new or old bicycle, whether or not he was wearing glasses." - Barney

*E*ach week Opie Taylor gets an allowance for doing his chores around the house. He earns twenty-five cents a week. In order to receive his allowance, he has to clean the garage, set the table every night, take out the ashes, and keep the wood box filled.

When Opie's new friend Arnold Winkler hears that Opie has to work for his allowance, he immediately tries to set things straight. He explains to Opie that an allowance means money that a kid is allowed to have. You don't have to work for it. He should know. He does not have to work for his allowance, and he gets just about anything he asks for, including a seventy dollar bicycle. In other words, he is one spoiled kid.

Opie tells Andy about the seventy-five cent rule that Arnold explained to him. Andy explains that there are no set rules as to how a father or mother should raise their children. Each parent raises their children as they see fit. He further explains to Opie that he sees fit that Opie will work for his allowance. So Opie's twenty-five cent allowance stays in place. Opie reports back to Arnold, and he gets further instructions on how to go about getting his way without having to work for it.

During all my years of teaching young children, I came across many different kinds of families. Each family had its own set of rules for their children. Many students I taught were Opie's age. Some had no responsibilities at home. Others had set chores to do within the home or farm. Some had every new toy or gadget that came along given to them, while others had to save their own money until they had enough to buy what they wanted. It was always rather interesting to find that those who had to save for things usually didn't get them because by the time they had enough money, they either no longer wanted the item or else some new product came along to take its place.

Teaching children responsibly and work ethics is not an easy task. But anything that is worth while is usually not obtained easily. One of the greatest things a parent can do for a child is to teach the value of money. This is exactly what Andy is trying to do. Andy could easily just give Opie some money to spend each week, but he truly believes it is important for Opie to work for his money. Opie is part of a family, and Andy believes that each member of the family has to share in the work. It is called "division of labor".

Arnold's father, on the other hand, gives Arnold anything he wants. Arnold learns very quickly in life that if he has temper tantrums, holds his breath, or rolls around on the ground kicking and crying, his father will give in and buy him what he wants. It is much easier than taking the time to teach Arnold the importance of working for what he wants in life. He makes excuses for Arnold by saying he is a "highly spirited child".

As it turns out, Arnold is the one who learns the value of working. Arnold's father begins to understand that he needs to change his

141

approach when it comes to raising his son. He begins that change in an old fashioned woodshed behind the courthouse.

"Now if we don't teach children to live in society today what's going to happen to them when they grow up." - Andy

Episode 85
"The Great Filling Station Robbery"

Wally's Gas Station at the Taylor Home Inn

"Oh you're making a mistake sheriff, a big mistake. This boy cannot be trusted. He's got sticky fingers." - Mr. Carter

*Y*oung Jimmy Morgan works for Mr. Carter. He is hired by Mr. Carter because Sheriff Taylor recommends him, and he thinks it will be good for Jimmy. Now Jimmy is accused of stealing a battery, and Mr. Carter wants Andy to arrest him. Rather than arresting him, Andy persuades Gomer Pyle to give Jimmy a temporary job at the gas station while Wally is out of town. He believes Jimmy's story that he was just borrowing the battery for a short time, and it broke when he accidentally dropped it.

One characteristic that makes Andy such a popular sheriff is that he believes in people. He likes to give people a second chance no matter what they may have done. So it is with young Jimmy Morgan. If Gomer gives him a job, Jimmy can earn enough money to pay for the battery, and Andy doesn't have to fill out all the paper work and Jimmy will not have to go to jail. Mr. Carter does not share this philosophy with Andy, and he warns Gomer that he is only asking for trouble. Andy says he accepts the responsibility for Jimmy, so

Gomer agrees to give him the job.   Gomer trusts Andy's good judgment.

Everyone makes mistakes. No one is immune from poor judgment. To penalize a person for a momentary lack of judgment or poor choice can have many consequences. Of course it depends on what is done because of the poor judgment. If poor judgment results in personal injury to an innocent party or the theft of someone's money or property, there naturally must be consequences of some sort. The difficult part is fitting the consequence to the crime. Much depends on the character of the person involved. Of course there is no question that certain crimes do not warrant second chances.

Andy apparently sees some good in Jimmy Morgan. He is not a bad kid. All he needs is some kind of positive pastime to keep him off the streets of Mayberry.   When Andy sees the excitement in Jimmy when he is talking about the patrol car's new carburetor, he also sees an opportunity to help a young man in trouble.   Jimmy loves cars and the thought of working in a gas station is something he will really enjoy.   So Andy takes a risk and accepts the responsibility of having him work at Wally's. He has faith in Jimmy, and perhaps that is all Jimmy needs; someone to have faith in him.

Shortly after Jimmy starts work, items disappear from Wally's. There are no signs of a break in, so whoever is stealing things is getting in through the front door. And the only people with keys are Gomer and Jimmy. All the evidence leads to an inside job, which also means Jimmy is a suspect. But somehow it just doesn't make sense to Andy

Barney decides to use some high tech surveillance equipment to help nab the thief. He sets up a camera in the garage and connects a string from the camera shutter to the front door. Whoever is coming in through the front door to rob Wally's will be photographed. However, the only person who has his picture taken is Barney.

Andy is a very good judge of character. His experiences as sheriff enable him to see things that the average citizen might not see. He does not see Jimmy as a criminal type. He trusts his instincts when he helps Jimmy, and his instincts prove to be right. His faith in young Jimmy just might result in an important turning point in a young man's life.

"It's him, it's Jimmy. We caught him red-handed." - Barney

Episode 86
"Andy Discovers America"

"Sheriff Taylor I'm surprised at you. How can I teach a class if the parents won't cooperate? How can I be expected to maintain discipline?" - Helen Crump

*H*elen Crump makes her first appearance in "Andy Discovers America". She is the new teacher in Mayberry, and Opie is in her class. She believes in strict discipline, and she expects her students to study hard. They raise their hands when they want to speak, and when she calls on them, they stand beside their desks. Miss Crump believes it is important for her students to understand history, so they will grow up to be citizens of which Mayberry can be proud. However the boys in her class disagree completely.

Teaching is a very difficult profession. I know; I was a teacher for thirty six years. Each year a teacher gets a class of new students. They vary in their abilities and in their willingness to learn. They come from different families with different sets of rules and values. Parents differ on their approach to homework and discipline. Each parent wants the best possible education for their child, and each teacher tries hard to provide it.

While complaining to Andy and Aunt Bee about Miss Crump, Opie somehow gets the impression that Andy is giving him permission to not do his homework. Andy says nothing of the sort, yet Opie twists the words that Andy says, and he uses it to his advantage. Opie tells Miss Crump what Andy says in front of the class, and before she knows it, she has a major problem getting the boys in her class to cooperate.

Adults need to be very careful what they say in the presence of children. Children can easily misunderstand or misquote what a parent or teacher might say. When I was teaching, I always sent a note home on the first day of school. It said, "If you believe only one half of what your child says about me, I will believe only one half of what your child says about you." While I meant it as a way to begin my year with new parents using a little humor, I was also sending them a subtle reminder that one cannot always believe the accuracy of what a child might say.

Andy believes education is very important for Opie. He understands that Opie is not an exceptional student. He does average work in school. He is a well behaved boy, and everyone likes him. So Andy is pleased with Opie. Yet he understands that he has created a problem for Miss Crump by inadvertently giving Opie some bad advice. So he decides it is his responsibility to rectify the situation. After all, he is the cause of it.

We all recall teachers we had as children. Some we remember with great fondness, and some not. When in college preparing to be a teacher more than forty years ago, I had a professor who gave me some very sound advice. I tried to incorporate his advice all through my teaching career. He said, "Later in life your young students will probably not remember one precise thing that you taught them, but they will always remember how you treated them." I think Opie and his friends will always remember how Miss Crump treats them. She is firm, yet she is kind. She expects her students to work hard and do well, yet she understands that not all students learn at the same pace.

Andy does something that is very important when dealing with a child and school. He talks with Opie's teacher. He realizes he has made a mistake and that it is his responsibility as a parent to be sure Opie becomes the best student that he can be.

"I reckon you do have to be careful what you say in front of young'ins; they pick up on the darndest things." - Andy

Episode 87
"Aunt Bee's Medicine Man"

"Oh Andy, I had one of the most extraordinary experiences of my life. Nothing happened to me like that since I was baptized." - Aunt Bee

*O*ne of the problems with the aging process is a person slowly begins to feel changes in one's body. There is not quite as much energy as there once was. It gets a little more difficult to get up after sitting for an extended period of time. Our hair begins to change color and our overall appearance begins to change. No one is immune from it. Not even Aunt Bee Taylor. But she discovers a rather unique way of dealing with ailments.

When Aunt Bee learns of the passing of one of her acquaintances, she begins to feel very faint and ill. Aunt Bee and her friend are exactly the same age and if it is her friend's time to leave this world, might not her time be next? Andy encourages Aunt Bee to see the doctor, but she doesn't want to hear the same thing he always says, "We're no spring chickens anymore." Certainly there is something better she can do?

We are bombarded with advertisements for health care items as no other generation has been. We cannot turn on the television or open a magazine without seeing an ad for some kind of medication that will take care of all our problems. There seems to be some kind of treatment available for everything from age spots to fungus of the toenail. All the products claim to be the best, and if we use them we will be happier and healthier. Of course they all come with fine print that is full of warnings, side affects, and cautions, often written so small we can barely read them.

Aunt Bee happens to come across a side show while walking home with Opie. A fascinating man by the name of Colonel Harvey is talking about Indians. Suddenly he turns to the subject of health and vitality, and before long he introduces his wonderful Colonel Harvey's Indian Elixir. He tells of its wonderful restorative powers. Use his elixir and you will no longer be tired and run down. Your energy will be restored and you will be full of pet. Indians use his elixir, and he asks if anyone has ever seen a tired Indian. This is just what Aunt Bee has been looking for – a quick cure for her ailments. At only one dollar per bottle, she cannot pass it by, so she eagerly purchases two bottles.

We can probably all identify with Aunt Bee. Who hasn't bought some kind of new medical treatment in the hopes that it would cure an ailment? With all the vitamins, supplements, over the counter remedies, and prescriptions available, one would think we would not have to worry about ever being sick. Yet we continue to have problems, and we continue to search for help. Our bodies have a definite mind of their own.

Colonel Harvey makes quite an impression with Aunt Bee. She invites him to dinner as a way to thank him for his great work. But before he arrives, Andy and Barney come home to find Aunt Bee playing the piano and singing like she has never done before. In reality, she is a bit gassed. As it turns out, Colonel Harvey's Indian Elixir is nothing more than plain old fashion moonshine.

We all need to be very careful when trying new products to treat illnesses. There are many excellent and legitimate products available. However Aunt Bee finds out a bit late that if it sounds too good to be true, then it probably is. But she and her friends have a good time, even though it does mean they have to suffer with some very bad headaches. Once again, Andy is very understanding about the entire situation.

"We're not spring chickens any more." - Aunt Bee

Episode 88
"The Darlings are Coming"

"Mr. Darling, as sheriff there's something I'd like to say to you. It's about parking your truck in front of the trough here and filling your radiator out of it." - Andy

The Briscoe Darling family makes its first appearance in Mayberry on a warm summer afternoon. They live up in the mountains, and when they drive into Mayberry, their old truck's radiator gets hot and boils over. Mr. Darling decides to fill the radiator with water from the horse trough, but he soon learns he is breaking one of Mayberry's many city ordinances. Being a firm believer in warning strangers first, Andy does not cite Mr. Darling, and the strange family goes on their way.

The Darling family is indeed a strange clan. They rarely enter Mayberry, and if they do, it is usually for an important event. When they do come to Mayberry, it is always a family outing. This means the entire family consisting of Briscoe and his daughter Charlene and his four quiet fun-loving boys make the trip. The important event that brings them to Mayberry on this occasion is they are meeting Dud Walsh at the bus depot. Dud has been away serving in the army, and he and Charlene are betrothed. Charlene can barely remember what Dud looks like, so she isn't very excited. Besides, a pretty new man has caught her eye; it's none other than Sheriff Andy Taylor.

It seems like every small town like Mayberry has some rather odd or eccentric citizens. I recall an old man who lived just outside our little town. He drove an old beater of a car, and he lived in an old tarpaper shack. His shack had no electricity or running water, and his only means of support was dealing in junk. Whenever he came into town people would stare at him. He didn't speak to many people, and most people avoided him as much as possible. He was dirty, and his clothes were old and tattered. Like the Darlings he came into town only when it was necessary. He was perfectly content living his solitude life out in the country away from everyone else. So are the Darlings.

Briscoe Darling and his family are not bad people. They are just very different from others. They do not understand the ways of the town people, so they often break the rules that they do not know. They believe in omens and spirits and are very superstitious. They eat foods like fish muddle, hoot owl pie, and hog backbone. So it isn't surprising that when they come into town they are bound to create a few problems for Andy. But Andy has no idea just how big a problem they really can be.

Andy, however, is very patient with the Darlings. He understands that their way of life is different. He overlooks some of their unusual habits, and when he removes them from the Mayberry Hotel for having too many people in a single room, he puts them up at the courthouse for the night. Aunt Bee even provides the food for the hungry family.

We can learn a lot from Andy's unending patience and tolerance that he has for the down and out people that frequent Mayberry. He never judges people or questions why they are in the situation they are in. He simply holds out a helping hand, and if it means overlooking a few of the rules and laws in Mayberry, so be it. In other words he does unto others as he would want them to do onto him.

"Andy, remember you've just eaten; don't run on a full stomach." - Aunt Bee

Episode 89
"Andy's English Valet"

"Well, I'm very sorry, I am, really. I can't think what came over me. I behaved like a proper Charlie and the bobby here is quite right. I do deserve a good dressing down." - Malcolm Merriweather

*M*ayberry is about to get its first visitor from across the ocean. Malcolm Merriweather is a very colorful individual. He is a gentleman's gentleman from England, and he certainly is one of the more interesting visitors who come to Mayberry. We first meet Malcolm in "Andy's English Valet", but he will return to Mayberry twice more in future episodes. He brings with him some very new experiences for the entire Taylor household.

Malcolm arrives in Mayberry while traveling the width and breath of the United States. While reading a map on his bicycle, Malcolm crashes into Fletch's truck. Not giving him a chance to explain, Barney quickly hauls Malcolm to the courthouse where he brings him in front of Andy. When Malcolm explains what happens, Barney immediately becomes suspicious because of his strange manner of speech. He is certain that Malcolm must be from "somewheres else", like maybe Canada.

Andy always is very understanding when the people of Mayberry get into trouble. He will bend over backwards to help them. But how will he react when a complete stranger from a different country causes an accident and then does not have the money to pay for the damages? Will he be as equally forgiving and understanding?

When Malcolm discovers that he does not have enough money to pay for the damage to Fletch's truck, Barney is all for locking him up? But tenderhearted Andy comes up with a better plan. He gives Malcolm a job at his house so he can earn the money to pay Fletch. The timing couldn't be better for Aunt Bee was just telling Andy that he needs to do some things around the house.

Malcolm isn't exactly a handyman around the house, and Andy soon discovers that he may be more trouble than he is worth. Seeing that Aunt Bee is away for a few days, Malcolm offers to clean the house and cook for Andy and Opie. After all that is what he does in

Ekmondwight, England. He is a gentleman's gentleman to the Colonel. Malcolm's true talents come to light quickly as the Taylor home is soon transformed to the customs and tastes of merry old England.

Despite Malcolm's efficiency and skill in the kitchen, Andy soon tires of Malcolm's constant attention. Malcolm overhears Andy telling Barney that he is a pest, and that he is going to have to come up with a way to tell him to leave. Once again, just like with Ellen Brown, Andy needs to find a way to undo the hurt feelings he creates by being overheard talking with Barney but the next morning Andy finds that Malcolm is gone.

That adage about words not hurting certainly is proven wrong in this episode. The words Andy speaks hurt Malcolm deeply. Thinking he is helping the Taylor family, Malcolm hears that he is nothing but a pest. This should send a strong message to each of us. Before we say something unkind about another person, we should ask ourselves, "How will this person feel if he overhears what I am about to say?" If we do this, I think we all might give a second thought to what we say.

"I'll tell you something. It's been the nicest part of my holiday, and I'm very thankful to you and your dad." - Malcolm Merriweather

Episode 90
"Barney's First Car"

"Oh well, I never drive the machine over twenty five miles per hour, and I also like to give it a ten minute rest stop every half hour." - Myrt Lesh

Isn't it amazing that in all the years that Barney and Andy have been working in Mayberry neither one of them owns a car? The squad car is used for everything. From Saturday night parking at the duck pond, to running errands for Aunt Bee, the Mayberry patrol car seems to always be available when needed. The rules for using an official vehicle for personal use must be very relaxed in Mayberry. But all of this is about to change. At least it is going to change for Barney. He decides to draw his life savings out of the bank and buy a car. But just what kind of car can he buy for three hundred dollars? He goes through the ads in the paper and finds just the right car. Not wanting to risk losing the car, he immediately sets up a time to take a look at it.

Purchasing his first car is a momentous occasion for Barney. It would be for anyone. My first car was a 1955 Ford, and it cost me two hundred and fifty dollars. It got about 50 miles to each quart of oil. It wasn't much, but it was my first car, and I was as proud of it as if it were a brand new one. Barney's first car is a 1954 Ford, and it cost him three hundred dollars. But that is as close as it gets when you compare the two purchases. Although my car was no beauty, I did buy it from a reputable local car dealer, while Barney buys his from a private party that he finds through a newspaper advertisement.

Barney is very inexperienced when it comes to buying a car. When Mrs. Lesh drives her car into Andy's driveway, Barney takes one look at it, and makes up his mind to buy it. The only question he asks is how much does Mrs. Lesh want for it? He refuses to take it for a drive or have a mechanic check it over, and when he hands over his nest egg, he doesn't even ask for a receipt. Then a strange thing occurs. Mrs. Lesh doesn't even have the registration papers with her, and she tells Barney she will mail them. This makes no difference to Barney, and within a few minutes Mrs. Lesh has his money, and Barney has his very own car. Both are very happy with the transaction.

Back when Barney bought his car, there were few regulations regarding the sale of automobiles. Many people purchased cars just like Barney. They made quick transactions with few questions asked. There weren't the laws to protect the consumer like there are now. Buying a car is a business transaction, and it needs to be thought of as such. There are unscrupulous people just looking for "buyers" who are ripe for the pickings. And poor old Barney is about as ripe as they come. He wants his first car so badly that he does not use any common sense, and he won't listen to Andy's advice.

Barney learns a very valuable lesson when he discovers the truth behind his car. But as usual, Barney carries it to extremes. He decides he will trust no one. We don't need to go quite this far when dealing with people. We simply need to be careful. We need to ask questions, get things in writing, and always know who we are buying from. Perhaps the best advice is that we should take our time and not rush into deals. Quite often when we sit back and think about the deal we are about to make, it often is not as good as it first appears. Apparently Barney decides owning a car is not worth all the hassle of buying one. He never does buy a car, and he continues to use the squad car all the while he lives in Mayberry.

"Who are you kiddin' sister? Who are you working with, Hubcaps Lesh, or do you got your own racket?" - Barney

Episode 91
"The Rivals"

Barney's Favorite Duck Pond

"Well, oh, I guess the best thing to do would be treat her as nice as you can and after that it's up to the love bug whether he's going to bite or not." - Andy

*B*arney and Thelma Lou see a lot of one another. Barney walks her to church every Sunday. On Tuesday night they have a standing date to watch a doctor program on TV at her house while eating a pan of homemade cashew fudge. They go out to eat, Dutch treat of course, and on occasion they are known to visit the duck pond.

Thelma Lou is always very true to Barney, while Barney has been known to step out with Juanita from the diner as well as a few other young Mayberry women. He seems to take his relationship with Thelma Lou for granted. Perhaps it is because Thelma Lou is so faithful, and he never feels threatened about losing her. So how will Barney react if some young good looking fellow suddenly starts paying attention to Thelma Lou? How will Barney behave if that same good looking young fellow starts to spend a lot of time with her, and what if he even goes to her house? And what will Barney do if that young good looking fellow is Opie Taylor?

Opie has a crush on little Karen Folker, but she doesn't want anything to do with him. He is heartbroken and he goes to Andy for advice. But Andy seems to think it is something that will pass, and he simply tells Opie to treat Karen as nice as he can. When Thelma Lou sees how dejected Opie is, she decides to cheer him up by making some chocolate brownies for him. This is all it takes for Opie to forget about Karen. He now has himself a new girlfriend – Thelma Lou.

Almost every young boy at some time or another has a crush on a girl. Most times it will be a classmate at school. But sometimes young boys develop crushes on much older girls. In fact they might be grown up woman like Thelma Lou. For the most part it is harmless, unless of course it is Barney Fife's girl a young boy happens to like. At first Barney goes along with Thelma Lou being with Opie, but before long he begins to lose his patience with Opie, and Andy's light hearted attitude doesn't help things either.

During my many years of teaching I have seen young crushes come and go. I have had many young children tell me about his or her special friend. I learned something important very early in my teaching career. What might seem like foolishness to an adult can be very serious to a child. Andy does not make fun of Opie and his girlfriend. He does not tease Opie and make it all sound like a bunch of nonsense. Andy treats Opie's problem with girls the same way he treats an adult's similar problem. Being the father that he is, Andy realizes that this is important to Opie, and if he doesn't take it seriously, then perhaps Opie will not come to him the next time he has a problem.

As Opie's crush on Thelma Lou grows, Barney gets more upset and frustrated. Andy knows that he is angry, and he knows that Opie is being a pest with Thelma Lou, but neither Andy nor Thelma Lou treats it lightly. They use a little psychology and a lot of patience to help Opie get through this difficult experience of "puppy love". Parents often tell their children to come to them with their problems, but unless those problems are taken seriously and dealt with accordingly, the next time their children just might go elsewhere for help. And that is what Andy does not want to happen with Opie.

"Sorry you're going to be busy at the movies, Barney. I was hoping we could drive up to the duck pond." - Thelma Lou

Episode 92
"A Wife for Andy"

"How long do you think you can do it? How long do you think you can be father and mother to that boy?" - Barney

*M*atch making is an age old custom in many societies. For centuries the aristocracy of England had arranged matches when their children were born. The matchmaker in the wonderful production of "Fiddler on the Roof" played an important role in society. Quite often young men and women were matched in order to benefit the wealth of the gentry. Romance and love would not even be a consideration. Wealth and power were the primary goals of many marriages. In some cases, the betrothed didn't even meet until the wedding ceremony; thus the custom of the bride wearing a veil to cover her face.

In today's modern society, matchmaking has taken on an entirely different look. We live in the age of technology, so it is to be expected that computers will do the matchmaking. There are countless websites on the internet that promise long lasting, fulfilling relationships. You answer some questions, and the computer does all the rest.

Mayberry has its own matchmaker by the name of Barney Fife. He is constantly on the look out for a suitable match for Andy, but more importantly, he is convinced that Opie needs a mother. So when Barney begins his search for a wife for Andy, can trouble be far behind? With Barney at the helm, we can be certain Andy is headed for big trouble.

There certainly is no shortage of attractive, single, women in Mayberry. When Barney decides to invite eligible girls to Andy's house to be scrutinized, an entire roomful shows up. Of course they have no idea they are being put through a screening process to become Mrs. Andrew Taylor. In fact, they have no idea why they are at Andy's house.

Barney tells Andy that he can look over all the girls and decide which ones are out and which ones are maybes. Barney seems to think choosing a wife is like selecting a head of lettuce at the market. All you have to do is just pick the one that looks the best.

Matchmaking can be a very risky business. No one likes to think they are being matched up with someone. Finding a mate is not that easy. Barney must not remember what happened with Jeff Pruitt. Now he is doing the same thing with Andy. Barney places a lot of importance on the outer beauty of a woman. He seems to forget that for any relationship to grow and blossom, it must be based on much more than beauty.

As usual, Barney's scheme for finding Andy a wife just does not work. Actually, it is a complete disaster. Not only does Barney invite a roomful of girls to Andy's house once; he does it a second time when Andy decides to take Helen Crump out to dinner. Isn't it strange that Barney wants a wife for Andy so badly that he will go to all the trouble he does to find one? Then when Andy finds someone he likes, Barney goes to a lot of trouble trying to end it. Andy just cannot win with Barney trying to help him.

Andy is not as vain as Barney appears to be. While he does appreciate the physical beauty of a woman, Andy understands the importance of inner beauty. He discovers Helen Crump is a fine person. She is intelligent, kind, witty, and most importantly, she is fun to be with. She is pretty, but that is not the most important thing. The most important thing is – Andy chooses her. Barney has had nothing to do with it at all.

"Well, I appreciate that Barn, and I'm glad you feel that way cause I've got something I want to tell you too. I've decided I'm gonna court Miss Crump." - Andy

Episode 93
"Dogs, Dogs, Dogs"

"Well, I said to myself. If I was a dog, where would I want to go? And I said to myself, I'd want to be out in the open. Out in the wide open spaces where I could jump and play and run with the wind in my fur." - Barney

When I was a young boy we had a dog. He had a rather unusual name. We called him Parachute. I have no idea why my father named him that. It wasn't because he was white. Parachute was all black with just a very little white throughout his body. He was a wonderful dog, and we all loved him very much. He was a mutt, yet we treated him as if he were a purebred. He would go along with us on our Sunday afternoon rides, and if we stopped for an ice cream cone, Parachute would get one too. His favorite flavor was vanilla. He was our first dog, and he was an important part of our family.

I always feel sorry for young boys who do not have a dog. Every boy should have at least one dog that will love him unconditionally. Dogs do just that. Opie Taylor does not have a dog. He has a pet bird named Dickie that we only see in the very first episode. After that Opie only has Andy, Aunt Bee, and Barney. He really would love to have a dog. It would give him a steady playmate since he has no brothers or sisters.

One day Opie appears at the courthouse with a little dog on a leash. Opie explains that the puppy followed him home. Andy feels sorry for the puppy, so he gives him some of Barney's lunch. After a discussion about why Opie should not have a dog, Andy agrees that Opie can keep him. A short time later, a sad Opie returns to the courthouse and tells Andy that his dog ran away. Andy assures him that he must have gone back to his owner, so Opie decides to go home. When he opens the door to leave a pack of yapping dogs run into the courthouse looking for food from Barney's lunchbox.

My wife and I are members of our county humane association. It is very disheartening to go to the shelter and see all the homeless and uncared for dogs and cats. It is even more upsetting when we see how many are euthanized each year because they cannot be placed in loving homes. We have been at the shelter a number of times when people have come to adopt a homeless animal. I never know who is happier – the family coming in or the dog that is being adopted. I suspect it is probably the dog.

Andy and Barney have a real problem with the dogs. An inspector is due, and if he finds all the dogs in the courthouse, he will most certainly deny the extra funds Andy and Barney are requesting. No one is going to give them additional money to take care of a pack of dogs. But what can they do with the dogs? Barney feels he has the solution when he takes the dogs to the country and sets them loose. Unfortunately what Barney does is often the reason there are so many homeless dogs. But Barney has a change of heart when a storm comes up, so he and Andy go and bring the dogs back. Now they are right back to where they started. What are they going to do with the dogs?

Pets deserve to be treated well. Being a responsible pet owner is important. All of the problems caused by the hungry dogs in the courthouse may have been avoided if they would have been taken care of in the first place. Eventually the owner of the dogs comes to claim them. He doesn't appear to be the kind of person who treats dogs very well, but I have a feeling Andy will visit the owner from time to time to check on the dogs.

"Someone was telling me that they'd seen you a while back with a whole pack of dogs. I've been hunting them critters high and low." - Clint Biggers

Episode 94
"Mountain Wedding"

"How about I fix you and your gun hand a mouthful to eat. I could heat up some nice hog backbone or some fish muttle." - Charlene Darling

The Darling family returns to Mayberry in their second appearance as they are in need of some help by Sheriff Taylor. It seems there is a strange man up in the mountain that refuses to accept that

Charlene and Dud Wash are married. Seeing Andy was the one who married them, the Darlings are asking that he come up to their cabin and set Ernest T. Bass straight. They had thought about killing him but they did not want to go that far. So Andy and Barney head to the mountains before sunup the next morning.

We meet Ernest T. Bass for the first time in "Mountain Wedding". He has decided that Charlene is not officially married because she was not married by a preacher. Andy shows him the marriage license, but Ernest T. is unmoved. As a way to avoid further trouble, Andy decides that Charlene and Dud will have a second wedding. This time it will be performed by the circuit preacher who will be arriving the next day. This does not discourage Ernest T. one bit, and he decides to court Charlene for the next twenty four hours. As it turns out, Ernest T. has a very strange way of courting the one he loves.

Weddings can vary greatly depending on where and when they are performed. Some people choose to have very elaborate ceremonies and receptions that cost many thousands of dollars. Others decide to have simple weddings with just a few family members and close friends in attendance. Others still select a simple marriage by a justice of the peace and a few witnesses in attendance. Whatever the manner one chooses for a wedding, the important thing is after the ceremony and celebration every couple is legally married. Whether the wedding cost ten thousand dollars or just twenty five dollars for a license, it is the promise made with the vows that truly unites a man and woman in matrimony. Ernest T. just does not seem to understand this concept at all.

Ernest T. does not recognize Charlene's marriage. He wants her all for himself, and the thought of her being married to another man is not easy for him to accept. For the next twenty four hours he tries to woo Charlene by serenading her in the middle of the night and by showing her how strong he is. When this does not help, he throws rocks through the window. On one rock is attached a message saying there just might not be a wedding. Andy decides this means Ernest T. is planning on stealing the bride. So a plan of action has to be put into place. Enter Deputy Sheriff Barney Fife, bride to be.

Dressed in Charlene's wedding dress, Barney is taken away by Ernest T., who is convinced that he has just stolen his beloved Charlene. Meanwhile the circuit preacher quickly performs a marriage ceremony for Doug and Charlene, and they are officially married for a second time. When Barney reveals himself to Ernest T. the truth finally sinks in, and Ernest T. accepts the fact that Charlene will never be his bride.

We get a glimpse of the simple life of the Darling family as we enter their humble home in the mountains outside Mayberry. They may be a backward group, but their family is a close knit family of love. They celebrate the joy of Charlene's wedding in a much different manner than most people. Yet Charlene and Doug are married, and even though he has lost her forever, Ernest T. Bass joins in the celebration. Perhaps he is thinking, "It is better to have loved and lost than to have never loved at all."

"If I ever hear you ain't good to her, I'm gonna call that lady sheriff." - Ernest T.

Episode 95
"The Big House"

"Yes sir, they sure run this place tighter than the state pen, except for one thing; the shakedown. We've been here for hours and not one shakedown." - Doc

The Mayberry Courthouse is the center of activity for Andy and Barney. While most of the prisoners housed in the Mayberry jail are local folks who have been incarcerated because they are unable to pay their small fines, occasionally we find professional criminals being housed within the courthouse cells. Such is the case when Doc and Tiny are brought to Mayberry for temporary housing while the police search for the remaining members of their gang. But will the Mayberry jail be secure enough for these two crooks? And will the Mayberry police force be able to guard the prisoners properly?

Some of the funniest scenes involving Barney are when he is in charge of guarding prisoners. This always seems to bring out both the best and the worst in Barney. For some reason when you combine prisoners and Barney Fife, the end result usually means trouble. And so it is with "The Big House", as Barney once again allows his ego to get in the way of common sense police work.

One of the reasons Barney Fife is so popular is because of his simple and rather naive ways. When one considers all the misadventures Barney has as deputy, it makes one wonder why Andy puts up with all his shenanigans. Well, the answer is rather obvious. Barney is Andy's best friend and cousin. Andy has a very special relationship with Barney, and he certainly could never find himself replacing him as deputy sheriff.

Barney Fife as a deputy is very challenging for Andy. Then when Barney decides to make Gomer Pyle a deputy to help guard Doc and Tiny, Andy's challenges are compounded. Barney gives Gomer a crash course on police work, issues him a badge and a gun, and then places him on the courthouse rooftop as a lookout man. Barney is Andy's number two man with an empty gun and a bullet in his pocket. Gomer is the number three man with a pistol and a shotgun sitting upon a roof. It doesn't take much imagination to figure out that this scenario is just a disaster waiting to happen. Imagine Gomer Pyle as an armed deputy. Gomer has enough trouble pumping gas and fixing flat tires. He is a gentle, simple person with a friendly, easy going manner. Not what one would say are the ideal qualifications for being a deputy.

I would have to say that Andy Taylor is the most patient man I know. He constantly has to bail out Barney whenever he gets into trouble. He allows Barney to take credit for things he doesn't do. Although Barney interferes in Andy's private life and often puts Andy in embarrassing and compromising positions, Andy stands behind his friend. Even when Barney endangers the safety of Mayberry, by allowing Doc and Tiny to escape several times, Andy gives him the credit for recapturing them, even though he is locked in a cell while the capture is made.

One can argue that in the real world, Barney's ineptness as deputy would not be tolerated for more than a few days. Yet he is by Andy's side year after year helping to prevent corruption and lawlessness in Mayberry. I wonder if Barney really knows how great a friend he has in Andy Taylor. You know, somehow, I think he really does know.

"If you don't know how to handle one of these things, you got no business carrying one." - Barney

Episode 96
"Opie the Birdman"

"You hear that? That's those young birds chirping for their mama that's never coming back. You just listen to that for a while." - Andy

*P*erhaps one of the most difficult functions of being a good parent is teaching one's child the difference between right and wrong. Children do not have the capacity to reason like adults. Many adults struggle with the concept of right and wrong. So is it any wonder children have a much more difficult time with it? Part of growing up and learning is making mistakes. We have all experienced consequences because of mistakes we have made. But if we learn from a mistake then it is no longer a mistake; it becomes a lesson. Opie learns a very important lesson about taking responsibility for one's actions.

In "Opie the Birdman" we see a very serious Opie Taylor. We usually see him doing humorous things. When he accidentally kills a songbird with a slingshot, we see a very touching and emotional side of Opie. We see a father who disciplines his child for doing something wrong. When Andy punishes Opie for killing the songbird, he demonstrates a very important rule for raising children. When you punish a child, punish out of love, not out of anger. When Andy finds it necessary to discipline Opie, it is always in a way to teach him a lesson, even if the lesson is learned at the seat of his pants.

Quite often adults punish children without giving thought to what they are doing. Out of frustration or anger, children are given consequences or punishments that do not fit the offense. When children are disciplined, there are two approaches one can use. A child can be disciplined as a way to punish the child, or he can be disciplined in a way that will teach the child. Hopefully, there can be ways to do both and do it effectively.

In this episode, Opie accidentally kills a song bird. Andy makes Opie listen to the baby birds chirping to help remind him of what he has done. Opie is very sorry that he has killed the bird's mother, but he still needs to be taught the gravity of what he has done.

Opie decides that since he is the one who takes away the birds mama, he will be the one to raise them. With help from Andy and Barney, Opie accepts the responsibility of taking care of the three birds until they are ready to be set free. He even gives them the names of Wynken, Blynken, and Nod. He takes this new responsibility very seriously.

An important aspect of Andy's disciplining Opie for killing the bird is that he is also very forgiving. He finds out Opie has done something wrong, he punishes him, and then he forgets about it. He does not keep reminding Opie about what he has done. When Opie takes on the responsibility of raising the birds, Andy encourages him and praises him for his fine efforts. He is proud of what Opie is doing, and he lets Opie know it.

Discipline was a big part of my teaching career. If a child did something that needed punishment and consequences, I tried to do it calmly. I tried to discipline my students in ways that would help change their behavior rather than merely be a punishment. I also tried to remember something very important when dealing with children. Just because a child does something bad, it does not make him a bad child.

"Wynken will tell Blynken, and Blynken will tell Nod, and Nod will tell Barney, and Barney will tell you." - Andy

Episode 97
"The Haunted House"

"All I'm saying is there are some things beyond the can of mortal man that shouldn't be tampered with." - Barney

*B*arney's superstitious ways are quite familiar to us. He believes Henry Bennett is a jinx. He uses chants to ward off bad luck, and he rubs a rabbit's foot and red hair. Now Barney will display his belief in ghosts, moving eyes, and floating axes, as he takes us through the old Rimshaw house, which in Barney's mind is really "The Haunted House".

Opie and his friend Arnold accidentally hit a baseball through a broken window at the old Rimshaw house. Word around Mayberry is that the old house is haunted because it is where old man Rimshaw tied his hired man in chains and then killed him with an ax. As the boys are about to enter the house to retrieve their ball, they hear strange moaning and groaning sounds. With no thought of their ball, the boys take off running to the courthouse to tell Andy about what they heard.

Andy has told Opie in the past that he does not want him playing around the old Rimshaw house. It is dangerous because of its run down condition. He tells the boys that he will get their ball for them. Otis happens to be visiting his cell during all this conversation, and he begins to tell tales about the haunting of the Rimshaw house. He has Barney's full attention, and when Andy tells Barney to go get the ball, he reluctantly agrees, but only after taking Gomer Pyle along. That way, both he and Gomer can show Opie that there is nothing to be afraid of in the Rimshaw House.

There are many people who believe in ghosts and spirits that float through the air. Barney is one of them. He always seems to let his imagination get the best of him. Many people enjoy going through haunted houses at Halloween time. It is even fun to get a good scare out of it. But for those of us who do enjoy this, we also realize that it is all just a game of make believe fun. It is when people really believe in ghosts and supernatural phenomena that problems can arise. So when Barney and Gomer enter the Rimshaw house, it can only mean there will be some kind of adventure.

I always find it amazing when I see Barney being superstitious. He is a trained police officer, and he is responsible for protecting the good citizens of Mayberry. Yet because of his wild imagination, he allows superstitious beliefs and nonexistent spirits to control much of his life. While Andy believes all the strange happenings within the walls of the Rimshaw house have a logical explanation, Barney sees spirits and the supernatural around every corner. He allows his fear of the unknown to control his actions.

Andy could go to retrieve the baseball himself. Instead he decides to send Barney. He knows of Barney's beliefs, yet he chooses to send Barney to the Rimshaw house. Does he really send Barney to retrieve the ball, or is his real purpose to get Barney to face up to his fears? How can he get Opie to overcome his fears when his own deputy has fears of his own? Leave it to Andy to come up with a plan to help both Opie and Barney.

Andy never passes up opportunities to teach Opie important lessons. Opie is a child and he thinks like a child. Andy never passes up opportunities to teach Barney important lessons. Why? Because Barney is a man, yet at times he thinks like a child.

"A still? Oh moonshines, so that's what it is. You know I thought it was something along those very lines." - Barney

Episode 98
"Ernest T. Bass Joins the Army"

"Yeh, that's me, able bodied man. I mean it means they're honored to get a man what could chin hisself twenty times with just one hand, what could dip in a barrel of water and pick out a watermelon with his jaws, or could chuck a full growed sick jackass across his shoulders and tote it five miles to the doctor." - Ernest T.

*E*rnest T. Bass makes another exciting visit to Mayberry. This time he decides to come out of the mountains on a very important mission. He is going to join the United States Army, and the army recruiter just happens to be in Mayberry. Imagine Ernest T. Bass in the United States Army. But what would make this strange man from up in the mountains want to join the army?

There are many reasons why young men join the armed forces. For many it is a matter of family tradition. Sons want to follow in the footsteps of their fathers and grandfathers. For others, it provides an opportunity to learn new skills and travel throughout the world. Many join as a means of earning money for a college education. Some are very patriotic, and they believe in the ideals of defending freedom and democracy around the world. Back in the 1960s many young men, enlisted in one of the branches of the armed forces rather than being drafted. They would then have a voice as to which branch they served. However, none of these reasons is why Ernest T. Bass tries to enlist. He simply wants to join the army so he can get a uniform.

Forget patriotism or family tradition or new skills. It's as simple as wanting to get a uniform.

Ernest T. has a rather unusual way of dealing with his anger management. Whenever he is angry with someone, he seeks his revenge by throwing his "bestest" rocks through their windows. Andy and Barney warn the army recruiter about Ernest T., but the army needs every able bodied man they can find, so the sergeant allows Ernest T. to take his physical. It doesn't take long, however, for the recruiter to find out that Andy and Barney are right. When Ernest T. is rejected, he immediately breaks the recruiter's window with a rock, and then he goes to the courthouse to do the same.

As we know, Andy always seeks the less confrontational method of solving problems. He basically has two choices when dealing with Ernest T. He can either lock him in jail, only to have him break windows again when he is released, or he can find a way to get Ernest T. into the army. Fortunately he has to do neither. Ernest T. admits he doesn't really want to be in the army, and that he only wants a uniform to wear so he can get a girl. He thinks if he has a uniform at least three or four girls back in the mountains will want him. Andy knows if he is going to get Ernest T. to go back to the mountains and quit breaking windows, he is going to have to find him a uniform. But just where he is going to find a uniform in Mayberry that will fit Ernest T.? Andy once again comes up with the perfect solution. He gives Ernest T. Barney's expensive custom made uniform.

Only in Mayberry can a lawbreaking trouble maker like Ernest T. be given another chance. Without making Ernest T. pay for replacing any of the broken windows, Andy sends him happily on his way back to the mountains wearing Barney's uniform. No one is too lowly or misguided to receive understanding and compassion by Sheriff Andy Taylor of Mayberry. Not even Ernest T. Bass, ex army man.

"Girls and love. You know what is the truth sheriff? As clever and good looking as I am, I just can't get a girl." - Ernest T.

Episode 99
"Sermon for Today"

"Consider how we live our lives today. Everything is run, run, run. We bolt our breakfast, we scan the headlines, we race to the office." - Dr. Harrison Breen

*V*isiting pastor, Dr. Breen, speaks the above words to the good people of All Souls' Church on September 30, 1963. The name of his sermon is "What's Your Hurry?" He believes that all people are living a fast paced life style, and everyone needs to slow down. Considering the people in Mayberry and their lifestyles, I would think "fast paced" and "Mayberry" is a classic oxymoron. There is perhaps no where else, anywhere, where the people are more laid back and relaxed than in Mayberry. Of course Dr. Breen is from New York, and he does not really know the people to whom he is speaking.

Perhaps the reason the people of Mayberry are loved by so many people for such a long time is because of the yearning there is for a place like Mayberry. Stay at home mothers are quickly becoming a thing of the past. Children as young as four years of age are in school, while even younger siblings are at daycare centers. Older children are shuffling their hectic schedules from one organized activity to another. Parents are working long hours developing careers or trying to make ends meet. Families rarely eat at a table together with a recent survey reporting that many families eat take out fast food on an average of four times a week. When Sunday morning comes around, people decide to sleep in rather than attend church. Sunday is the only time they have to spend together. With malls and many businesses now open seven days a week, Sundays are fast becoming the day when family members all go their separate ways; each doing his own thing. There are very few opportunities for entire families to be together as one.

After hearing Dr. Breen's inspiring sermon, the Taylors return home for a relaxing Sunday. Andy and Barney are found sitting on the porch after enjoying one of Aunt Bee's wonderful Sunday dinners. Andy suggests that he and Barney should run down to the drugstore for some ice cream, but Aunt Bee quickly puts a stop to that idea. Soon Gomer Pyle joins the group, and together they begin to reflect on Dr. Breen's message. Recalling the wonderful days when

Mayberry had a band concert in the open air, they decide if they all work hard they will be able to organize a band concert for that very evening. But everyone is going to have to pitch in, and they are going to have to work fast. There is a lot to be done, and there isn't much time to do it all.

I am very fortunate to live in a community where a free band concert is performed at an outdoor band shell along a beautiful slow moving river. Every Thursday night during the summer months the municipal band has a one hour concert. People bring their lawn chairs, dogs, and young children. A young man sometimes sells ice cream treats from his old fashioned ice cream vending bicycle. For an hour each week we go back to the past and enjoy a wonderful evening of music. It is a tradition that has been going on now for many years, and we all hope it continues for a long time to come.

When the Mayberry band concert fails to emerge, everyone is very disappointed. However, the most disappointing part of the entire venture is that Dr. Breen does not listen to his own words. When he is asked to stay for a cup of coffee, he has to decline the invitation because he needs to rush off to preach a sermon. As he gets in the car to depart, Andy asks him a very poignant question. "What's your hurry?"

"Look at you all, so nice and relaxed; a picture of contentment. Yes, you all look as serene and relaxed as if, ah, well, as if you have just finished listening to a pleasant band concert." - Dr. Harrison Breen

Episode 100
"Briscoe Declares for Aunt Bee"

"Miss Bee, I never dreamed that anything so beautiful could be said to me. It was your heart talking to my heart. Now my heart is answering. Miss Bee, I'm declaring for you." - Briscoe Darling

The Darling family returns to Mayberry. Being the kindhearted man that he is, Andy invites Briscoe and his family to supper. Upon hearing the Darling boys are terrible cooks, Aunt Bee makes sure Briscoe gets extra food and attention. Not knowing that Aunt

Bee treats all her guests this way, Briscoe gets the notion that she is interested in him. When Aunt Bee recites a beautiful poem about a rose, Briscoe misinterprets her intentions and suddenly announces that he is declaring for Aunt Bee.

Andy knows that every time the Darlings visit Mayberry there is bound to be misadventure. It certainly is no exception on this visit. Briscoe woos Aunt Bee with words and music. He fails to understand her rejection. He offers her a sturdy cabin, his undivided love, and the devotion of four fun loving sons. When Aunt Bee makes it perfectly clear that she is not interested, Briscoe does the unthinkable. He kidnaps Aunt Bee and takes her to his cabin.

Kidnapping brides appears to be a common tradition with the mountain folk around Mayberry. First Ernest T. Bass kidnaps a bride to be, and now Briscoe Darling kidnaps Aunt Bee. Apparently Briscoe has forgotten that Sheriff Taylor does not tolerate kidnapping in Mayberry; especially when it involves his own family members. Kidnapping is a very serious offense everywhere. Does Briscoe overdo it this time to a point where he will find himself locked up in the cells of the Mayberry jail?

Andy and Barney immediately go to the Darling cabin where they find Aunt Bee safely sitting on a chair. Briscoe is shocked when Andy asks Aunt Bee if she is hurt. He informs Andy that he would never hurt a beloved. Andy tries without success to get Briscoe to understand that he just can't steal a person and expect her to marry him. Briscoe insists that he is not giving up. He is determined to make Aunt Bee his bride.

Andy could arrest Briscoe for kidnapping and false imprisonment. But as we well know, Andy always tries to avoid arresting people whenever possible. Even though it is his own beloved Aunt Bee who Briscoe Darling abducts, Andy refuses to arrest him. Why doesn't he take Briscoe back to Mayberry and lock him up? Perhaps it is because Andy knows that Briscoe is basically a good person, and he has no intentions of harming Aunt Bee. He simply lives by a different set of beliefs and customs, and Andy knows he must use an unusual approach if he is going to resolve this problem.

Because Briscoe Darling lives by his own set of rules and customs that go back many years, Andy uses a bit of basic psychology on Briscoe. Briscoe is set in his ways, so what will happen if his beloved

Bee starts to change him? Will she still be the desirable woman he believes her to be? After scrubbing the floors, taking a bath, and getting his hands hit with a spoon, Briscoe decides it is not worth the pain to have Aunt Bee become his wife. Andy's plan works, and once again a very delicate situation is brought to a peaceful end. Can you just imagine Aunt Bee living in the Darling's mountain cabin cooking for Briscoe and his fun loving boys?

"Well Miss Bee, your kisses are awful nice and highly valuable, but to be perfectly honest with you, they just ain't worth the pain." - Briscoe Darling

Episode 101
"Gomer the Houseguest"

"You know, Wally's a strange man. He just done the funniest thing. He fired me from my job." - Gomer Pyle

*g*omer Pyle is a very lovable character. His simple, childlike manner has a way of creeping into our hearts every time we see him. His greasy cow licked hair and nasal voice help to create this image. He lives in a little room behind Wally's Gas Station where he cooks his meals on a one burner hotplate. His lack of social graces often causes embarrassment to those around him; yet the people of Mayberry accept Gomer for who he is. In fact, he is a very popular and valuable employee at Wally's Gas Station. The only problem is Wally does not fully appreciate that simple fact.

Growing up in a small town in the late 1950's and early 1960's, I knew quite a few guys like Gomer. Some were classmates while others were just fellows who were living in town. Some were the high school drop outs that for one reason or other just could not make it academically. However, back then they had no difficulty finding jobs. One of the things we were always told was that if we quit school we would just end up pumping gas. Even our little town of under five hundred people had four gas stations, and each one needed someone to pump gas and check the oil. My very first job out of high school was at our local Chevrolet dealer pumping gas and washing cars. I worked just two days before I quit. I hated smelling like gas and oil all the time.

Gomer loves his job at Wally's. He looks forward to pumping gas and putting air in tires. Most of all he loves telling stories while pumping gas for his friends who stop in. Wally, on the other hand, thinks Gomer is being inefficient in his duties, so he fires him. This means that Gomer loses his place to live. Once again, being the kind old softy that he is, Andy invites Gomer to stay at his house until he can find a place to live. But it doesn't take long for Andy to realize that he has made one very big mistake.

Andy faces a problem with Gomer that many of us have to deal with at some time or other. How do we tell a friend something that will result in hurt feelings? Gomer does not understand what it is like to live within a family. He has lived by himself for so long that he fails to realize that his actions are upsetting the Taylor household. Should the Taylors continue to tolerate Gomer's unintentional inconsideration because he is a friend, or has the time come to tell him he must leave? This is Andy's dilemma.

It turns out Andy does not have to do either. When Gomer's personal followers find out he is living with Andy, they begin to bring their cars to him. Andy finds his driveway full of cars leaking oil and making noise. He decides enough is enough, so he leads the parade of vehicles back to Wally's Gas Station. Wally realizes that Gomer is his business, and he readily agrees to give Gomer his job again as well as fixing up his little room in back. Gomer may get things done at a snail's pace, but Wally's customers don't seem to mind. While waiting, they can always hear another one of Gomer's wonderful tales.

We can all learn a lesson from this touching episode. The next time we need to say something that might create hurt feelings, perhaps we won't have to say anything at all. Perhaps, like Andy, we can find another way. At least it won't hurt to try.

"I just come by to thank you for helping me get my job back." - *Gomer Pyle*

Episode 102
"A Black Day for Mayberry"

"Something's come up; pretty important. No, I'd tell you about it, but I can't. Hah, hah, it's nothing like that. This is something big." - Barney

*B*arney fife is indeed an excitable person. In today's terms he might be classified as being hyperactive. He is easily agitated, highly imaginative, quite impulsive, and very spirited. It doesn't take much to get him upset. This is especially true when it comes to police work. Many times Andy has to calm him down and prevent him from doing something irrational. So how does Barney react when he finds out a gold shipment worth over seven million dollars is coming though Mayberry on its way to Fort Knox?

Keeping secrets and police matters confidential is not one of Barney's strong points. He spreads false rumors countless times because he fails to keep privileged information to himself. Andy often has to chastise him for repeating things that he vows to keep secret. In most cases the results are embarrassment or inconveniences for a few people. But when Barney lets it slip that the gold shipment is coming through Mayberry, he disrupts the entire secret plan developed by the Treasury Department. It is perhaps Barney's most serious mistake as Mayberry's deputy sheriff.

When a person is entrusted with privileged information, it is imperative that the right of privacy prevails. I volunteer in a local hospital three days a week, and I often am privy to privileged information regarding patients and employees. Because of federal privacy laws, I am not allowed to discuss it with anyone. I am not allowed to say who I see in the hospital. It is grounds for immediate dismissal if I should violate a patient's right to privacy in any way. Barney could learn a few things by sitting in on some of our meetings dealing with consequences of divulging privileged information.

Barney spills the beans about the gold shipment when he gets to bragging about his important work he has to do. His ego gets in the way of his duty as a police officer, resulting in the entire town of Mayberry knowing about the shipment. What is supposed to be a secret pass through Mayberry is turning into one big three ring circus.

171

It is amazing how often Andy tolerates Barney's ineptness as his deputy. Time and time again Barney makes a major blunder and serious consequences result. But time and time again Andy covers for Barney and allows him to continue as deputy. He never disciplines Barney except for occasionally taking away his gun. Is Andy doing the right thing when he allows Barney to continue making mistakes? Is he endangering the lives of Mayberry's citizens by allowing Barney to carry a gun that he accidentally discharges? Does Andy's friendship with Barney overshadow his responsibility as Barney's boss? I often wonder if Andy would tolerate such action by a deputy who was not his best friend and cousin. Will this latest mistake result in Barney's departure as deputy sheriff?

For whatever reason, Andy does tolerate Barney's mistakes. Whether he is right in doing so is not important to me. What is important is that I see an example of true friendship. Barney's mistakes are not intentional. If he is guilty of anything, he is guilty of poor judgment. Andy knew what Barney is like when he made him his deputy. Despite his bumbling performances, Andy continues to stand by his friend. He looks out for Barney and protects Barney whenever he can. After all, isn't that what being a friend is all about? But I wonder if the Treasury men will be so understanding and forgiving?

"Barbarians, worshipers of Hammond." - Regis

Episode 103
"Opie's Ill-Gotten Gain"

"Bad news, huh? I hate to tell you I told you so, but I did you know." - Andy

*H*ave you ever thought about what it must be like for Opie to have Miss Crump for a teacher? He is in a rather precarious position. Not only is Miss Crump his teacher, but she is also his father's girlfriend. In all my years teaching I don't think I have ever known a teacher who was dating one of her student's parents. It must be very difficult for Opie to have Miss Crump as a teacher and also as a prospective mother. It must be equally as difficult for Miss Crump because Opie is in her class every school year.

Opie is an average student in school. He has occasional problems with some subjects as do many students. He struggles at times and he does very well at times. Andy never puts undo pressure on Opie in regards to his school work. He expects him to study hard and to do the best he can. When Opie does this, Andy is satisfied.

It is report card time for Opie, and when Andy comes home after a hard day at work, Opie presents him with his card. Expecting bad news, Andy is flabbergasted when he discovers all A's on the report card. Aunt Bee bakes a special cake, and the family is celebrating the event when Barney comes to call. Of course once Barney hears the news, his expertise in education takes over, and he tells Andy that he should get Opie's IQ tested. He says he might be a genius like "Einsteen". Andy decides he is going to have a picture taken of Opie holding the report card so he can send it to relatives. Suddenly the average student Opie is elevated to the status of straight A student.

When school begins the next day Miss Crump informs Opie that she made a mistake on his report card. He did not get all A's. In fact one grade was an F. Opie tries to tell Andy about the mistake, but Andy is so proud of Opie's report card that he just can not bring himself to do it. Then when he gets home from school, Andy presents him with a brand new bicycle as a reward. Opie refuses to ride the bike, however, and decides to study instead. He cannot bring himself to ride a bike he knows he did not earn.

Opie is a very unhappy child. His father suddenly is very proud of him and all because he thinks Opie has earned straight A's on his report card. Opie is put in a very difficult situation for such a young boy. Why does Opie have to tell his father? Miss Crump is the one who makes the mistake. She is the one who put all the A's on his report card. When a teacher makes a serious error such as Miss Crump does, it is the teacher's responsibility to inform the parent; not the child's. Eventually Miss Crump does explain things to Andy, but not before Opie decides to run away from home.

Andy learns a valuable parenting lesson from the report card mistake. When Opie explains why he is running away, Andy realizes how important it is for parents to tell their children they are proud of them all the time. A child should not have to earn straight A's in order to receive praise from a parent. Andy places so much importance on Opie's report card that Opie feels there is no way he can live up to his new image. An average student like Opie who works hard and does the best he can deserves just as much praise as the student who is gifted and earns straight A's.

"Well, I was going away someplace and not come back until you was proud of me again." - Opie

Episode 104
"A Date for Gomer"

"Andy's got hot knees." - Barney

*J*ust because Mayberry is a small town, it doesn't mean there aren't important social events. The Chamber of Commerce Dance is one of the biggest dances held in Mayberry. Barney waits all year for it to come around so he can get all dressed up to take Thelma Lou. He polishes his hat and has his old salt and pepper suit cleaned. It is just perfect for the dip. The flowers are ordered, all the plans are made, and the big night is almost here. Nothing will stop Barney from taking Thelma Lou to this exciting dance; nothing that is unless Thelma Lou gets company on the day of the big event.

Thelma Lou's cousin, Mary Grace, unexpectedly calls and tells Thelma Lou that she will be coming for a short visit. Thelma Lou is delighted until she remembers the dance. How can she go to the dance with Barney and leave her cousin home alone? She knows Mary Grace will not agree to tag along with them alone, so Barney and Thelma Lou have just two choices. They can either forget about going to the dance, or they can find a date for Mary Grace. According to Barney finding a date for Mary Grace will not be easy because she is a "dog". They decide they will ask Andy to take Mary Grace, but much to their disappointment, Andy is already planning to take Helen to the dance.

Dances can be a lot of fun; especially if you are a pretty girl with a bubbly personality. It is exciting to get all dressed up for a date and enjoy an evening of dancing and fun. But what happens if you are not a pretty girl with a bubbly personality? How much fun can a dance be if you are a rather plain looking girl without a fancy dress or an outgoing personality? For many girls like this, it is just easier to not go to dances at all.

Not wanting to miss the dance, Barney and Andy persuade Gomer Pyle to take Mary Grace to the dance. At the same time, Helen and Thelma Lou are talking Mary Grace into going with Gomer. So the problem is solved and the three couples are going to have a wonderful time together. So far everything is going along just perfectly.

Neither Gomer nor Mary Grace knows much about going on a date. They are strangers to one another, and both are very quiet and shy. Unfortunately our society caters to the "beautiful people". Television and magazines feature young, attractive, sophisticated people in their ads and promotions. The Gomer Pyles and Mary Graces of the world must feel really left out. But they want the very same things as everyone. Both Gomer and Mary Grace are kind and considerate people. They want to be having fun and they want to be accepted. They may not know all the social graces, and they may not wear the latest fashions, but in reality they are no different from anyone else.

When the boys arrive to get the girls, Gomer shocks everyone when he suddenly leaves with no explanation. He sees that Helen and Thelma Lou are wearing flowers; so he leaves to buy a corsage for Mary Grace. He thinks it is wrong for Mary Grace to attend the dance unadorned. When he returns, he finds Mary Grace home alone. The others have gone to the dance. Not having a way to get to the dance, Gomer and Mary Grace enjoy a wonderful evening together away from the limelight. They find they don't need a fancy dance in order to have a good time. They have each other.

"Your flowers, your corsage, when I come in I noticed the other girls had one and you didn't. It wouldn't be right for you, Mary Grace, to go to the dance unadorned." - Gomer

Episode 105
"Up in Barney's Room"

"My mother's dresser; this dresser came all the way from Fort Lauderville. Oh Mr. Fife, how could you?" - Mrs. Mendlebright

*B*arney Fife is a single man who lives very frugally. He does not own a car, and he owns just one suit. He has few expenses, so one might think he'd have a nice apartment or a house like Thelma Lou or Helen Crump. Instead he chooses to live in a five dollar a week room at Mrs. Mendlebright's rooming house. He is not allowed to cook in his room, and he cannot use a light bulb larger than forty watts. But Barney likes Mrs. Mendlebright very much, so he is quite content with his living arrangements.

When I began teaching in 1967, I lived much like Barney. I rented a room from an elderly couple that cost me six dollars a week. Like Barney, I could not cook in my room, and I had to share a bathroom. I could have found something better, I suppose, but my landlords were very nice. Breakfast was included each morning, and we often spent quiet evenings playing board games. It fit my needs perfectly, and I felt right at home.

Barney can not cook in his room, so he has to eat most of his meals at the diner. I too had to eat all my evening meals at the only diner we had in town. It didn't take long for me to get tired of eating at the same place. Before long all the food began to taste alike. I suppose that is how Barney is feeling when he cooks his chili on a hot plate on that fateful night. Andy delivers his check, and while they are talking, the chili begins to burn. Smelling the smoke, Mrs. Mendlebright quickly arrives on the scene, and when she finds the smoking hotplate hidden in her mother's bureau; she tells Barney he must leave. For one who so strictly enforces Mayberry's laws, Barney does not have any qualms about breaking Mrs. Mendlebright's rules.

Upon leaving Mrs. Mendlebright's house, Barney temporarily moves into the back room of the courthouse. It doesn't take long for Barney to admit that he has made a bad mistake. Where will he ever find another place like the one he had with Mrs. Mendlebright? She treats him like her own son. She even shampoos his hair. On warm summer evenings the two of them often sit on her front porch counting cars. Barney is very lonesome, and he wants to go home.

When I changed jobs after two years at my first school, I once again chose to rent a single room rather than an apartment. My second experience was very similar to my first. I rented from a very nice elderly lady, and it again cost me only six dollars a week. The rules were the same, yet I was extremely satisfied. Perhaps like Barney, I needed to be mothered by my landlady. She often did extra things for me, and on occasion she would invite me to have dinner with her. Once again, it was like living at home.

Rooming arrangements have changed drastically since the days of Mrs. Mendlebright. I doubt if too many young teachers or deputy sheriffs would even consider the kind of arrangements that Barney and I had. But as I look back over my life, I can honestly say that those four years I spent living in the rooming houses were four of the happiest years of my life. Perhaps that is why this episode is one of my all time favorites.

"Barney, I'd like to have you come back. You're a tidy person. Nobody leaves the wash basin the way you do." - Mrs. Mendlebright

Episode 106
"Citizen's Arrest"

"Now my oath stipulates that I'm to uphold the law. If my mother made a U turn I'd give her a ticket." - Barney

*B*arney makes a point to never overlook any violation he encounters. Whether it is jaywalking, littering, or parking in front of a fire hydrant, if Barney sees it, Barney issues a citation. It doesn't matter who the perpetrator is; whether it's Andy, or even the governor of the state, they are treated like any ordinary citizen. So it comes as no surprise when Barney issues his friend Gomer Pyle a ticket for making an illegal U turn.

In "Citizen's Arrest" we see another fine example of what sometimes happens when people in positions of authority think they are above the law. Barney doesn't hesitate in issuing Gomer his citation. The fact that Gomer is his friend doesn't make a bit of difference. If he breaks a law then he must face the consequences. But when Barney makes the very same illegal U turn, and Gomer makes a citizen's arrest, Barney justifies it by saying he is a police officer driving an official vehicle.

The concept of a citizen's arrest goes back many years. Historically, the citizens arrest originated under Anglo Saxon law in medieval England. English sheriffs encouraged and relied upon citizens in the towns and villages to make citizen's arrests. From this long standing tradition originated the concept of the "posse comitatus" which is a part of the United States legal tradition as well as that of the English. The law allows a common citizen to make virtually the same types of arrests as a sheriff or constable could. In our country today, the right to make a citizen's arrest is a constitutionally protected right under the Ninth Amendment. Barney must have skipped over that part in the sheriff's manual. He knows nothing about a citizen's arrest and it sure gets him into trouble.

Barney does not adhere to the principal of a citizen's arrest. Andy persuades him to issue himself a ticket to quiet the on looking crowd who are cheering Gomer's actions. When Andy and Gomer return to the courthouse to settle their differences, Barney refuses to pay the ticket and decides to lock himself up in jail. He is sure this will make Andy look foolish. Barney continues to put pressure on Andy by resigning as deputy, but Andy accepts his resignation. Barney has resigned several times in the past.

A police officer's job is very demanding. While most people might think the worst place for a police officer to work is in a large city, some police officers will say it is much more difficult in a small town. In a large city the police carry out their duties mostly among strangers. However, a small town police officer has to deal with his own friends and family. No matter what the situation, the small town officer will most likely have some sort of personal involvement with either the victim or the perpetrator. This can make things very difficult indeed; especially when it involves a very good friend.

Both Gomer and Barney expect special treatment when given citations, so they are equally at fault. Gomer feels he should be exempt from penalty because he is Barney's friend. Barney feels he is exempt because he wears a badge. But in reality, neither is exempt. Our laws are made to protect everyone, and they must be obeyed by everyone.

"Actually, what I want to say is that I realize I made a dang fool of myself, and I'm sorry." - Barney

Episode 107
"Opie and His Merry Men"

"You see Ope; it ain't only the materialistic things in this world that makes a person rich. There's love and friendship. That can make a person rich." - Barney

*F*ood begins to mysteriously disappear from some of the homes in Mayberry. Half a turkey, fruits, vegetables, an apple pie, and a whole ham are missing. It is a strange coincidence that all the places where food disappeared from are the homes of Opie's friends. Is it possible that Opie and his friends have something to do with it all?

There are a great many homeless people in the world today. For reasons that vary greatly, many people have neither shelter nor food. Many are elderly. Some suffer from mental illnesses or physical disabilities which prevent them from working. For whatever the reason, homeless people are a part of our society that needs assistance. There are government agencies, church organizations, and private groups that spend many hours and dollars trying to help these people who are so desperately in need.

Homeless is a relatively new term. When Opie and his friends are out playing in Crouch's woods, they come across a man living in a shack. He is a hobo. He does not have a home because he chooses not to work. He lives his life moving from town to town living off what he can get from others. In some ways he is very similar to Opie's friend Mr. Dan. Neither man likes the idea of work. They would much rather spend their days in idleness. They are alike too in that they both take advantage of Opie's kindness.

Opie and his friends decide to help their hobo friend. They are playing Robin Hood, and they know that Robin Hood and his band of merry men steal from the rich and then give to the poor. Compared to their new friend, Opie and his friends appear to be rich. So they take food from their homes and bring it to the hobo. They are just like Robin Hood. They take from those who have a lot, and they give it to someone who has little.

When Andy discovers that Opie is responsible for some of the missing food, he explains that it is wrong to steal; no matter what the reason. Opie does not understand how it can be stealing when he is simply taking something from someone who has so much and then giving it to someone who is so needy. After all, he did not take it for himself. Andy and Barney explain that stealing is stealing no matter what the reason.

Andy realizes he once again has a situation very similar to Opie's friendship with Dan Browne. He wants to find a way to show Opie how wrong he is about his hobo friend. He knows that showing him is much better than telling him. Actions speak much louder than words, or so the old saying goes. So Andy wisely decides on a plan of action.

When Andy offers the hobo jobs which really do not exist, the hobo makes all kinds of excuses why he cannot work. No sooner does Andy suggest that he can stay at the courthouse when Wary Willy takes off running. Opie and his friends see first hand that their hobo friend has made up the entire story about not being able to work. So Andy's plan works, but he has now created a new problem. How does he tell Opie that he was lying when he told the hobo about all the jobs he didn't really have for him?

"Petulla oblongata. He gave himself away as a phony right from the start. The petulla oblongata ain't in the leg; it's in the brain." - Barney

Episode 108
"Barney and the Cave Rescue"

"Barney Fife, you are really something. You really are......
Some picnic; sitting around with a wet blanket way out in the
middle of nowhere." - Thelma Lou

*P*oor Barney, even when he does something really brave and
wonderful, he still has a way of getting things all wrong. Most of
the time when Barney gets himself into trouble it is because of his
ego or impulsiveness. But in "Barney and the Cave Rescue," Barney
takes charge of a very serious and dangerous accident involving
Andy and Helen Crump. He performs very well under pressure while
getting the entire town involved in rescuing Andy and Helen from a
cave-in. The only problem, there are no Andy and Helen to rescue.

After Barney pulls his gun on Mr. Meldrim while mistaking him for a
bank robber, he becomes the laughing stock of Mayberry. To make
matters worse, it is the day of the big town picnic. Barney decides he
is not going, but when Andy promises that they will go off somewhere
by themselves, he reluctantly agrees to attend the big event. While
at the picnic, Andy and Helen decide to explore the old caves.
Shortly after they enter the cave, Barney and Thelma Lou follow. A
loud rumbling sound is heard, and suddenly the roof of the cave
collapses trapping Andy and Helen. When Barney realizes they are
still in the cave, he organizes a massive rescue operation with the
help of the very same people who poked fun of him earlier in the day.
Meanwhile Andy and Helen discover a way out of the cave, so they
head back to town to change clothes. When they hear on the radio
that Barney has organized a rescue, Andy decides they had better be
in the cave for him to rescue. If the rescuers were to discover they
were not in the cave, Andy knows Barney will never be able to live
down the ridicule he will face.

Barney has no idea that Andy and Helen are safe. He believes for
good reasons that his best friend and Helen are in the cave and the
cave has collapsed. His instincts take over, and nothing is going to
prevent him from saving their lives. During his rescue attempt we do
not see the nervous, shaky, bumbling Barney Fife. We see a very

concerned and capable deputy sheriff. We see one friend who bravely and without any concern for his own safety enters a dangerous cave with only one thing on his mind. He must find Andy and Helen. He refuses to let other's doubts stand in his way.

None of us knows when we might be called upon to do a heroic deed. We don't know how we will respond when it happens. We may come upon a tragic auto accident late at night, and we may be the only person who can render assistance. Someone may suffer a serious medical crisis while in our company, and we may have to respond immediately. If such a thing were ever to happen, we might be amazed at how we react. For some reason, human beings seem to receive inner strength and courage when facing danger. I think this is especially true when the danger is to those people we care about so much. For Barney Fife, knowing his best friend is in serious trouble is enough for him to rise to the occasion and act with the courage needed to do what he has to do. Forgetting about all his failures in the past, Barney will do whatever is necessary to save Helen and Andy. How wonderful to see all the people cheer and applaud Deputy Sheriff Barney Fife. It is certainly something we do not see often enough.

"I got 'em Barney; all the papers they had left. Here's the change from the ten dollars you gave me." - Opie

Episode 109
"Andy and Opie's Pal"

"Yah, that's what I call two real buddies. I like to see that. You know it's the friendships you start early in life. Them are the ones that really last." - Barney

*O*pie makes friends very easily. He has made friends with two hobos who pass through Mayberry. When Tex runs away from home, it is Opie who befriends him. He has a little girlfriend named Karen and a spoiled friend Arnold Winkler. Perhaps the reason others befriend Opie so easily is because Opie is the kind of boy who knows how to share. He shares his money to help buy a winter coat for his little girl friend, Charlotte. He shares his baseball while playing with Arnold.   Sharing is sometimes very difficult with children; especially when it comes to sharing friends. So how will Opie react if he suddenly has to start sharing his father with a friend? Remember the difficulty he had sharing Andy with Peggy?   Will Opie have problems now if Andy spends time with a new friend?

Opie is an only child and as such he has never had to share his father's time with a sibling. He gets all Andy's attention when he is home. He gets to go fishing with Andy, and he doesn't have to let an older brother or sister do something first. If he needs help with his homework or has a problem, it is easy for him to get Andy's help. And when Andy wants something done at the courthouse, Opie knows that he is the one who will get to do it. In fact the only person Opie has to share his father with is Barney, but Opie doesn't mind because Barney is just like a second father to him.

A new boy by the name of Tray Bodin arrives in Mayberry, and immediately he and Opie become great friends. They are about the same age. Tray has no father, and Opie has no mother. They enjoy playing the same things, so it would appear that this new friendship will be one that will blossom and grow. Andy takes an immediate liking to Tray, and he begins to give him the attention that he usually only shares with Opie. It doesn't seem to bother Opie at first, but when Andy tells Tray he can use his fishing pole, and when he takes him along to check the cabins by the lake, Opie decides enough is enough, and he sets out to end his new friendship.

Children often view friendships quite differently than adults. All of us have many acquaintances, but we probably have few very close friends.   Friends are the special people in our lives with whom we spend quality time. We share our joys and sorrows with them. We overlook their little idiosyncrasies that seem to get on our nerves because they are friends. We stick with them and help them if they get in trouble. And they stick by us through thick and thin. They are the special people in our lives.

For children a friend often means someone they enjoy playing with. They may meet someone for the first time, and within a few minutes they become "best friends". Opie is not willing to share his father with Tray, and Tray likes to spend time with Andy. Perhaps Opie does not think about Tray being fatherless. He is not willing to share his father because he may be afraid of losing him to Tray. But when Andy uses Barney to show Opie what it is like to hurt a friend, Opie realizes how wrong he is. Andy is a wonderful father and friend to Opie. In fact he is such a great father and friend that there is enough of him for two boys to enjoy ; maybe even enough for two boys and Barney.

"He's got something even better than that, son. Now he's got a genuine, full sized, regulation friend to match." - Andy

Episode 110
"Aunt Bee the Crusader"

"You could if you wanted to. Maybe you stay around jails too much. Maybe you should go to church more often." - Aunt Bee

*A*unt Bee is usually a very mild mannered stay at home homemaker. She attends church each Sunday and she sings in both the church and town choirs. She enjoys her garden club and other social activities. Her cooking talents are known throughout Mayberry, and she enjoys having entries in the country fair. She isn't a very political person, and generally speaking not too many things get her riled. But if Aunt Bee happens to take up some important cause, watch out. She is not someone to mess with.

Aunt Bee learns that the county has condemned the property of Mr. Frisbee, the egg man, so she immediately confronts Andy. The county needs Mr. Frisbee's land so they can extend the highway. Being sheriff, it is Andy's duty to serve the eviction notice to Mr. Frisbee. When Aunt Bee learns the reason for the eviction, she immediately decides to take up the cause against Andy and the county. We have seen how Andy dislikes the idea of evicting people. He hated serving papers on the Scobys and Frank Myers. But this time it is different. This time Andy believes the county is right in evicting Mr. Frisbee.

When Andy serves Mr. Frisbee the eviction notice for the County of Mayberry, the county is invoking the power of eminent domain, a legal term meaning the government's authority to force people to sell their homes for a price the government decides is fair. Andy tries to explain this concept to Aunt Bee, and he tells her Mr. Frisbee is being paid more than the property is worth. But Aunt Bee will not condone the throwing of a man off his property for any reason, much less for money. She forms a protest group, and they are determined to see Mr. Frisbee's property rightfully returned to him.

The power of eminent domain has been around for a long time. Governments have used it many times for the development of important roads, parks, or public buildings. At first it was used only for developing public projects. However, recently the Supreme Court ruled that the power of eminent domain can now be used to seize property for commercial use. This decision has created major problems for many communities around the country. People are now losing their homes for entirely new reasons.

If it were not for the power of eminent domain we would not have many of our great highways and public parks. It is always a delicate issue when the government tries to seize the property of one person in order to benefit others. Whether this is right will probably be debated for generations to come as prime real estate becomes scarcer.

Aunt Bee truly believes that Mr. Frisbee should be allowed to stay on his land. It has been in his family for generations. But what will Aunt Bee do when she finds out that Mr. Frisbee's land is being used for something illegal? Imagine her dismay when she finds out that Mr. Frisbee is running a still. Next to fighting unfair evictions, perhaps Aunt Bee's greatest passion is getting rid of moon shiners. So Andy ends up having to protect Mr. Frisbee from a very angry Aunt Bee.

"But you can understand why I rushed to Mr. Frisbee's defense. He seemed like a poor man who needed a friend. I had to do something." - Aunt Bee

Episode 111
"Barney's Sidecar"

"Don't wear my hat Ange, I can't stand to wear a hat after it's been on somebody else's head. My mother was the same way." - Barney

The good citizens of Mayberry are rather used to Barney's various shenanigans. They aren't overly concerned when they hear a gunshot coming from the sheriff's office. They assume Barney has accidentally discharged his gun again. If they hear someone yelling for help as they pass the courthouse, they most likely know Barney has once again locked himself in a cell. Or if they happen to see Barney driving down Main Street with the siren blasting and the lights flashing, they know he is probably giving a pretty young girl an escort to the post office. So why should they get too concerned when Barney shows up one day wearing a helmet and goggles, driving a World War 11 motorcycle?

Barney is forever complaining to Andy about the lack of modern crime fighting equipment in Mayberry. They have no teargas, no sub machine guns, and no riot gear. They don't even have a second patrol car to help catch the speeders out on the highway. Well, if Andy isn't going to anything about it, Barney sure will.

When Barney attends a police auction, he returns to Mayberry driving an old World War 11 motorcycle, complete with a sidecar. We never do know just where the money comes from for this purchase. Andy never questions the cost of the motorcycle; but he does question its use. Barney assures him that it will be ideal for patrolling the highway, running errands, and as far as the sidecar, it will be perfect for carrying things from the store. Barney also tells Andy that he won't even be noticed, but when he puts on his goggles, helmet, and gloves, Andy knows that Barney will indeed by noticed.

Change is quite often very difficult for some people to accept. The people of Mayberry are a slow moving, quiet, easy going people. Things have not changed much in Mayberry for many years. Barney's presence on his "motorcycle" is a bit more than the people can take. One of Barney's shortcomings is that he generally does not do things in moderation. He just kind of jumps into things and goes full speed. When he gets his motorcycle, Andy advises him to be inconspicuous. But it is difficult for Barney to be inconspicuous with his white helmet, goggles, white gloves, flags, and leather jacket. Add to this the speed in which he drives around town, and it is more than the people can tolerate. Even Aunt Bee suggests they string a wire across the road to get Barney when he speeds down the street. She saw the Nazis do it once in a movie. It really worked too. But Andy squashes that idea; he would like to hurt Barney a little, not kill him.

Andy knows he must find a way to rid Mayberry of the dangerous motorcycle. But how? He also knows Barney is very sensitive, and there is no way he will agree to give up his cycle; unless there is a way to do so without hurting his feelings. As usual Andy is able to come up with a plan that not only gets rid of the motorcycle, but also spares Barney hurt feelings and pride. True friendship once again guides Andy through a difficult situation with his best friend. Although it saddens Barney by having him give up the motorcycle, Andy once again makes the streets of Mayberry safe for everyone.

"Al, Bert, the Marlow boys; it's theirs Barn." - Andy

Episode 112
"My Fair Ernest T. Bass"

"He stuck his hand in the punch bowl, and he ate every bit of the watermelon rind. And if that wasn't enough he soaked the paper napkins in the punch, and then he threw them at the ceiling." - Mrs. Wiley

*E*rnest T. Bass once again comes to Mayberry. He crashes a party given by Mrs. Wiley, and when he is told to leave, he throws a rock through her window. Andy and Barney are called to investigate, and when Andy hears the description of Ernest T, he knows immediately who he is dealing with. Upon returning to the courthouse they find Barney's uniform on the desk and Ernest T. in a cell. Why has Ernest T. returned his uniform? It was supposed to help him get a girl back in the mountains. But it did not work, so now Ernest T. still does not have a girl, and he is back in a very nasty rock throwing mood.

Despite his backward ways and his inability to read and write, Ernest T. is just like the rest of us in one important way. He wants to be loved. He explains to Andy and Barney how he tried to court Hoggette Winslow, Hog Winslow's daughter. But according to Ernest T., it just didn't take. It came to an abrupt end after he hit her on the head with a rock, and she decided to marry the taxidermist who sewed her up. The only reason he went to Mrs. Wiley's party was so he could get a girl. So Andy and Barney are right back to where they were the last time Ernest T. came into Mayberry.

Contrary to Barney's warnings, Andy decides he will try to clean up Ernest T., teach him some manners, and try to pass him off as a cousin at Mrs. Wiley's next party. When Barney comes to check on Andy's progress, he does not even recognize Ernest.T. He is clean, well groomed, and wearing a suit and hat. Andy is even able to teach Ernest T. how to speak without twanging through his nose so much. But has Andy really done such a good job that he will be able to pass Ernest T. off as his cousin Ollie?

I can remember when I was younger and I was invited to various social activities where I just knew I did not fit in. Basically I am a simple person with simple tastes, and when I was put into a situation where the people were more sophisticated, I was very uncomfortable. I attempted to act and speak like the people I was with. In most cases I just did not pull it off. I did not share their interests or life styles at all, and I am sure I was as transparent as glass whenever I tried to be like them. I ended up not enjoying myself at all. How could I possible have a good time if I had to constantly be worried about what I was saying or how I was acting?

Ernest T. is in a situation much like I was. Andy has the best of intentions when he tries to help Ernest T. But he is trying to change him into something he is not. He can change Ernest T.'s appearance, and he can change a few of his mannerisms, but he can not change who Ernest T. is. If a person wants to improve one's self for the better, so be it. But can one person really change another person, especially into something the person can never really be? Ernest T. is Ernest T. He is a man from the mountains, and when he is in Mayberry, he doesn't have the social skills to fit in. But that should not stop him from pursuing his dream of finding a girl. For someone once said, "For every man there is a woman." And as we see in this episode, it is true even for Ernest T. Bass. And Ernest T. finds his girl when he is the real Ernest T. Bass, not Cousin Ollie.

"Let's talk about me. You want to know about me? I don't spill at the table, I don't throw food, and I try not to talk through my nose." - Ernest T.

Episode 113
"Prisoner of Love"

"Sheriff, thank you. It's what you didn't do. You didn't ask me why or how come I'm here. And you've given me an evening in which the only one asking questions was myself." - Female prisoner

*P*risoner of Love" is an episode quite different from most others. We see the normally very level headed Sheriff Andy Taylor take on one of the characteristics we most often see in Deputy Barney Fife. Andy allows his attraction toward a beautiful young woman prisoner to somewhat interfere with his duties as sheriff.

An attractive female jewel thief is brought to the Mayberry jail for an overnight stay. Both Andy and Barney are enamored with her beauty. While we would expect Barney to act rather foolishly in this situation, it is Andy who is most affected by the newest visitor. We see a very human side of Andy that we haven't seen before in this unusual story line. Andy already has a steady warm relationship with Helen Crump. Since meeting Helen, he has not been attracted to another woman in Mayberry. Yet for some reason, this attractive female prisoner gets to Andy, and he cannot stop thinking about her.

Andy and Barney are both so smitten by this attractive prisoner; they practically fall over each other trying to cater to her needs. They create such a ruckus that Otis begins to complain. Barney and Andy flip a coin to decide who gets to take Otis home. When Barney and Otis leave, the prisoner asks Andy to sit with her and just talk. Andy finds her a very good listener, and he enjoys telling her stories about the folks in Mayberry. He is non judgmental with the prisoner and never once does he talk about her situation. We know that Andy treats all people like this. He accepts people for who they are, and while he sometimes tries to change them, he doesn't usually judge them

Barney returns to the courthouse, and Andy realizes that perhaps it would be better if Barney were to stay. Andy goes home for a while, but after a short time he decides to rush back to the courthouse. Perhaps the thought has occurred to him that just maybe the prisoner was being especially sweet with him for a purpose. Just as he enters the courthouse door, he runs right into the prisoner on her way out. In the cell is Barney desperately trying to open the prisoner's overnight case. It appears that both Andy and Barney were duped by the "prisoner of love."

Andy once chastised Aunt Bee and Barney for allowing Gentleman Dan Caldwell to charm his way out of the cell. Now the very same thing has happened to Andy. He allows a beautiful woman to use her charm to weaken his resistance. But this just illustrates that Andy is no different from most men. We all sometimes turn to putty when in the presence of a beautiful and charming woman. I like to think Andy realizes his mistake while sitting on the porch, but we will never know for sure. Does he rush back to the courthouse because he realizes he was being used by a beautiful woman, and he fears the same thing will happen to Barney? Or does he rush back to the courthouse because he really wants to spend more time with "the prisoner of love?" I will leave that for to you to decide.

"Well, you can't blame a girl for trying." - Female Prisoner

Episode 114
"Hot Rod Otis"

"I took on a night job. I've been at it a month to earn some extra money. And today, today is the day I finally got enough to buy something I've always had my heart on." - Otis Campbell

*O*tis Campbell is once again staggering into the courthouse. It is Friday night, and he has his usual "snootful". But something very different happens this time. Otis asks Andy and Barney to wake him up at eight o'clock the next morning. But Andy doesn't believe Otis because he always sleeps late after a night of drinking. When Barney comes to work the next morning, he decides to wake up Otis to teach him a lesson about saying foolish things. But to their surprise, Otis thanks them for waking him and announces that he is going to finally buy something he has always wanted.

When it comes to Otis Campbell, "Hot Rod Otis" gives us a very clear picture of the kind of man he is. Otis is basically a good person. The only time he indulges in his drinking is on weekends. During the week he works hard as a glue dipper at the local furniture factory. As we see in this episode, he is even willing to take on a part time job to earn the extra money he needs to buy something. Apparently Otis does not like to buy things on credit. Or perhaps no one will give him credit. So even if it means waiting a while to make his important purchase, Otis is going to use his savings to pay cash.

Andy and Barney cannot figure out what Otis could possibly buy that has him so excited. They are in the process of ruling things out when they hear the sound of a car horn outside the courthouse. When they investigate the noise, they discover, much to their horror, Otis behind the wheel of an old car. Now they know what Otis wanted.

Barney is convinced that Otis driving a car will be a disaster for Mayberry. But Otis has a license, so as long as he doesn't drive while drunk, there is nothing Andy can do. Barney decides to give Otis a refresher course on the rules of the road. Otis thinks it is a big joke, and before long, Andy sends him on his way. They decide to keep a close watch on Otis to make sure he follows the rules of driving and doesn't drink and drive.

Otis attends a party that night, and when he leaves he is staggering and singing. Just as he reaches his car he passes out across the front fender. Horrified that Otis is about to drive, they take him to the courthouse and devise a clever scheme that they hope will convince Otis to get rid of the car. After throwing water in Otis' face, Andy and

Barney pretend that Otis has drowned after driving his car into the river. Otis hears their story and begins to cry and cry. When Andy and Barney wake Otis, they learn that Otis believes he just had a bad nightmare. He then lets them know that he had sold the car before he took his first drink at the party. So their entire little act was all for naught.

We learn another important thing about Otis in the last scene. Despite his serious drinking problem and being the town drunk, Otis knows himself well enough to give up his car on his own. He understands how his weakness might cause him to drive while drunk, and Otis does not want to harm himself or anyone else in anyway.

"You know Otis really is a nice man and the way he goes around, something could happen to him and we never would see him again." - Barney

Episode 115
"The Song Festers"

"Gomer, you sure have a high roof to your mouth. No, I knew you had a strong speaking voice but I had no idea you could sing like that." - Andy

*B*arney loves to sing and he is back in John Masters' choir. In episode 52, "Barney and the Choir", Barney leaves the choir because he was given a prize for his performance. Now he is back in the choir, and he is about to be the soloist for an upcoming concert. John Masters is not satisfied with Barney's performance, so he tells Andy if he can find a better soloist, he is going to replace him. Of course Andy knows how Barney will feel if he is replaced, so he feels he should at least forewarn him of that possibility.

Not only does Barney love to sing, he also believes he has great talent. Much of the reason is due to Eleanora Poultice, Barney's voice teacher. She has told Barney he has the potential to be another Leonard Blush, "The Masked Singer" on station WMPD. Both teacher and student are convinced Barney will be the soloist, and he will do Mayberry proud. With praise like this from Eleanora, no wonder Barney is full of confidence.

An important part of being any kind of teacher is to always give praise. Praise helps to motivate students to work hard and improve. But false praise can be very detrimental to a person as we see in this episode. Whether or not Eleanora truly believes Barney has great talent, she gives him constant praise. It doesn't take much for Barney's ego to be lifted, and when he hears Eleanora sing his praises, he believes no one will beat him out for the soloist part. Unfortunately she is setting Barney up for a big disappointment. For little do they know, a wonderful new singing talent is about to be discovered.

After being overheard singing while changing a flat tire, John Masters selects Gomer Pyle as Barney's replacement. Even an untrained ear can understand his choice. Gomer's rich, perfectly pitched voice is far superior to Barney's, and Andy is the one who has to tell him the bad news. When Barney hears the news, to say he is disappointed would be an understatement. Then when he hears that Gomer Pyle is the one who will be singing in his stead, he really feels bad. Gomer is one of his good friends. But that isn't what bothers Barney the most. The fact that he loses out to someone like Gomer, a gas station attendant who has never had a singing lesson, is a real blow to Barney's pride. Yet the fact that Gomer is Barney's friend will result in Barney's singing after all.

Gomer Pyle is about to experience something very unusual. He has just been chosen to sing a solo at a concert that will be attended by a great many Mayberry people. Perhaps for the first time in his life he will be the center of attention. People will talk about his wonderful voice, and new doors will be open for him. He is about to show all his friends that he can do something besides pump gas and put air in tires.

After rehearsing with John Masters, Gomer learns of Barney's great disappointment. Rather than seeing his friend hurt, Gomer decides to give up his solo so Barney can sing. He knows Barney has pride, so he cannot just quit. He needs to find a way that will enable him to step down gracefully and allow Barney to sing the solo. Gomer shows his true character when he sacrifices his own fame for the sake of a friend.

"Now Andy, let me finish. We'll find a catch name for you, like the Three Bells." - Eleanora Poultice

Episode 116
"The Shoplifters"

"Well, I guess this proves you were right sheriff. I probably was robbed during the night. Well, it's easy enough with Rip Van Winkle here on guard." - Ben Weaver

Weaver's Department Store is being robbed. Ben is adamant that Andy do something about it immediately. Andy assures him that he and Barney will do all they can. Barney decides to take charge, and he goes to the store at night. Unknown to him, Ben is also at the store. Finding the back door unlocked, Barney enters the store, and within minutes he and Ben are playing a game of cat and mouse in the dark. Before long Andy enters the scene, only to find Barney and Ben running around yelling about a burglar. Of course there is no one in the store except for the two of them and old Asa, the night watchman, who is fast asleep in a chair. Andy tells Ben that his store is not being robbed at night. Someone is walking off with the goods in the middle of the day. The thief is a shoplifter.

Shoplifting is a common crime in the United States. While often times we think of shoplifters as people who steal small items from retailers, in reality it is a multibillion-dollar crime. Statistics state that shoplifters steal over $20 billion worth of goods each year. Shoplifting is America's number one property crime. There are approximately 23 million shoplifters in the United States with one in eleven citizens who shoplift. Someone must absorb the costs related to shoplifting, and that someone is you and I. We invariably end up paying higher prices to cover the loss of shoplifted merchandise.

Ben Weaver is very angry and concerned about his lost merchandise. Ben lets Andy know that he cannot afford the losses.

If the shoplifting continues, Ben will do what every other merchant does when shoplifting occurs. He will raise his prices, and the good folks of Mayberry will be the ones to suffer. But who could be stealing from Ben? Is it one of Mayberry's own good citizens, or is it an out of town stranger who thinks it will be easy pickings in Mayberry? Well, Barney is about to go into action to find out.

Barney decides to keep watch in the store incognito. He dresses in one of the hunting outfits Ben has in his store and pretends to be a dummy. Now, some people might argue that Barney need not pretend, but that is another story for another book. In any event Barney decides he has spotted the thief and he persuades Andy to let him make an arrest. He accuses a little old lady of shoplifting, but when she empties her large bag, all it contains is her knitting and family bible. After threatening to sue the store, she is let go, and Andy and Barney leave the store. It appears Barney has made another blunder.

I have seen several shoplifters in action. The first time I informed the store manager, and they caught the person. Another time I saw a young boy steal a toy. Because of his age I decided not to inform the store. Instead I followed him outside and I stopped him. I said to him, "Don't you think it would be a good idea to return that toy you stole?" I followed him back to the store and watched as he put the toy back on the shelf. I often wonder how Barney would handle a case of shoplifting by a child. I imagine he would resort to his philosophy to "nip it in the bud". By the way, Barney was right all along. It was the little old lady who was stealing from Ben Weaver.

"A little time behind bars may cure you of your taken ways lady." - Barney

195

Episode 117
"Andy's Vacation"

"Well, the 302 disturbing the peace for both, and for Maudy, the 710; assault with a deadly weapon. She threw a chicken at him." - Barney

*R*arely do we see Andy lose his temper or hear him say a bad word about Mayberry. In "Andy's Vacation" he decides he has had enough of everything. He tells Barney that, "In a friendly sortta hope you'll understand way", that he is sick of him too. It does not sound like Andy at all. He is tired, irritable, and sick of being sheriff. In other words he is experiencing that very common phenomenon known as "job burn out". I would imagine each of us has gone through the exact same thing at one time or other.

Americans are often accused of being an overly hard working people who do not know how to relax. Most workers in many European countries receive five weeks of paid vacation a year. With considerably much shorter vacations, is it any wonder American workers experience work related stress problems? While on a vacation in Sweden a few years ago, my relatives could not believe that my wife was using her entire year's two week paid vacation on our visit. They boasted of their four to five week vacations after being on a job for only one year. They couldn't imagine having only two weeks.

Andy hasn't taken a vacation all year. He has an entire week coming, and he finally agrees to take the week off. Barney suggests he go to a beach house in Florida, but Andy decides to lie around home enjoying his time reading the National Geographic and doing a little gardening. But after being home less than a day, he decides to go to the mountains to escape the constant phone calls and problems with Barney.

It seems whenever there is a need for a third deputy in Mayberry, Andy and Barney call upon Gomer Pyle for help. One would think that in a town the size of Mayberry there would be at least one person who might be a little more qualified than Gomer. But Gomer is a friend to both Andy and Barney, and most of the police duties are dealing with minor offenses. Certainly Barney and Gomer can handle the job for just one short week. But what will happen if the state police should bring a hardened prisoner to the jail? Will Barney and Gomer be up to the challenge of guarding him?

The prisoner is in the Mayberry jail for less than five minutes when he manages to escape. Rather than call for help, Barney decides he and Gomer will go after the escaped prisoner so that no one would need to know of the escape. However, as one would expect, their attempt to recapture the man only leads to more problems and hilarity. Not only does Andy capture the prisoner, but Barney and Gomer release him again, and he is off and free for a second time in one day. But once again Andy comes to the rescue, and the prisoner is finally captured for good. Even with the prisoner's double escape, the *Mayberry Gazette* gives Gomer and Barney the full credit.

Does Andy ever get his week's vacation? Certainly he does. He finds the perfect formula for a relaxing stress free week. Andy gives Barney a one-week vacation, and he returns to the office. Andy's vacation away from Barney is about to begin.

"Now old Hugo Hotflash might have been on the wrong team back in '18, but he was a heck of a soldier." - Barney

Episode 118
"Andy Saves Gomer"

"Shazam! An oil fire! Sure a lucky thing you came by here Andy. Why flames could a come shutting out there any minute and then the whole place would a gone up and it would of spread to the gas pumps and then kaboom." - Gomer

When Andy stops at Wally's filling station one day, he doesn't expect to walk away a hero. At least he is a hero in the eyes of Gomer Pyle. As Andy walks into the station, he smells smoke. He finds Gomer sound asleep in a chair with smoke coming out of the trash barrel. Andy wakes Gomer and while he runs around in circles,

Andy calmly puts out the little fire with sand. Gomer immediately becomes indebted to Andy for saving his life. From a little smoke on an oily rag, Gomer's imagination has the entire station engulfed in flames. Gomer decides to be eternally grateful to the man who risked his life to save his. Andy has no idea how his actions are about to change his life.

There are all types of heroes; war heroes, firefighters, and doctors to name a few. Sometimes we even label great athletes as heroes. Some people enjoy being labeled a hero. Barney Fife bought every newspaper in town when people called him a hero after his daring cave rescue. But some do not. Otis Campbell said he wasn't a hero just because he descended from one. Andy certainly doesn't think of himself as a hero after putting out Gomer's fire. He unintentionally hurts Gomer's feelings when he says what he did was really nothing. Poor Gomer thinks Andy is saying his life is worth nothing.

In many cases people are given medals after doing a heroic deed. Andy is about to receive far more than a medal. Gomer presents him with fresh fish, huge piles of firewood, and constant and undivided attention. He even transfers his gratitude to Opie who is the "firstborn son of the man who saved his life." Gomer takes time off from work so he can show his gratitude to the Taylors. From helping Aunt Bee bake a cake to picking up Opie whenever he falls, Gomer is there to be of assistance.

Andy had a similar problem with Gomer in Episode 101 "Gomer the Houseguest". Gomer was underfoot all the time, but Andy could not bring himself to ask Gomer to leave. Andy is such a kindhearted person. He wouldn't hurt people for anything. But Gomer is just getting to be too much. Andy, Aunt Bee, and Opie even take to eating their meals in a cell hidden behind a blanket. There must be some way for Andy to get Gomer to understand that he has paid his indebtedness to Andy. Fortunately for all the Taylors, Andy does come up with an idea where he makes it look as if Gomer has saved his life. He puts the plan into action, and it works to perfection. Or so Andy thinks.

Gomer is like many people. He has a difficult time accepting help from others. He feels Andy deserves more than just a simple "thank you." But in reality, a nice thank you is the only thing most people do want when they help someone in need. A nice hand written thank you card, a telephone call, or a personal visit is the best way to show one's gratitude. Most people don't expect anything more nor do they want anything more. Now if someone could just get this idea across to Gomer Pyle.

"And all's well that ends well. Gomer feels like everything's even between us and we can go back to living without fish every morning." - Andy

Episode 119
"Bargain Day"

"Now Miss Bee, what do you want with hamburger with all that beef?" - Mr. Foley

*A*unt Bee has always been a thrifty person. She appreciates the value of a dollar, and she knows how hard Andy works for his money. It isn't clear where Aunt Bee gets her money. It is very likely she receives some from Andy for doing all the housework. Most likely she had money of her own when she first came to Mayberry. In any event she makes the day-to-day decisions on the household budget, and she pays for the food and other things needed. But she doesn't spend money foolishly, and if there is a bargain to be found, Aunt Bee will find it. But as she discovers, a bargain is not always a bargain.

It is a very hot summer day in Mayberry. The Taylors are at the breakfast table, and Opie comes to breakfast wearing new shoes that squeak. Aunt Bee bought them on sale even though they are too big for Opie. She says he will grow into them, and besides she bought them because she saved money. Aunt Bee fills the sugar bowl from an oversized cumbersome sack and spills sugar all over the table. She bought the largest sack because it is more economical that way. Andy reminds Aunt Bee that she goes to way yonder too much trouble trying to save a penny or two. Besides, according to Andy, "a penny earned is a penny taxed."

When my wife and I first married we had to watch every single penny. Everything we bought was either used or on sale. We always had to buy the least expensive model of toaster, coffee maker, or piece of furniture. We always looked at the bargain aisles first whenever shopping. Even though we usually saved a lot of money shopping this way, our purchases didn't always turn out to be such bargains. Because we bought generic brand coffee, it remained in the cupboard never brewed. The used color television we bought from a neighbor had a sickly green color to it all the time and then died a slow death shortly thereafter. My five-dollar lawnmower that I bought at a thrift sale left large wet clumps of grass all over the lawn which I had to rake after each mowing. Oh we saved money all right, but not for very long. We would have been money ahead if we would have bought better things in the first place.

Aunt Bee has an old unused freezer that she bought at an auction. It has been sitting on the back porch ever since. According to Andy the only thing that has ever been in it was a mouse, and he went in to keep warm. Determined to prove Andy wrong, Aunt Bee buys one hundred and fifty pounds of beef from Mayberry's new butcher. It cost ten cents a pound less than Mr. Foley charges, so she just cannot pass up a bargain like this. Now she would have a use for her freezer, and she can show Andy how smart a shopper she is. She'll surprise him with a nice roast beef in the middle of the week.

Things don't go quite the way Aunt Bee plans. The beef turns out to be tough, and the freezer breaks down shortly after filling it with beef. The days are getting warmer, and Aunt Bee needs to find somewhere to store the meat. She reluctantly asks her good friend Mr. Foley if he will store it. Andy refuses to allow Mr. Foley to be troubled for their mistakes, and he ends up buying a new freezer. The repairman just happens to have it on his truck, and it just happens to be the very best one. But how will Aunt Bee react?

"Oh Andy, Clara knows a discount house, thirty percent off. They have bankrupt stock, everything, washers..." - Aunt Bea

Episode 120
"Divorce – Mt. Style"

"Beak of owls, strip of swine. Tooth of comb, take mine from thine. Kenobba in, kenobba out, kenobba in and round about."
- *Charlene Darling*

*D*ivorce is a rarity in Mayberry. It is mentioned briefly several times in all the episodes. Most married folks in Mayberry appear to be quite happy. Of course there are those who have problems, but yet they choose to remain married. Andy certainly would be unhappy if anyone he knows is about to be divorced. But how would he feel if he found out he was actually helping a newly married young couple get a divorce?

Charlene Darling makes a surprise visit to Mayberry late one night. She asks Andy if he will take her someplace, but she doesn't say where. They end up out in the country by a large oak tree. She borrows a shovel from the trunk of the squad car, digs a hole, buries a cloth sack, and recites a strange incantation with Andy at her side. Thinking she is performing a ritual to heal someone back in the mountains, Andy goes along with the procedure. Little does he know he has just helped Charlene perform the mountain ceremony for a divorce? Charlene is now "officially" divorced from Dud Wash, and she is free to marry Andy.

As we have seen in earlier episodes, the Darlings live by a unique code of rules. Tradition, magic, omens, and incantations influence much of their lives. Andy doesn't even try to explain that divorces are granted by the court system. He knows the Darling family will never accept that. So when Briscoe and his sons learn that the divorce ceremony is done and complete, they accept the fact that Andy will now be the new member of their fun-loving family.

Barney decides it is up to him to save Andy. He takes it upon himself to find a peaceful solution to Andy's dilemma. He goes to the library and finds a book on mountain folklore. He learns that if the divorce proceedings are dug up before the light of a full moon, the divorce becomes null and void. However, Briscoe and the boys also

201

know this, and they are at the burial site to prevent the removal of the sack.

Unfortunately divorce is a common event in our modern day society. According to statistics the divorce rate in the United States doubled between the years 1960 -1980. At the current time divorce ends about half of all marriages. Perhaps the stable family life we see in Mayberry is one of the reasons so many people long to live there. If only we could be content with a much simpler life, perhaps marriages would stand a much better chance to survive over the long run.

Getting the Darlings to accept the divorce proceedings to be null and void is no easy matter. However, Barney reads the folklore book again and discovers another ritual that just might get Andy off the hook. Andy gets Barney to dress in a black suit, which makes him look so thin, and then he rides a white horse from east to west in front of the bridegroom. This curses Andy and the union becomes cursed. The Darlings head back to the mountains and Andy is a free man once again. Andy once saved Aunt Bee from a marriage to Briscoe, and now he saves himself from a marriage to Charlene.

"Yah, yah, all we need is somebody willing to dress up in a black outfit and ride a white horse; Some patsy." - Barney

Episode 121
"A Deal is a Deal"

"Sure they do, but they sleep light. See, they're alert even when they're asleep. He'd wake up just like that if anything happened." - Opie

*A*s a child there were two things that I hated; taking a bath and selling things. Taking a bath was the lesser of the two evils. Selling was absolutely awful. I not only disliked it, I was terrible at it. Even to this day whenever I am asked to sell something, my blood pressure increases, and I get a knot in my stomach. All those memories from selling as a child come rushing back to my mind. I failed at it then, and I am going to fail at it now.

Opie and his friends are trying to win a pony. They are all running around Mayberry trying to sell jars of Miracle Salve. It cures crows' feet, prickly ash, and all sorts of other common ailments. The only problem; it just doesn't sell. Andy and Barney have both bought some, but those are the only jars Opie has sold. He is very discouraged, and he decides to send the salve back to the company. But when Tray Boden sends his back, he gets a letter from the Miracle Salve Company saying they are going to put him on a blacklist. Deciding the owners of the salve company are crooks, Barney enlists Gomer's help, and they go to Mt. Pilot with a plan to help Opie and his friends.

Children are easy targets for sales companies. They often offer great prizes and rewards as a way to get children to sell their products. I remember as a child going door-to-door trying to sell Christmas cards as a way of getting some great prizes. The cards were usually overpriced and they were not the best quality, and if I did manage to sell enough for a prize, the prize rarely turned out to be like the ones pictured in the ads.

Barney and Gomer make a visit to the Miracle Salve Company pretending to be Opie Taylor Sr. and Dr. Pendyke, D.V.M. They concoct a story about the salve being able to cure the mange, and how Dr. Pendyke would like to buy all their salve and sell it to other veterinarians. When Barney asks if they can get the salve back from the boys in Mayberry, the men at Miracle Salve say they will see what they can do. Several days later Barney and Gomer see the two men collecting all the salve from the boys and giving them each a dollar. Barney is certain that his brilliant plan has worked perfectly.

Quite often children come to my door selling various products. It is always good when I find out they are selling through legitimate fund raising organizations. Few children sell things for their own personal gain. Most often they are trying to raise money for their church, school, soccer team, or some other organization. Our kitchen cupboards contain numerous cookies, candy bars, and popcorn tins that were all bought in order to help out a needy group. But the one thing I have never been offered is a jar of salve. And if I ever am, I don't think I will buy it; especially if it is called Miracle Salve.

Barney has the best intentions when he goes to Mt. Pilot. He goes to help Opie and his friends, and because of Barney's effort they no longer have to sell Miracle Salve. And besides that, they are each one dollar richer. Opie learns that the selling business is a difficult way to make money, and Barney learns that you cannot fight fire with fire.

"It didn't work like you said it was going to Barney. They're supposed to sell all that stuff to veterinarians." - Gomer

Episode 122
"Fun Girls"

"You know I've never been in a jail before except to visit friends." - Daphne

After more than forty years, "Fun Girls" continues to be one of the all time favorite episodes ever aired. It features the first of two appearances of those zany fun-loving blondes, Skippy and Daphne, from Mt. Pilot. The girls are old friends of Barney, and they unexpectedly turn up in Mayberry one Friday night.

Andy and Barney are working late taking inventory. While Barney goes to get sandwiches, Goober and Gomer arrive at the courthouse, and Andy cannot get any work done. No sooner do the boys leave when Helen and Thelma Lou show up. Andy explains they have to work late, so they decide to meet at the diner after the movies. Barney finally returns without the sandwiches and presents Andy with more unwelcome visitors. He had run into a couple of old friends at the diner, and they insisted on coming back to the courthouse so they could see a jail.

Barney's old friends turn out to be Skippy and Daphne. The girls are all dressed up and are looking for a fun time. Andy tries to politely tell them that they are too busy to entertain them, but he learns Barney has promised to drive them back to Mt. Pilot. Helen and Thelma Lou see Barney, Andy and the" fun girls" getting into the patrol car driving off. Helen and Thelma Lou break their dates for the dance and end up taking Goober and Gomer, while Barney arranges the "fun girls" to be dates for Andy and him.

Forgiveness is vital to any relationship. Harboring anger and failing to forgive one's mistakes leads to mistrust and bitterness. Thelma Lou is a very forgiving person. Time and time again she forgives Barney. Despite all his faults and indiscretions, she loves him for who he is, and she always finds it in her heart to forgive his mistakes.

Andy, too, is most forgiving. For years Barney has bumbled and fumbled his deputy duties, yet Andy always overlooks it. He forgets the many false rumors Barney has spread throughout Mayberry. Now he needs to forgive Barney once more. This time Barney almost brings about an end to his relationship with Helen. When Helen refuses to listen to Andy about the "fun girls", he decides to stay home and perhaps give Helen some time to "cool off." But Barney can not let matters rest. He arranges to take the "fun girls" to the dance knowing it will only infuriate Helen and Thelma Lou more.

Using games and childish tactics to get back at someone seldom works. Barney seems to do things the hard way. Rather than sitting down with Thelma Lou and talking things over, he goes through his scheme of taking the "fun girls" to the dance. He not only leads the "fun girls" on, he also makes Helen and Thelma Lou more jealous. However, both Thelma Lou and Helen come to believe that Barney and Andy are victims of one big misunderstanding. All ends well when Andy and Barney take Helen and Thelma Lou home from the dance. What about the "fun girls"? How will they get back to Mt. Pilot? Perhaps they will find some other eligible bachelors to give them a ride home. Certainly Barney and Andy won't, will they?

"There you go. See, everything turned out for the best. It was a little adventure but it turned out all right." - Barney

Episode 123
"The Return of Malcolm Merriweather"

"I don't know how she does all she does. Cooks, cleans, sews, shops, takes care of Opie. I wonder if she knows how much we really appreciate everything she does for us." - Andy

*M*alcolm Merriweather makes a surprise return visit to Mayberry. He makes his usual entry into town peddling his bicycle down the middle of the street causing all sorts of traffic problems. This time however, he manages to avoid getting hit by a truck. He has been traveling around the country visiting historical sites and has decided to revisit Mayberry.

Andy wonders if Aunt Bee knows now much she is really appreciated. Since coming to live with them, her number one concern has always been Andy and Opie. Their needs are always her top priority. Perhaps they haven't told her often enough how important she is to them. Maybe we all need to ask ourselves a similar question. Do the people who care for us really know how much we appreciate them? There are many people who care for us in many ways that it is easy to take them for granted. Think about the people who care for our children. Do we remember to thank the school bus driver or crossing guard for their roles in making sure our children get to and from school safely? Do we thank coworkers or employees? Do we thank the health care workers who care for our elderly parents or grandparents? Do we ever thank our own family members for all the things they do for us?

Andy thinks that it is time he does something to show Aunt Bee his appreciation. He decides to give Malcolm a job to help take some of the workload off Aunt Bee. She will now have time for all her club meetings and social activities. She will have more leisure time than she has ever dreamed possible. No longer will she have to rush about with her housework, cooking, and shopping. She won't even have to bother bringing lunch to Andy and Barney. Malcolm will do it all. Aunt Bee is about to become a lady of leisure.

Andy has the best intentions when he gives Malcolm a job. He truly believes Aunt Bee will enjoy her leisure time. She will be able to watch her favorite doctor television program without missing a single stitch. Her breakfast will be waiting for her when she gets up in the morning. Yes, Aunt Bee's new lifestyle will be wonderful. Andy has certainly thought of everything – except for one small detail. He forgets to ask Aunt Bee if it is what she wants. Will Aunt Bee really be happier with so much more free time?

As Malcolm goes about his duties in the Taylor home, a change occurs in Aunt Bee. While Malcolm is creating elaborate lunches for Andy and Barney, Aunt Bee is at a club meeting. Rather than preparing supper and doing dishes, she sits on the porch. Even Opie notices a change. He tells Malcolm that Aunt Bee always sings when she is working. It is at that point that Malcolm realizes that he has never heard Aunt Bee sing. He understands why and decides to do something about it. Malcolm has found a place where he feels useful and is truly happy. But Aunt Bee's happiness is more important, so Malcolm unselfishly finds a way to return her to her rightful place among the Taylor family. Malcolm is right when he says people are happiest when they are busy.

"Just a Cornish pastry that's all. Well, you see there's meat and potatoes in one end and plum pudding in the other. So you start with the meat and potatoes and work your way to the dessert." - Malcolm Merriweather

Episode 124
"The Rumor"

"Come on Thelma Lou, put two and two together, read the handwriting on the wall, blow away the smoke and look at the fire." - Barney

*T*hings are not always what they appear to be." "Looks can be deceiving." These are two very familiar sayings that we hear quite frequently. They are sometimes used to help teach an important lesson. It is too bad Barney doesn't think about these things before he gets all excited and starts "The Rumor."

By the time Episode 124 comes along, we are well aware that nothing will make Barney happier than to see his best friend, Andy Taylor, married. Barney has tried many times to get Andy to enter into the happy state of holy matrimony. But nothing has worked. Barney once organized a big party when he told everyone Andy and Mary were getting engaged back in Episode 59, "Three's a Crowd." Of course he was wrong. So one would think he would be more careful in the future. But Barney just never seems to learn from his past mistakes. Once again he finds himself getting things all mixed up.

Barney jumps to a wrong conclusion when he sees Andy kissing Helen in the jewelry store right on Main Street. To Barney it can mean only one thing. Andy and Helen are picking up an engagement ring. Barney wastes no time telling Thelma Lou and Aunt Bee. Before long a big celebration is planned. Aunt Bee cannot decide what to give for a wedding present. She finally comes up with the idea of having everyone chip in to redecorate Andy's bedroom, which she describes as an "elephant's nest". So Andy's room is redecorated for the bride, and everyone is looking forward to the big event. Barney is not too keen on the gift. He thinks a bed with a fringe is "kissy" looking.

If you have ever lived in a small town, you know how fast rumors can spread. Gossip seems to be the most popular activity among many small town folks. It doesn't seem to matter whether it is good news or bad news, it travels with incredible speed. When the rumor is about a well-known citizen, such as a sheriff or teacher, it seems to travel even faster. If it is about a sheriff and a teacher, you can only imagine how fast it travels.

The good people of Mayberry seem to forget the many times Barney has spread stories about Andy. They accept this new rumor without question, and everyone gets involved with the planning of the party and buying the gift. Perhaps everyone is so happy to hear that Andy and Helen are finally getting married, they don't stop to consider the source of the rumor. If they did, perhaps they would not be so anxious to believe it.

How do rumors such as Barney's get started? False rumors quite often begin just like Barney's rumor does. A person sees something and repeats what is seen. Unfortunately what one sees is not always what one thinks it is. From buying a bracelet for a niece's graduation, and and little kiss, it takes Barney less than an hour to start the rumor that Andy and Helen are engaged. When Andy and Helen are presented with their gift, their embarrassment is very understandable. They are not ready for marriage, and if the day does come for them to get engaged, I wonder who will be the first to know. If I were Andy, I would be sure to tell Barney first, just to make sure he gets things right.

"Wait a minute; I saw you kiss her in the jewelry store right on Main Street. You're engaged; you stop kidding me and tell me you're engaged." - Barney

Episode 125
"Barney and Thelma Lou, Phfftt"

"I mean there's a lot of things in this world I might be worried about, but losing Thelma Lou is not one of them. I got that little girl right in my hip pocket." - Barney

*B*arney and Thelma Lou have lovers' spats occasionally, but they always make up. They argue over Barney's inexpensive dates, his acting like a love sick school boy when he meets pretty girls, and of course the "Fun Girls". But this time their disagreement reaches a new level, and it has nothing to do with Barney and other girls. But it has everything to do with Barney Fife.

The conflict between Barney and Thelma Lou begins when Gomer takes Thelma Lou to a dentist appointment in Mt. Pilot. On the drive Gomer tells Thelma Lou how nice a guy Barney is and how everyone talks about Thelma Lou and Barney. He tells her how pretty she is, and that Barney isn't worried about losing her because he heard him say just that morning how he has her in his hip pocket. From that moment on, Thelma Lou gets very interested in what Barney has been telling Gomer, and when she finds out everything, she decides to teach Barney a lesson in no uncertain terms. Barney has made

Thelma Lou jealous in the past by playing games, so now it's Thelma Lou's turn.

People often resort to mind games and foolish tactics as a way to deal with problems. This is especially true when relationships are having difficulties. Rather than going to Barney to talk about how she feels, Thelma Lou decides to make Barney jealous by taking Gomer to the movies. She breaks her standing Tuesday night date with Barney. Every Tuesday night since starting to date, they have spent the evening at Thelma Lou's watching a doctor program on TV and eating a pan of cashew fudge. When a dejected Barney goes on the rounds with Andy, they see Thelma Lou going into the movies with Gomer – the same movie Barney and Thelma Lou saw together the night before.

Thelma Lou is embarking on a rather dangerous scheme to teach Barney his lesson. She plays up to Gomer to make Barney jealous, and her plan is working. But her plan backfires when she kisses Gomer on the jaw, and Gomer sees it as an obligation for him to marry her. Gomer comes from a family with a very strict code of conduct, and when two people kiss, it means they have to get married. So now Thelma Lou has compounded her problem, and good old Andy is forced to come up with a solution.

When Thelma Lou starts out to teach Barney a lesson, she certainly does not have any intentions of hurting Gomer. He is an innocent victim of her scheme. Gomer is kind enough to drive Thelma Lou to Mt. Pilot, and he is pleasant and proper the entire time. He knows perfectly well Thelma Lou is Barney's girl, and he would never do anything to hurt his good friend. By her actions, Thelma Lou puts Gomer in a very tenuous situation, one which he does not deserve. Thankfully, Andy is able to resolve the matter, and everyone returns to the way they once were. But, as we see at the end of this episode, Barney does not learn a single thing during this entire unfortunate episode with Gomer.

"Why rush? We've got nothing but time. I'm not going anyplace; she's not going anyplace. What am I worried about; I got that little girl right in my hip pocket." - Barney

Episode 126
"Back to Nature"

"Thus ways both the sheriff and I will be able to pass along to you our skills as woodsmen in order that you in turn can pass it along to your children, and your children's children." - Barney

*G*rowing up in Mayberry, Opie and his friends have lots of fun. Most of their activities are the kind that can be classified as "free play". Nothing is really organized for them. If they want to go fishing, they go fishing. If they feel like playing football or baseball, Opie and his friends get together and play somewhere. Bike rides, swimming, or just fooling around are often spur of the moment ideas that result in a lot of fun.

On occasion, an activity is planned and organized for Opie and his friends. In "Back to Nature", Andy, Barney, and Gomer plan to take the boys on a camping trip. They hope to get the boys more interested in the great outdoors. At seven o'clock in the morning, the group heads out to the woods for their overnight adventure. Everything goes fine the first day and night. The boys enjoy setting up camp, cooking outdoors, and listening to Andy's campfire tale of the man with the golden arm. The problems begin the next morning when Opie is missing, and Barney and Gomer go off searching for him. Opie returns shortly, but it is a long time until Barney and Gomer find their way back to camp.

Whenever an activity involves children, it is essential to establish rules. It is the only way to insure things will go smoothly. Andy takes on a big responsibility when he takes a group of boys camping. He has a rule that everyone must stay together. No one is to go off on his own. But when Opie decides to go off by himself to look for some berries, his actions create a big problem. Gomer and Barney get lost while out looking for him.

As we might expect, Barney lets everyone know that he is an expert when it comes to being an outdoorsman. But when it becomes necessary for him to live up to his talk, it is evident that nothing is further from the truth. He is unable to build a snare that works; his attempt at starting a fire without matches fails, and as far as knowing directions, he ends up walking around in circles. Even after all his failings, he refuses to listen to Gomer, and he insists that he knows exactly where they are.

Andy is unable to look for Barney and Gomer because he must stay with the boys, and he does not want them to know that they are lost. He waits until Fletch arrives with some food and archery equipment, and then he goes off in search of the lost woodsmen. When Andy comes upon Gomer sitting by Barney's unlit fire, he thinks of a way to help them return without making Barney look foolish. He knows how kids are. If they find out Barney, the great outdoorsman was lost, there will be no end to their teasing, and Andy does not want that to happen to his best friend. Barney has had his share of ridicule.

Andy's devotion to Barney's well being is such an admirable quality. He is forever looking out for Barney. Andy may pull some practical jokes on Barney to make him look silly or feel foolish, but they are almost always done in private. Andy does not like to see his friend belittled or humiliated, even if it is by children. Wouldn't the world be a better place if each of us could have a friend like Andy Taylor, Sheriff of Mayberry?

"Well, he's not one to hang around the cooking fire. He's out somewheres doing his nature studies." - Andy

Episode 127
"Gomer Pyle U.S.M.C."

"Well, I got word from the draft board saying my number was coming up and I was gonna be expected to serve a term of military duty. You see every young man between the age of 18 and 35 is expected to serve a term of military duty. Did you know about that?" - Gomer Pyle

Episode 127 brings Season Number Four to a close, and with it we say good-by to Gomer Pyle. Gomer leaves Mayberry when he joins the United States Marine Corps. It is an episode that blends together the humor of Gomer Pyle trying to make it as a soldier, and the reality of young men being drafted into the armed forces.

Gomer Pyle U.S.M.C. was originally aired on May 18, 1964. At that time, the United States was involved in the Viet Nam War. It was a difficult period for our nation, as thousands of our countrymen lost their lives. Perhaps the Viet Nam War was one of the very reasons why Mayberry came to be loved by so many people. It was an escape from reality, and for a short time each day, viewers could sit back and visit a place where there was no hate, injustice, or war. So it was only fitting, that the final episode of 1964 should touch upon a military theme. It was also in that year when I turned 18 years of age, and I became eligible for the military draft. However, I never did serve in the military because of serious vision problems. Unlike Gomer, they turned me down.

Andy attempts to dissuade Gomer from joining the Marines, but Gomer is adamant about serving his country. Not thinking the Marines will accept him; Andy drives Gomer to the military base, just in case he needs to return home. Gomer of course is confident that he will make it. He read about a General Lucius Pyle, so Gomer figures if one Pyle can make it, so can he. Gomer gets off to a bad start with Sergeant Carter, when they arrive late. He ends up doing KP duty for three weeks, and things go from bad to worse when fellow Marines tricks him into wearing Sergeant Carter's dress uniform.

We see a very serious and compassionate side to Gomer that we have never seen before. Gomer talks about how his daddy told him one time that he was going to be tested to see if he were a man. Gomer believes the Marine Corps is that very test his daddy spoke about. When Andy asks him if he would be disappointed if he were told to go home, Gomer answers by saying it would break his spirit. Andy knows now that he must do all he can to help Gomer. But after that, Gomer will be entirely on his own.

Each of us is tested numerous times during our lifetime. Some tests are self-imposed, while others are tests that we cannot control. Like Gomer, I believe these tests help us to become who we are. Gomer is not the image of your typical soldier. He does not have great physical strength, high intelligence, or a killer instinct which is sometimes needed with a soldier. But Gomer does possess honor, inner courage, loyalty, and self-respect, and if I had to choose which kind of Marine I would want to be, I would choose the Gomer kind. For then I would know; I am truly a man. Andy leaves Gomer and returns to Mayberry to a place full of love, security, and peace. Hopefully, the things Gomer has learned and experienced while living in Mayberry will help to guide him through his time in the Marines.

"Well Gomer, whenever I see a man sitting by his self in a Quonset hut with a bucket on his head, I've got to ask, "What's wrong?" - Andy

A Visit to the Taylor Home Inn Bed & Breakfast

I was fourteen years old when I first visited Mayberry. It was the beginning of what was to become a lifelong passion for the wonderful make believe town of Mayberry, North Carolina. Little did I realize that forty-five years later, I would enter the Andy Taylor home to the whistling theme song, "The Old Fishing Hole", and that I would be welcomed with a big kiss from Ellie Walker, a delightful three year old black schnauzer.

Dave and Marsha Scheuermann, who live in the small town of Clear Lake, Wisconsin, have created a very real part of Mayberry by replicating Sheriff Andy Taylor's home. Nestled among six acres, located in the quiet countryside, just outside Clear Lake, the Scheuermanns own and operate the Taylor Home Inn, Bed & Breakfast.

Taylor Home Inn Bed & Breakfast

I had been communicating with Dave and Marsha since they first began their dream of recreating the Taylor home. From our many emails we shared, I got the impression that they were two very special and unique individuals. I was not mistaken. Recently my wife Linda and I had the pleasure of spending a night at the Taylor Home Inn. It was truly one of the most wonderful experiences of my life.

From the moment we walked into the Taylor Home Inn, we were treated like family, and not like just paying guests. It is difficult to express the feeling one gets when first entering the Taylor living room. It was as if we were stepping back in time, and we were really entering a

215

part of Mayberry. The first thing I noticed was the beautiful stone fireplace that is an almost exact replica to the fireplace found in the television Taylor home. In fact, everything in the living room and dining areas were either exact replicas, or as close to being exact as possible. The pictures on the wall, the ceramic pelican that Opie won at the county fair, the vintage black and white television, and a guitar were all there. It was a surreal feeling to just sit on that sofa and see everything that Andy, Aunt Bee, and Opie saw for over forty-five years.

Owners Dave and Marsha Scheuermann

Walking into the Taylor Home Inn kitchen was a very emotional experience for me. I almost expected to see Barney come in through the back door for his morning cup of java. I have spent many wonderful hours in the Taylor kitchen over the years, through the wonders of television, but I never expected to one day be there. Everything was there, except for the crack in the ceiling. Dave and Marsha did a wonderful job of hiding that slight little flaw in the Taylor home. Seeing Aunt Bee's white china cabinet filled with blue willow dishes really made that kitchen come alive as no other kitchen could. The canister set and cookie jar

Aunt Bee's Kitchen at the Taylor Home Inn

on the countertop were exactly like those used by Aunt Bee, Andy, and Opie.

That much loved kitchen in the Taylor Home Inn produced the most scrumptious breakfast that Linda and I have ever eaten and it was

Aunt Bee's Cupboard at the Taylor Home Inn

served on blue willow dishes by a charming waiter named Dave. We knew it was breakfast time when Marsha did her "call to breakfast", a wonderfully performed rendition of old *14A* on the living room piano. I almost began singing "Welcome sweet spring time we greet thee in awe," but seeing Marsha was a music teacher, I decided against that. Our breakfast began with Marsha's own specialty dish of vanilla yogurt, covered with sweet and crunchy Minnesota granola, mixed with home made Clear Lake maple syrup, and topped with numerous large fresh sweet blueberries. Add to that, a tall glass of fresh orange juice, and we were finished with course number one. Next on the menu came freshly baked pecan and apple pancake, sprinkled with powdered sugar. The third course was an expertly prepared

fluffy omelet with ham, cheese, green peppers, and cilantro. To make the breakfast complete, we shared the Taylor table with a delightful family from Canada, who were visiting Clear Lake before returning their mother to her native Brazil. How fitting that we should share the wonderful food and hospitality of Mayberry

Sharing a Wonderful Breakfast at the Taylor Home Inn

with nice friendly folks from another country. Aunt Bee would have welcomed them to her table, just as Marsha and Dave did.

The guest rooms at the Taylor Home Inn were again replicas of the three Taylor bedrooms. The beds and other furnishings were once again close replicas to the television set furniture. Viewers rarely saw the inside of the Taylor bedrooms, so Dave and Marsha had to be very creative with their decorating skills. The only difference from the television bedrooms was that each bedroom had a beautiful, large, modern private bathroom which fit in with each bedroom's décor perfectly. Linda and I had the honor of spending the night in Andy's room, which is the largest of the three.

An added feature to the upstairs level of the Inn was a beautiful guest lounge. Here we could relax while watching reruns of "The Andy Griffith Show". There was a small refrigerator which contained bottles of water and pop for the guests. Coffee, tea and fresh baked cookies were provided in the evening as we traveled back to Mayberry for a few hours. We chose to sit with Dave and Marsha to watch several reruns and just share stories about our passions for Mayberry.

I would be remiss if I didn't say more about Ellie Walker. She was an absolute delight. We were even encouraged to play the roll of Ernest T. Bass. The Scheuermanns conveniently have rocks lying around near the porch. Dave and Marsha demonstrated that if you throw the rocks out into the fields, Ellie Walker would chase after them and retrieve them. She kept us entertained for quite a while with this favorite activity. I am happy to say that at no time did we break any windows with the rocks. Ellie was also an excellent lap sitter.

Of course on the television series Andy, Aunt Bee, and Opie spent many evenings sitting on their front porch, just as we did during our stay. Dave, Marsha, Linda, Ellie Walker, and I spent several hours just sitting on the porch talking. We talked mostly about Mayberry. We drank coffee, shared our favorite episodes and Mayberry moments, and what better place to do so than out on a beautiful front porch. Just like in Mayberry, when Dave and Marsha's neighbors passed by, there would always be a honk of the horn and a friendly wave. Those two hours of quiet time, spent with two new special friends, were perhaps some of the best two hours of my life.

There is much more I could tell you about our visit, but I want you to discover a few things for yourself when you visit the Taylor Home Inn. Do we plan to return to Clear Lake? Well, just try to keep us away. We are already making plans for return trips each year to celebrate our wedding anniversary. It is truly a wonderful experience. We all have our dreams, but for many of us, they just never do come true. Dave and Marsha had a dream, and it did come true for them. They took a small part of make believe, and they transformed it into reality. They are truly two very fortunate people.

Ken and Linda Anderson relaxing with Ellie Walker

A Tribute to Don Knotts

H ow does one begin to say farewell to a living legend? For people of all ages and from every walk of life, February 26, 2006, was a very sad day. It was the day when the world lost a great and gifted performer. For more than forty-five years Don Knotts has touched the hearts of millions as he portrayed that bumbling, nervous, and loveable Deputy Barney Fife.

We first met Barney Fife and the wonderful people of Mayberry back on October 3, 1960, when the very first episode, "The New Housekeeper" was aired. It was at that time when we were first introduced to Mayberry, North Carolina and Barney Fife. Television and comedy would never be the same again.

Ken's Personal Tribute to Don Knotts

My friends and I grew up watching The Andy Griffith Show. It didn't take long for me to realize that Mayberry was a very special place, and the people who lived there were very special people. However, many people considered Mayberry to be a totally unrealistic and phony town. But growing up in a small town very similar to Mayberry, I can attest to the fact that there were towns like Mayberry. I use the past tense were because those days of Mayberry and the Andy

221

Griffith Show are no longer here. Gone are those simpler and much slower times when virtues such as innocence, caring, modesty, respect, and simplicity were the norm in countless small towns throughout this great land. However, because of reruns and DVD's, Barney Fife will continue to be a part of our lives for many years to come, and generations of people yet to be born will be able to meet and enjoy those loveable folks from Mayberry.

People who know me well often call me Barney. All you have to do is look at my license plate on my car and you will understand why. It is B FIFE. I wear a Barney Fife collector's wristwatch, and I carry a Barney Fife driver's license in my wallet. When I dress up for a special event, I quite often wear one of my beautiful Barney Fife ties. If I am out for a leisurely walk you may see me wearing one of my favorite Mayberry sweatshirts or t-shirts. I drink soda from a Barney Fife stein, and we often serve food on our Barney Fife dishes. I have a Mayberry pennant hanging in my den, and I have numerous pictures of Barney Fife around the house. My bookcase contains books about Mayberry and several specifically about Barney Fife. And last but not least, my model train collection slowly travels through my complete collection of all the important buildings of Mayberry. So you might say I am rather a fanatic when it comes to Don Knotts. And you are right; when it comes to Don Knotts I have a special place in my heart just for him.

When I retired early from teaching because of medical issues I had a difficult time accepting my final day of teaching. On that very momentous day, the teachers at Fall Creek Public Schools dressed up as Barney Fife. They presented me with a large poster of Barney Fife. However, it had one alteration. Instead of Barney Fife's face on the poster, it had mine. They knew how to make my final and difficult day of teaching a very special one. They included Barney Fife in my farewell.

Television today is unlike television when Barney Fife and Mayberry first debuted. Standards of conduct and decency were quite different. To this day, families can gather around the television and know that for the next thirty minutes they will share in good clean humor without any embarrassment.

Through his portrayal of Barney Fife, Don Knotts taught me many things; some of which I carried with me throughout my thirty-six years of teaching. In one of his most memorable scenes, Barney was defending Andy when he was removed from the office of sheriff. In defense of Sheriff Taylor, Barney said, "When you are dealing with people instead of going by the book, it is better to go by the heart." How much better the world would be today if each of us could live by that simple philosophy.

There will always be a special place in my heart for Don Knotts. Unfortunately I never had the privilege of meeting Don. But if I had, I know what I would have said. It would have been, "Thank you Mr. Knotts. Thank you for giving me forty-six years of laughter. Thank you for making my life just a little bit better by having entered my home for so many years. Thank you for setting a standard for others to follow."

Ten-four Barney. Over and out.

Farewell, Don Knotts. Farewell, Barney Fife. Farewell to a comedian whose likes we shall never see again. Thank you for all the memories.

Also Available

It's All About You, Lord
a collection of Christian
poetry straight from the
heart of **Wayne Irwin**,
retired businessman
and former member
Colorado National
Guard
ISBN 1-933912-29-4
$10.99

A Tribute to Mayberry,
a wonderful collection of
poems written about the
people, places, and
storylines of the great
television series.
Compiled by
Kathryn Darden
for Christian
Activities Publications.
ISBN 1-888061-11-1
$9.95

Both books available through **www.westviewpublishing.com**

*For more information on self-publishing your book,
contact Kathryn Darden at kathryndarden@westviewpublishing.com*

About the Author

Ken Anderson was born in Evanston, Illinois and is a Graduate of University of Wisconsin-Eau Claire, with a degree in Elementary Education. He also did Graduate Studies at University of Wisconsin – Eau Claire. He spent 36 years as an elementary teacher in Wisconsin, was listed in 1994's *Who's Who Among America's Teachers*, and received An Outstanding Wisconsin Elementary Teacher Award in 1974.

Very active in his community, he is a former board member for Eau Claire County Humane Association and received their Humane Education Award in 1997. He also served on Eau Claire County Selective Service System Board for five years and is a current member of the board for Sacred Heart Hospital Volunteer Partners in Eau Claire, Wisconsin. Currently a member of Trinity Lutheran Church in Eau Claire, Wisconsin, he has served as a youth mentor for confirmation students; is one of the lectors for scripture readings on Sunday mornings; has done individual volunteer student tutoring at an elementary school in Eau Claire; served on numerous church committees and church councils over the years; and currently volunteers about 40 hours a month at Sacred Heart Hospital at the Regional Cancer Center.

He is an avid reader of English mysteries; enjoys driving his 1966 restored Chevrolet convertible in area parades; writing poetry; model trains; attending bible studies; listening to Celtic music; attending plays and concerts; and watching Andy Griffith Show Reruns.

He is a collector of various Mayberry collectible items including the entire Hawthorn Mayberry Village Collection. The organizer of a Mayberry Memories Fan Club in Eau Claire, he teaches Back to Mayberry Bible Study, a mini-class on Mayberry, and is a faithful member of the WBMUTBB Group on the internet.

Ken thinks that it is important for today's readers to understand that the values that were found in Mayberry are as important today as they were back when Mayberry first aired. He wants to give readers some things to reflect upon as they watch the wonderful episodes that show life as it was in Mayberry.

His published writings include short stories and articles published in the Lutheran Digest and Family Life Today, poetry included in an anthology, Earthshine, published by Poetry Press, and a number of articles published by various newspapers. He also has a number of poems that were included in the anthology, *A Tribute to Mayberry*.

Printed in the United States
200014BV00002B/367-417/A